# The Intentional Teacher

## Choosing the Best Strategies for Young Children's Learning

Ann S. Epstein

National Association for the Education of Young Children
Washington, DC

Photographs copyright © by: Nancy Alexander—107; Susan Klein—1; Jean-Claude Lejeune—i; Lois Main—front cover (top left); Elisabeth Nichols—front cover (top right), front cover (bottom left); Ellen B. Senisi—front cover (bottom right), back cover, 41; Michael Siluk—23; Renaud Thomas—9, 67, 87; Francis Wardle—127.

National Association for the Education of Young Children
1313 L Street NW, Suite 500
Washington, DC 20005-4101
202-232-8777 or 800-424-2460
www.naeyc.org

**The Intentional Teacher: Choosing the Best Strategies for Young Children's Learning**

Through its publications program the National Association for the Education of Young Children (NAEYC) provides a forum for discussion of major issues and ideas in the early childhood field, with the hope of provoking thought and promoting professional growth. The views expressed or implied in this book are not necessarily those of the Association.

Carol Copple, *publications director*; Bry Pollack, *managing editor*; Malini Dominey, *design and production*; Lisa Bowles, *editorial associate*; Natalie Klein Cavanagh, *photo editor*; Susan A. Liddicoat, *consultant editor*; Laura Power, *indexer*.

Library of Congress Control Number: 2006939553

ISBN: 978-1-928896-41-8

NAEYC Item #165

# About the Author

**Ann S. Epstein** is director of early childhood at the High/Scope Educational Research Foundation in Ypsilanti, Michigan, where she has worked since 1975. There she develops curriculum materials, as well as child and program assessment tools. She also directs a team of early childhood specialists who conduct in-service training around the country and abroad; supervises implementation of the NAEYC-accredited High/Scope Demonstration Preschool; and evaluates federal, state, and local programs.

Dr. Epstein is the author of several books and articles for professional and practitioner audiences. She has a doctorate in developmental psychology from the University of Michigan and a master's degree from Eastern Michigan University.

# Contents

# Acknowledgments

Writing a book as ambitious in purpose and wide-ranging in scope as *The Intentional Teacher* entails the help and encouragement of many people. First and foremost, I want to thank Carol Copple. As I groped my way toward defining the problem I take up in this book and identifying a balanced solution, Carol and I engaged in lively discussions about the terms of the debate and how much we could push the field forward by honestly addressing our concerns and critics, as well as by embracing the latest developments from research and practice. *The Intentional Teacher* was consequently the most difficult but also the most rewarding book I have ever written. I owe that satisfaction to Carol's unflagging faith that I could do it and her support during the lengthy process of research, reflection, and creation.

A major reason for the simultaneous hurdles and satisfactions in this process was learning about each content area in greater depth, particularly the knowledge and skills that preschoolers acquire primarily through child- or adult-guided learning experience. As I explain in the preface, one source of information was a group of consultant researchers, curriculum specialists, teacher-educators, and practitioners with expertise in one or more areas. These individuals responded to an informal written survey, talked me through the issues in their domain and in early childhood as a whole, and some reviewed manuscript drafts. Although I thank each of them below according to their main area of expertise, many offered ideas across developmental domains. Their excitement about the project helped sustain my own commitment to completing the task I set for myself.

For helping to frame the issues up front and synthesizing the general principles and lessons learned at the end, my sincerest appreciation goes to Sue Bredekamp and Larry Schweinhart. In the area of literacy, I extend thanks to Linda Bevilacqua, Cathy Calamari, Jim Christie, Andee DeBruin-Parecki, Mary Hohmann, Lesley Morrow, Susan Neuman, and Linda Ranweiler. Those who provided input on mathematics and scientific inquiry were Beth Casey, Rosalind Charlesworth, Doug Clements, Juanita Copley, Sue Gainsley, Charles Hohmann, Stuart Murphy, and Polly Neill. The consultants on social skills and understandings were Maury Elias, Betsy Evans, Alice Galper, Debbie Handler, Lilian Katz, Shannon Lockhart, Sherri Oden, Bob Pianta, Emily Vance, and Julie Wigton. Expertise in physical development came from Frances Cleland, Rhonda Clements, Joy Kiger, Rae Pica, Steve Sanders, Karen Sawyers, Sharon Schneider, and Phyllis Weikart. The art chapter benefited from the insights of Ursula Ansbach-Stallsmith, Chris Boisvert, Margaret Johnson, Beth Marshall, Kay Rush, and Eli Trimis. Their knowledge of theory and research, and the examples they provided from their own experience as practitioners, made everyone in this group a valued contributor. I thank them for their interest in the project and their insights into how intentional teachers can best help young children learn.

I also want to thank the rest of the editorial and production staff at NAEYC, particularly Bry Pollack, who, along with Carol, helped to shape and clarify the major messages in this book. It was evident from Bry's author queries that she sometimes knew better (or at least earlier) than I did what I was trying to say. I also appreciated her patience as I balanced, somewhat precariously, the schedule imposed by the editorial process with the other demands of work and life.

Finally, I thank the many teachers and young children with whom I have shared a love of learning in my 40 years as a developmental psychologist and educator. My admiration for their dedication, enthusiasm, and delight in discovery was the inspiration for the writing of this book. I hope that *The Intentional Teacher* is only one of many joint adventures on our journey to learn more about the human mind and how it understands and appreciates our wonderful and complex world.

Preface

# Why "The Intentional Teacher"?

When publications editor Carol Copple encouraged me to write a book for NAEYC, I took the opportunity to explore the difficult but timely issue of how to purposefully and effectively teach content to young children, particularly preschoolers. Although the ideas and strategies presented here apply across the early childhood spectrum, the book's main focus is preschool because these years are currently the subject of most active reconsideration, and my own work and experiences are primarily in this age range.

Questions about the best way to teach young children are hardly new. The subject waxes and wanes in public interest, but since 2001—and the passage of the federal No Child Left Behind Act—it has received renewed attention in the popular press as well as in the professional literature. The current controversy pits extreme interpretations of "child-initiated learning" (passive teacher) against "adult-directed instruction" (scripted lessons). Given the intensity of the battle, with young children often caught in the middle, finding a balanced position is in their best interests. Such a balance is also supported by research, as the Committee on Early Childhood Pedagogy, in its report *Eager to Learn*, concluded:

> Children need opportunities to initiate activities and follow their interests, but teachers are not passive during these [child-]initiated and directed activities. Similarly, children should be actively engaged and responsive during teacher-initiated and -directed activities. Good teachers help support the child's learning in both types of activities. (National Research Council 2000a, 8–9)

In the intermediate stance I advocate in this book, both young children and their teachers have active roles in the learning process.

In addition to raising questions about *how* to teach young children, educators are also rethinking *what* to teach them. They are debating what content, or subject matter, belongs in an early childhood curriculum. Most early childhood educators are now convinced that certain learning domains not prominent in early childhood education a decade ago, notably literacy and mathematics, should be essential parts of the preschool curriculum. But they remain committed to also meeting young children's needs for meaningful social, physical, and artistic experiences. Above all, teachers want to interact with children in ways that respect the children's different personalities, varying levels of development, diverse cultural backgrounds, and individual modes of inquiry and learning.

This book, then, is written for teacher-educators and reflective practitioners who, in grappling with the issue of how and what to teach young children, seek a balance between extremes.

Drawing on the latest theory and research, *The Intentional Teacher* sets forth the rationale for a blended approach that combines what I am calling "child-guided" and "adult-guided" learning experience.

I use the term *child-guided* to refer to experience that proceeds primarily along the lines of children's interests and actions, although teachers often provide the materials and other support. The term *adult-guided* I use to refer to experience that proceeds primarily along the lines of the teacher's goals, although that experience may also be shaped by children's active engagement. For example, children develop ideas about sinking and floating or what can be done with clay largely through exploration and investigation; but to learn the names of letters requires adults to provide this information. Regardless of whether children are engaged in child-guided or adult-guided experience, however, teachers always play a vital educational role by creating supportive environments and scaffolding learning.

Further, a central premise of the book is that from what we currently know about how young children learn, within each content area certain of its objectives or skills seem to be acquired or best acquired in the course of child-guided experience, whereas certain other objectives and skills seem to require adult-guided experience. But these two learning contexts are not mutually exclusive.

## This book's objectives

My first objective was to take a reasoned and reasonable look at the instructional divides in early childhood and attempt to find common ground in these heated debates. Proponents at the extremes may not be satisfied with where I come out. But for those focused not on ideology but on when and how various approaches and strategies are most effective, the material I present here should help us move forward in this endeavor. This book is therefore intended to *encourage reflection about our principles and our practices*.

The second and related objective is to *broaden our thinking about appropriate early curriculum content and related teaching strategies*. The new focus on early literacy, mathematics, and science is beneficial and essential; but we must still keep social-emotional, physical, and creative development in the curriculum too. Children need to acquire important information and skills in *all* these content areas, with teaching strategies pegged to how they can best understand and apply what they are learning.

Recent and past NAEYC publications, including the classic *Reaching Potentials: Appropriate Curriculum and Assessment for Young Children* (Bredekamp & Rosegrant 1992), emphasize that "child-initiated" learning never meant that teachers didn't teach. "Good early childhood programs are, of necessity, highly organized and structured environments that teachers have carefully prepared and in which teachers are in control. The difference is

that children are also actively involved and assume some responsibility for their own learning" (5).

While rejecting narrow drill-and-practice methods, NAEYC stresses the importance of setting learning objectives and does not believe curriculum should emerge solely from children's interests. To enable children to achieve the desired outcomes, teachers must keep these outcomes always in mind and plan on that basis. It is a grave misinterpretation of developmentally appropriate practice, as articulated by NAEYC, to think, for example, that by just letting children play, they will emerge literate in grade 3. Play and other contexts in which children explore and construct ideas are vital to their development and learning, but teachers must know what to do to enhance the quality of these child-guided experiences. Equally important, teachers must know what other experiences and what instruction children require in order to learn to read and write, as well as to acquire important knowledge and skills in other learning domains.

My third and primary objective for this book is to *provide specific ideas and strategies* for interacting with children in key subject areas. I will attempt to address the question of what content learning is likely to occur from children's own activities and what content usually requires direct adult instruction. As emphasized above, these are not mutually exclusive. For example, children's solitary and peer play present many opportunities for teachers to promote learning, and teachers can plan explicit instructional activities based on the interests they observe in children's spontaneous play. Nevertheless, an awareness of what content young children are more likely to acquire through one mode or the other can give adults a leg up as they strive to be planful, thoughtful, and intentional in their teaching.

## Basis for the book

Three sources of information provided the basis for the ideas in this book regarding how and what children learn and how adults support that learning. First and foremost, I undertook an extensive review of the literature in key subject domains. The publications I consulted covered child development theory, current research, and recommended preschool practices.

A second valuable resource was input from some 40 "informants." These project consultants included researchers, curriculum specialists, teacher-educators, and practitioners with expertise in one or more content areas. (Their names are listed in **Acknowledgments.**) In an informal written survey, conversations, or both with these individuals, I asked them to identify which content children seemed most likely to acquire in a child-guided learning context and which in an adult-guided context. I also solicited concrete examples from the respondents' own research, training, and teaching experiences. At least two informants in each domain then reviewed the chapter drafts.

In undertaking the survey, I frankly anticipated some resistance to my request to classify the content areas of each domain into those primarily acquired in child-guided experience and those largely acquired in adult-guided experience. Yet all the consultants thought the question was legitimate and were intrigued by the challenge it posed. Also surprising was the amount of consensus in their responses. Despite occasional differences in degree, I was never faced with the dilemma of resolving diametrically opposed answers. So, while the material derived from the surveys requires further systematic research, input from these consultants nevertheless provided "face validity" for the book's basic premise.

The third source of information was my own 35 years of professional experience in curriculum development, staff training, and educational research. Trained as a developmental psychologist, I cannot claim to be an expert in every content area covered in this book. However, in addition to input from the literature and helpful colleagues, I have through my association with High/Scope access to a library of observational data, anecdotal notes, audiovisual records, and commentary from diverse research, training, and program sites around the country and abroad. These resources provided a rich archive from which to draw real-life examples.

Given these multiple data sources, I trust the information presented here is an accurate reflection of current thinking and agreement in the field—at least until the field discovers that our current thinking about a particular content area needs to be revised.

## Scope and organization

To keep the project manageable, I did not undertake to consider all the domains in the early childhood curriculum in this volume. I wanted to offer this way of thinking about the intersection of content and pedagogy and explore it within a number of curriculum domains, but it was not my purpose to be exhaustive.

One area that I do not include is music and dance; instead I focus on the visual arts. Two areas that I deal with selectively but far from comprehensively are science and social studies. Because of the similar and parallel processes in math and science, I included scientific inquiry in **Chapter 4,** but I did not attempt to capture the full scope of science content. In the case of social studies, key aspects are subsumed within the area of social skills and understandings, but I have not tried to go beyond these to a fuller analysis of social studies content in **Chapter 5.** Also, "approaches to learning," rather than being treated as a separate content area, is embedded throughout the discussion of the various disciplines.

*The Intentional Teacher: Choosing the Best Strategies for Young Children's Learning* has two main parts. The first chapters lay out the meaning of "intentional teaching." **Chapter 1** introduces the concept of intentional teaching and explains the rationale for promoting children's learning of knowledge and skills in a blend of both child-guided and adult-guided experience. These terms and others used throughout the book are defined and discussed, in particular *intentional, teaching,* and *content.* **Chapter 2** briefly reviews the best practices that underlie all developmentally based programs as teachers engage children with content across diverse areas of early learning.

Next, curriculum chapters address the intentional teaching of content. They constitute the bulk of the book, exploring young children's learning and the intentional teacher's role in that learning in five domains: **Chapter 3, Language and Literacy; Chapter 4, Mathematics and Scientific Inquiry; Chapter 5, Social Skills and Understandings; Chapter 6, Physical Movement;** and **Chapter 7, The Visual Arts.** Each chapter begins with an overview of the area, and then identifies the knowledge and skills children seem to acquire primarily through child-guided versus adult-guided learning experience.

Many practical teaching strategies are presented and illustrated with anecdotal examples. The teaching strategies I offer here certainly do not constitute a complete list. Based on your own personal observations and teaching experiences, you will add your own strategies and continue to learn more about those recommended by other researchers and expert practitioners.

Because this book intends to explore new ground, each chapter ends with **Questions for Further Thought.** It is hoped these questions spur ongoing debate and inspire teacher-educators and practitioners to continuously examine their ideas and practices.

The book closes with the chapter **Reflections on Intentional Teaching.** First I offer general guiding principles of intentional teaching to help practitioners apply these ideas across all learning domains and situations. Finally, sharing a series of thoughts and beliefs that crystallized in my own mind while writing this book, I invite you to consider the value of intentional teaching in imparting knowledge and skills to young children.

To encourage you to continue exploring on your own, a **Resources** section is also provided.

I hope *The Intentional Teacher* opens minds, inspires further research, and spurs the sharing of ideas. If you develop a renewed appreciation for content and think about how you can intentionally engage young children with the world of knowledge and skills in each domain, then I will have accomplished my objectives in writing this book.

# Introducing Intentional Teaching

Preschoolers Tony and Salima are sitting on the floor, playing with the acorns Salima collected at outside time. Salima divides the acorns evenly between them. Their teacher sits on the floor next to them. Tony piles his acorns together, while Salima forms a large circle with hers. Tony says, "Hey, you got more than me!" Salima responds, "No, I don't. We each got the same." The teacher wonders aloud how they could find out whether they have the same number, and the children suggest counting the acorns.

**Tony:** 1, 2, 3, 4, 5, 6, 7, 8, 9, 10, 11, 12, 13, 14. (He lines up his acorns in a row as he counts.)

**Salima:** 1, 2, 3, 4, 5, 6, 7, 8, 9, 10, 11, 12, 13, 14. (She also lines up her acorns in a row.)

**Teacher:** You each have 14.

**Tony:** Yeah. We got the same.

**Teacher:** (Spreads Tony's acorns across the floor and puts Salima's in a pile.) Now who has more?

**Tony:** (Smiles.) I do!

**Salima:** No, you don't. We each got the same. See? (She counts her acorns and puts them in a row, then counts Tony's acorns and puts them in a row as well.)

**Teacher:** (This time she puts Tony's in a pile and spreads Salima's out across the floor.) Now who has more?

**Tony:** (Thinks for a moment.) Nobody's got more. We got the same!

**Salima:** (Smiles.) That's what I said!

This book is about how the *intentional teacher*, like the teacher in this opening vignette, acts with knowledge and purpose to ensure that young children acquire the knowledge and skills (content) they need to succeed in school and in life. Intentional teaching does not happen by chance; it is planful, thoughtful, and purposeful. Intentional teachers use their knowledge, judgment, and expertise to organize learning experiences for children; when an unexpected situation arises (as it always does), they can recognize a teaching opportunity and are able to take advantage of it, too.

Intentional teaching means teachers act with specific outcomes or goals in mind for children's development and learning. "Academic" domains (literacy, mathematics, and science) as well as "traditional" early learning domains (social and emotional, cognitive, physical, and creative development) all have important knowledge and skills that young children want and need to master. Intentional teachers therefore integrate and promote meaningful learning in *all* domains.

Intentional teaching requires wide-ranging knowledge about how children typically develop and learn. Teachers must have a repertoire of instructional strategies and know when to use a given strategy to accommodate the different ways that individual children learn and the specific content they are learning. At some times or for some content, children seem to learn best from *child-guided experience*—that is, they acquire knowledge and skills through their own exploration and experience, including through interactions with peers. At other times and for other content, children seem to learn best from *adult-guided experience*—that is, in set-up situations in which their teachers introduce information, model skills, and the like. (See the box opposite.)

The division between what is child-guided and what is adult-guided experience is not a rigid one. Rarely does learning come about entirely through a child's efforts or only from adult instruction. In any given subject, how a child learns will vary over time. For example, young children begin to build their speaking and listening skills through spontaneous and natural conversations (child-guided experience). However, they also learn syntax and vocabulary from the adults around them, and teachers often make a point of introducing new words and structures (adult-guided). Children also differ individually in how they like to learn. Some do a lot of exploring and thinking through problems on their own, while others very readily ask adults for information or help. But every child learns in both modes.

Similarly, the division of content into the knowledge and skills that seem to be best acquired primarily through child-guided experience versus those through adult-guided experience is not an exact process. For example, in typically developing children, basic language abilities clearly are acquired largely through child-guided learning experience (albeit, with linguistic input from the adults around them); children are born with the capacity to hear and reproduce the sounds of speech and are inherently motivated, as social beings, to communicate with others. By contrast, identifying the letters of the alphabet is something that children cannot do intuitively; as arbitrary creations of a culture, letter forms and their names clearly are learned in adult-guided experience. In other content areas, the division is not so clear. But even in cases where assignment to "primarily child-guided" versus "primarily adult-guided" is more difficult, knowledgeable

educators can make a determination that most will agree on. I found this consensus in consulting with my expert informants for this book.

These divisions are imprecise. But it is still useful for teachers to consider when and how to support children's own discovery and construction of knowledge, and when and how to convey content in teacher-guided activities and instruction. That consideration is a major focus of this book. *The Intentional Teacher* asks which type of learning experience is likely to be most effective in which content areas, and what teachers can do to optimize learning in that mode. It also emphasizes that regardless of whether children engage in child- or adult-guided experience, teachers always play a vital educational role by creating supportive environments and using instructional strategies to advance children's thinking to the next level.

In other words, both child-guided and adult-guided experience have a place in the early childhood setting. It is not the case that one is good and the other bad, or that one is developmentally appropriate and the other not. Intentional teachers understand this and are prepared to make use of either or both in combination, choosing what works best for any given subject, situation, or child.

# Intentional teaching terms

At the top of the daily message board, the teachers write the sentence: "Who is here today?" Underneath they draw a column of stick figures, and next to each figure they write the name of a child or adult in the class. Each day the teachers indicate who is absent that day by making an erasable X in front of that name. Each day they also draw stick figure(s) and write the name(s) of any guest(s) who will be visiting the classroom. If the guest is free to play with the children, they draw a toy, such as a ball or book, in the stick figure's hand. If the guest is there only to watch or observe, they draw a clipboard in the hand.

Each morning the class begins by talking about who is "present" and who is "absent." Then, together with their teachers, the children count the number of stick figures with no mark (in school) and those with a mark (not in school). They also discuss any guest(s) who are coming and whether that person will be a

# Child-guided experience + adult-guided experience = Optimal learning

An effective early childhood program combines *both* child-guided and adult-guided educational experiences. The terms "child-guided experience" and "adult-guided experience" do not refer to extremes (that is, they are not highly child-controlled or adult-controlled). Rather, adults play intentional roles in child-guided experience; and children have significant, active roles in adult-guided experience. Each takes advantage of planned or spontaneous, unexpected learning opportunities.

| | Child-guided experience . . . | |
|---|---|---|
| is *not* entirely child-controlled (with the teacher passive) | proceeds primarily along the lines of children's interests and actions, with strategic teacher support | is *not* entirely adult-controlled (with the children passive) |
| Example: Two children want to divide a bowl of beads equally between themselves. | | |
| The teacher does not get involved, even when the children become frustrated and begin to get angry at each other over who has more. | The children first try to make two equal piles by eyeballing them, but they are not satisfied. The teacher suggests they count their beads. They do so, and then move beads between their piles, count again, and make adjustments until the piles are equal. | The teacher counts the beads and divides by 2, telling the children how many beads each should take. |

| | Adult-guided experience . . . | |
|---|---|---|
| is *not* entirely child-controlled (with the teacher passive) | proceeds primarily along the lines of the teacher's goals, but is also shaped by the children's active engagement | is *not* entirely adult-controlled (with the children passive) |
| Example: The teacher wants the children to learn about shadows and their properties. | | |
| The teacher allows the children to deflect the focus from shadows to a discussion of what they want for Christmas. | The teacher plans the lesson and leads a small group in exploring shadows with flashlights and a sheet. The teacher encourages and uses the children's input; for example, when they want to make "animal" shadows. | The teacher controls all aspects of the lesson and delivers it to the whole group. |

"player" or a "watcher." Sometimes the teachers ask the children to "predict" whether an absent child will be back the next day. For example, after informing the class that Tommy had left yesterday for a three-day vacation, a teacher asks, "Do you think he will be here tomorrow?"

These teachers are acting with intention throughout this daily activity. They take advantage of both child-guided and adult-guided experience. The children are naturally curious about the members of their classroom community, and using a daily message board helps to solidify their social awareness. The children know everyone's name and notice when a peer is missing from their small-group table. This awareness the children come to on their own, that is, through child-guided experience. For adult-guided experience, the teachers use the children's knowledge and interest to introduce literacy ideas and processes—writing each person's name on the message board.

They also embed mathematical concepts and processes into using the board. There is classification (present versus absent; players versus watchers), counting (one-to-one correspondence of names and stick figures; tallying those with and without marks), and relational time concepts (yesterday, today, tomorrow). Children are asked to predict, a process used in science; later they see whether their prediction is confirmed.

Throughout the activity, adults and children engage in conversation, which enhances language development. Using adult-guided strategies, the teachers intentionally introduce new vocabulary words, such as *present* and *absent*. And the natural flow of talk, in which adults capitalize on the child-guided desire to communicate, boosts fluency.

Earlier in this chapter, I introduced the concept of "the intentional teacher" and organizing idea of "child- versus adult-guided experience" using three terms that reappear throughout the rest of the book. They are *intentional, teaching,* and *content,* and because they play such a key role in understanding

the chapters that follow, let me clarify now how I define them and how they fit together.

## The meaning of *intentional*

To be "intentional" is to act purposefully, with a goal in mind and a plan for accomplishing it. Intentional acts originate from careful thought and are accompanied by consideration of their potential effects. Thus an "intentional" teacher aims at clearly defined learning objectives for children, employs instructional strategies likely to help children achieve the objectives, and continually assesses progress and adjusts the strategies based on that assessment. The teacher who can explain just *why* she is doing what she is doing is acting intentionally—whether she is using a strategy tentatively for the first time or automatically from long practice, as part of an elaborate set up or spontaneously in a teachable moment.

Effective teachers are intentional with respect to many facets of the learning environment, beginning with the emotional climate they create. They deliberately select equipment and materials and put them in places where children will notice and want to use them. In planning the program day or week, intentional teachers choose which specific learning activities, contexts, and settings to use and when. And they choose when and how much time to spend on specific content areas and how to integrate them. All these teacher decisions and behaviors set the tone and substance of what happens in the classroom.

Intentionality refers especially to how teachers interact with children. Pianta defines intentionality as "directed, designed interactions between children and teachers in which teachers purposefully challenge, scaffold, and extend children's skills" (2003, 5). Berliner (1987; 1992) emphasizes that effective teaching requires intentionality in interactions with students, with an understanding of the expected outcomes of instruction. He summarizes research on the relationship between classroom environment and learning outcomes in a list of elements characteristic of good intentional teaching:

▶ **High expectations**—Teachers assume children are capable of achieving meaningful educational goals. Teachers who *expect* children to learn will deliberately engage in instructional activities to enhance children's knowledge and skills. Teachers' high expectations are also transmitted to children and parents, who then see themselves as active and capable participants in the learning process.

▶ **Planning and management**—Teachers have concrete plans to introduce subject matter and sequence children's learning. They can manage both individual behavior and group dynamics. While guiding the class toward defined objectives, teachers remain open to pursing related topics that arise and capture children's interest.

▶ **Learning-oriented classroom**—Children, as well as teachers, value the classroom as a place where learning occurs. When adults act with the intention of teaching, children can act with the intention of learning.

▶ **Engaging activities**—Teachers understand how children learn and that activities and ideas connected to children's own experience are more likely to capture their interest. They understand also that tasks pegged too far above or below children's current capabilities can undermine children's self-confidence in their ability to learn.

▶ **Thoughtful questioning**—Teachers pose questions to get insight into what children are thinking and to stimulate their thought processes. Rote questions and the thoughtless recitations they evoke, by contrast, not only fail to further children's learning but can derail it through boredom, resentment, or discouragement.

▶ **Feedback**—Children naturally look to teachers for supportive and evaluative feedback, and effective teachers know when and how to provide it. Presenting information, making comments, asking questions, identifying contradictions in children's

thinking, and posing "what if" challenges are hallmark strategies of intentionality. Unlike praise or criticism, which merely indicates "right" or "wrong" and may be interpreted as a sign of the teacher's personal (dis)approval of the child (e.g., "I like the way you solved that problem"), evaluative feedback focuses on learning rather than judgment ("Your idea to carry the cup on a tray solved the problem of water spilling on the floor").

# The meaning of *teaching*

Teaching is the knowledge, beliefs, attitudes, and especially the behaviors and skills teachers employ in their work with learners. An effective teacher is competent in three areas:

▶ **Curriculum**—the knowledge and skills teachers are expected to teach and children are expected to learn, and the plans for experiences through which learning will take place. Effective teachers know the subject matter covered in their program's curriculum and how children typically develop with regard to each domain addressed. Efforts to specify what preschool children need to know and be able to do have been made by states in their standards and by specialized professional organizations such as the International Reading Association (IRA & NAEYC 1998), Council on Physical Education for Children (NASPE 2000; 2002), and the National Council of Teachers of Mathematics (NCTM 2000; NAEYC & NCTM 2002).

▶ **Pedagogy**—the ways teachers promote children's development and learning. Effective teachers ensure that children experience a learning environment that promotes their development and learning in all areas of the curriculum. For starters, teachers establish a nurturing environment in which children are healthy and safe and feel secure. Beyond this basic responsibility, teachers respect children's differences, are inclusive with respect to special needs, relate to families, and use instructional approaches and strategies effectively to support children's learning and thinking. The essential elements of this component are highlighted in the

Teaching standard of NAEYC's Early Childhood Program Standards and Accreditation Criteria (2005) and in its book *Basics of Developmentally Appropriate Practice* (Copple & Bredekamp 2006). A quarter of a century of research, summarized in the panel report *Eager to Learn: Educating Our Preschoolers* (National Research Council 2000a), establishes that how adults interact with children is a significant determinant of developmental outcomes. More than any other variable, instructional interactions define a program's quality and its impact on children's intellectual and social development (Pianta 2003).

▶ **Assessment**—the process of determining how children are progressing toward expected outcomes of learning and development. Effective teachers know how to administer, interpret, and apply the results of assessment as they plan learning experiences for individual children and the class as a whole, and to monitor individual and group progress. Teachers share assessment results with parents to ensure home and school work together to support children's early development. (Assessment also is increasingly used for program and teacher accountability.) Some assessments are dictated by administrators or policy makers, then administered by teachers or outside specialists; other assessments are developed by individual teachers to fit their classroom needs. Guidelines for appropriate assessment of early learning are defined in a joint position of NAEYC and NAECS/SDE (2003) and in the Assessment standard of NAEYC's Early Childhood Program Standards and Accreditation Criteria (2005).

## The meaning of *content*

Content is the substance or subject matter that teachers teach, and therefore the object of children's learning. For the purposes of this book, *content* refers more specifically to the knowledge (certain vocabulary and concepts) and skills in an area of learning:

▶ **Vocabulary**—the language used in a content area. For example, reading vocabulary includes the names of the letters in the alphabet as well as words such as *alphabet, book, author,* and *rhyme.* Social development vocabulary includes words for feelings *(angry, happy)* and the language used to invite someone to play or to tell someone to stop throwing blocks. Visual arts vocabulary includes descriptors for color, shape, and texture, as well as names of artists, genres, and techniques.

▶ **Concepts**—the important ideas or principles within a content area, its "big ideas." For example, basic reading concepts include that books are read front to back, that print on a page is read from top to bottom and left to right, and that a relationship exists between spoken and written language. In social development, basic conflict resolution concepts include that it is better to solve problems by talking than hitting, and that solutions should be fair to everyone. Visual arts concepts include "big ideas" such as realism versus abstraction, and how cultural beliefs and values are represented through art.

▶ **Skills**—the specific abilities needed within a domain of learning and development. In reading, skills include recognizing the component sounds in words and the letters of the alphabet from their written shapes. Conflict resolution skills include expressing feelings, listening to others, and negotiating a compromise. Examples of visual arts skills are manipulating a paintbrush to make art, and observing and comparing the work of two artists.

Of course, there are knowledge (vocabulary and concepts) and skills that cut across one or more content areas, and early childhood education strives to maximize such broad and general learning. Because this book is organized by content area, however, the challenge for the intentional teacher is presented as identifying the "what" and "how to teach it" in each content domain. But, while this book looks at content in area-specific ways, in the classroom the cumulative result of a comprehensive and integrated education should be developing children's total vocabulary, enhancing their overall conceptual understanding of the world, and expanding their full repertoire of skills.

The field of early childhood education is sometimes accused of being anti-content. If the accusation has some truth to it, it's partly carryover from a time when much of the emphasis in early education was on sharing, cooperating, and playing nicely in order to transition children from home to a group setting. It's also partly developmental appropriateness misinterpreted, typified by well-meaning teachers who insist they cannot display the alphabet because it pressures young children to memorize their ABCs.

If early education has been criticized for neglecting content, primary education is accused of going the opposite way and ignoring social and emotional development (and, in response to current academic pressures, of reducing support in other domains such as physical development and the arts). This tension prompted NAEYC and NAECS/SDE to develop a joint position on curriculum for children birth through age 8 (1991; 2003). The 1991 statement aimed to address two basic problems of the time: "the 'early childhood error' (inadequate attention to the content of the curriculum) and the 'elementary error' (overattention to curriculum objectives, with less attention to the individual child)" (Bredekamp & Rosegrant 1992, 3).

Today, curriculum that meets the needs of young children is "comprehensive" (NAEYC & NAECS/SDE 2003):

> [It] encompasses critical areas of development including children's physical well-being and motor development; social and emotional development; approaches to learning; language development; and cognition and general knowledge; and subject matter areas such as science, mathematics, language, literacy, social studies, and the arts (more fully and explicitly for older children). (2)

Each of these content areas has its own vocabulary, concepts, and skills for children to master. Because young children typically are encountering these content areas for the first time, they need their teachers to "set the foundation for later understanding and success" (NAEYC 2001, 39).

\*     \*     \*

> If all children are to succeed, teachers need to create an effective balance between learning that's child initiated and learning that is guided by adults. (Hyson 2000, 60)

This book advocates a balanced approach, acknowledging that children learn through both child-guided and adult-guided experience and that teachers are most effective when they are able to choose among and apply any of a range of teaching approaches without going to the extremes. As shown in the box on page 3, that approach is neither laissez-faire, in which all learning is left to the child, nor entirely top-down, in which the child is seen as an empty vessel into which the teacher pours knowledge. Interactions between teacher and children are neither overly teacher-directed and didactic nor overly child-centered and left to chance. Instead, intentional teaching means systematically introducing content, in all domains, using developmentally based methods and respecting children's modes of learning.

Naturally, there will be individual differences. What some children get on their own or through interactions with peers, other children will encounter only through direct adult intervention. Therefore, the suggestions offered here cannot substitute for teachers observing and knowing the experiences and learning styles of the individual children in their classrooms.

At present, the early childhood field lacks a label for such a balance between child-centered and adult-directed approaches. "Eclectic" seems too random. "Combination" or "middle-of-the-road" are vague. In this book, I have suggested a term not original to me, but useful in this context, I believe. I suggest *intentional teaching*—because it says teachers play a thoughtful role during both child- and adult-guided experience. Whatever label we use, it is important that the words convey our commitment to child development principles as well as to educational content.

Defining and following such a balanced approach may help us to get past polarizing debates and reach more effective practice. Further, this approach will inspire us to continually update our knowledge and reflect on our practices—that is, to be intentional teachers whose methods ensure successful outcomes for young children.

## Questions for Further Thought

**1.** What terms other than *intentional teaching* might describe the kind of thoughtful, multifaceted instruction advocated in this book?

**2.** In what contexts does *child-guided* experience seem to predominate? In what contexts does *adult-guided* experience seem to predominate? In what situations do adults themselves learn primarily through their own efforts and in what situations is their learning primarily guided by others? How can understanding adult modes of learning inform how we intentionally teach children?

**3.** How can the early childhood field reverse public perception that it is "anti-content"?

**4.** How can the early childhood field educate the public that "content" for young children should cover all areas of learning, not just literacy, mathematics, and science?

**5.** What strategies, in addition to writing books such as this, can the early childhood field employ to encourage the adoption of intentional teaching?

# Best Practices for Intentional Teaching

2

"We haven't recorded many anecdotes lately about seriation," Peter, a teacher, says in daily team planning. "Let's plan an activity to encourage children to arrange things in a series or pattern."

Later that day Peter provides each child in his small group with flat ribbons in three widths and several colors, along with paper and a glue stick. He asks, "What could you do with these ribbons?" Amy makes a border on her paper that repeats the pattern red/white/red/white, but in random widths of ribbon. Namen makes a "wild man" whose hair alternates thin green and wide blue ribbons. Michael glues ribbons together in a long line in no particular pattern and says, "This is Snakey."

Josh announces he's going to make a snake too. He uses three thin red ribbons for the head, three medium red ribbons for the body, and three wide red ribbons for the tail because "It's got a big loud rattler at the end."

Peter is being an intentional teacher. He thinks about a content area (seriation—an aspect of mathematics) where not much is happening in the classroom. Then he plans a small group activity to focus children's attention on the topic. What is also noteworthy is how Peter chooses to engage children in learning about seriation. He doesn't just tell or show them that things come in different widths; he doesn't give them worksheets to copy ready-made patterns. Instead, he provides them with materials that lend themselves to being arranged in series or patterns, and then lets the children explore the materials.

As they worked, Peter also offered the children appropriate comments, questions, and challenges to stretch their thinking about all the ways that graduated sizes and patterns turn up in their lives. He did not see children's investigations into seriation as a one-time experience. Through the materials Peter made available daily and in subsequent group activities, children continued to explore these mathematical concepts through both child- and adult-guided experience.

Peter's teaching exemplifies early childhood education "best practices." That is, he had a goal in mind for the children's learning, he provided interesting and open-ended materials, he encouraged children to explore the materials and concepts at their own developmental level, he interacted with them to support and extend their discoveries, and he recognized the importance of repetition in mastering new knowledge and skills. These practices are based in child development theory, educational research, and the reflections of generations of teachers. We use them because we know they work. We value them because they reflect common ideals and beliefs about human development. And we advocate their use in every classroom, regardless of curriculum.

With the increased focus on early childhood programs in the past decade has come increased professional and public concern about teacher quality. Some policy makers have called for "teacher-proof" methods of instruction, and some curriculum developers have responded with packaged or scripted lessons that can be implemented with little training and almost robotic consistency. Understandably, many educators resist the idea that good teaching can be so mechanical or superficial: "Teachers must have a deep understanding of how children learn, as well as what is important for children to learn" (Espinosa 1992, 163).

Ready-to-use resources should not be dismissed out of hand, however, if the curriculum is designed with an understanding of how young children learn and it gives child as well as teacher opportunities to provide input. Such materials can offer a welcome and useful starting point for the novice teacher, or even an experienced teacher approaching an unfamiliar subject area. But they do not relieve teachers of the need to be intentional. Teachers must still decide how to apply the curriculum to individual and groups of children. And with time and experience, most teachers are able to bring more of their own creativity to teaching.

# An overview of best practice

Best practices require us to always be thinking about what we are doing and how it will foster children's development and produce real and lasting learning—the definition of intentional teaching. Much has been said about what constitutes early childhood best practice and the principles underlying it (particularly Bredekamp & Copple 1997; Hyson 2003; NAEYC 2005), too much to be covered thoroughly here. What this chapter does provide, however, is an overview of how intentional teachers use these best practices in the classroom.

Intentional teachers apply best practice principles in six key areas of responsibility. One of them, planning *curriculum* (the content of learning), is dealt with extensively in **Chapters 3–7**. Three others—structuring the physical learning *environment*, *scheduling* the program day, and *interacting* with children—concern how teachers implement the curriculum in the classroom. These are each reviewed below, comprehensively but through the focused lens of intentional teaching.

The remaining two areas—building relationships with *families* and *assessing* children's development—are also reviewed, but even more narrowly with regard to their intentional aspects. The section on families discusses communicating with them about your program's balance between adult-guided and child-guided experience, as well as encouraging families to also be intentional in providing their children with both kinds of experience outside the classroom. With respect to assessment, the focus in this chapter is on using results to intentionally plan for children's learning and to identify areas for your own professional development. (For further guidance on families and assessment, as well as the other topics addressed in this chapter and the book, see the **Resources** list.)

# Structuring the physical learning environment

The first thing a teacher does, even before the children arrive, is set up the classroom. Creating this setting should be undertaken with careful consideration of children's development, curriculum goals, and teaching strategies. The setting must promote not only children's learning but also their pleasure in learning and the motivation to pursue it. Because the classroom is a teacher's main work space, it should be welcoming and inspiring to her, too.

## 1. Provide a safe and healthy indoor and outdoor environment

To be licensed, a program must comply with applicable standards for sanitation, ventilation, lighting, and temperature control. This is a primary responsibility of the teacher as well as the program (NAEYC 2003; 2005). In particular, children's safety depends on teachers being able to see and hear what is happening from anywhere in the room.

The classroom and outdoor play area should have adequate space to move freely. Programs commonly consider the children's need for space and mobility, but teachers also must have space to move with children, join their play, and take advantage of learning opportunities as they arise.

## 2. Organize the space in interest areas or centers

Distinctive areas encourage different types of activity and expand the range of content children are enticed to pursue. They also promote thoughtful decision making, as children survey the room and choose where, with what, and with whom they want to engage. Taken together, a program's indoor and outdoor areas should address all aspects of children's development and allow groups of various sizes to play in each area. It should accommodate activities of different noise and physical energy levels, including offering places where children can find quiet and solitude during the day. Relative position should also be considered; for example, art area near a sink, quiet and noisy areas separated from each other.

Typical indoor areas might include books (and other materials for early reading and writing); blocks (and related building materials); house; visual art; music; dress-up; mathematics; science; sand and water; puzzles, games, and toys; computers (although these may be in the writing area). Outdoor spaces might include exercise equipment (climbers, slides, tricycles); open areas for moving in various ways; areas for gardening, investigating wildlife (plant and animal), exploring art in nature.

## 3. Supply plentiful and diverse equipment and materials

Good teachers provide sturdy, open-ended materials that children can use in many ways and that reflect the diversity of their homes and communities. While most materials should be present each day to encourage in-depth exploration, some may be rotated periodically to expand children's experiences. Reintroducing familiar materials can also inspire new uses. Items should not only look attractive but also have different textures, smells, sounds, and tastes. Materials that can be handled ("manipulatives," such as blocks, beads, shells, puzzles, dough) allow children to *explore* with all their senses, *transform* (change), and *combine* (put together and take apart). Teachers should label and store equipment and materials so they are visible and easily accessible to children. It encourages

---

### How the Learning Environment Affects the Complexity of Play

When teachers set up their classrooms, they commonly worry about matters of health and safety. Less obvious, but no less true, is that creating a safe and secure learning environment can also affect how children play in the setting. Children's feelings of security and confidence in a space affect the complexity and length of their play:

> When children are in a large space, they feel small in comparison to their surroundings, and time seems to pass more slowly for them. When children are in a playhouse, in a play yard tent, or under a table, they feel large in comparison to their surroundings, and attention seems to be sustained. . . . Perception of the size of the space in which children play affects the quality of the play and thus the potential for learning. Altering space to make children feel large in relation to their environment may enable children to enter complex play more quickly and to continue complex play for longer periods of time. (Tegano et al. 1996, 136, 138).

---

children's initiative and independence when they can find, use, and return supplies on their own.

Often it is better to have fewer different types of items, but more of the same or similar things. (An obvious exception is large or expensive equipment, such as computers.) Young children are eager to get started on an activity, and waiting for a turn is difficult for them. Boredom, loss of interest, and frustration from waiting can make for unhappy and unproductive play. Multiple sets of materials also have other advantages. Children who are all working with the same materials are more likely to compare and share observations about their experiences. The exchange promotes social interaction and provides insights, as children note what their peers do, see, and say.

## 4. Display work created by and of interest to children

Seeing concrete reminders of their own work prompts children to recall and reflect on what they and their peers have done. It can also lead them to expand on their ideas and pursue an interest or project on subsequent days. Walls, shelves, and pedestals are all places to display examples of children's artwork and emergent writing, products of their science experiments and discoveries such as models or simple charts, rules they create for a game they invent, family and class photographs, mementos of field trips, turn-taking lists for distributing snacks or choosing a song, and so on. The displays should be changed periodically, so "children's recent works predominate" (NAEYC 2005, Criterion 3.A.06). Displays that have been up too long cease to attract attention.

Displays should focus on the activities, products, and interests of the children, not the adults, which means information for parents and teachers should be posted somewhere other than the classroom. But displays of children's work are an excellent way to share with parents, administrators, visitors, and others what is happening in the program.

---

### Reflecting Cultural Diversity in Classroom Materials

Reflecting cultural diversity in the classroom isn't just displaying unusual objects that set one group apart from another or celebrating holidays. Here are some ideas for making sure all the areas of your classroom are as diverse as the children and families in the program.

Art area—Crayons in different skin tones; materials that showcase and encourage children to make the arts and crafts found in their community (e.g., ceramic bowls and statues, clay to make pottery; woven wall hangings and placemats, yarn and frame looms)

Block/construction area—Animal figures representing typical and unusual pets (e.g., dogs and cats, snakes, pigs); toy vehicles representing different types of jobs (e.g., construction equipment, farm tractors, taxicabs); diverse building materials used locally (e.g., wood, bricks, thatching grasses, boards made of recycled plastic)

Book area—Books in languages spoken at home; books depicting a variety of family constellations, races and ethnicities, cultures, and ages (including the elderly); books showing men and women engaged in different activities at home, work, and leisure; books depicting children and adults with various disabilities

House area—Multiracial boy and girl dolls; kitchen utensils and food packages reflective of those in children's homes; dress-up clothing with items from different cultures and occupations; child-size disability aids (e.g., walkers, crutches, eyeglasses with lenses removed)

Music area—Tapes with songs reflective of children's cultures; musical instruments used in different cultures

Science area—Real examples and/or photos of plant and animal wildlife native to the area; tools and other items related to local weather patterns (e.g., for snow removal, sun protection, rainy season, hurricane preparedness)

---

# Scheduling the program day

The intentional teacher's goal here is to offer children a rich and varied mix of learning opportunities, within a supportive framework of routine.

## 1. Establish a consistent yet flexible daily routine

Routine provides young children with emotional stability and security. They know what will happen, when, and what is expected of them. Routines such as morning greetings can soothe any anxiety young children might feel in separating from their parents: "[It] may seem like an obvious ritual, but being fully greeted in a conscious, sincere way sets a positive tone for a child's day" (Evans 2005, 50–51).

The number and nature of the day's components should be carefully chosen, in the same way that areas and materials should strike a balance between too much and too little. Dividing the day into a few meaningful blocks of time avoids too frequent transitions, which can be disruptive for young children. The sequence and length of activities also provide children with important experiences in temporal relationships and helps to develop early mathematics concepts. A reasonable amount of flexibility is also needed to allow teachers to capitalize on spontaneous teaching opportunities and extend children's interests.

Finally, recurring routines let children revisit materials and repeat activities. In our eagerness to broaden their experiences, we sometimes forget children need to deepen their understanding of familiar materials and subjects too.

A consistent routine also gives teachers a framework for planning, as they think about how to integrate content into each component of the day. For example, children can explore number through one-to-one matching at greeting time (counting the number of children present), choice time (tallying how many children are playing in each area), and small group (charting how many children use each paint color). The daily structure also prompts teachers to think about content broadly so they can include the full range of cognitive domains (introducing different subjects across activities) and social components (altering group size and composition; creating "communities" of shared interests and experiences) over the course of a day.

Every day some parts of the schedule should offer children options, allowing them to share control with teachers. Even during adult-led activities, they should be able to count on having choices; for example, in how to use the materials or with whom to partner.

## 2. Allow for a variety of types of activities

Teachers should schedule each program day to offer opportunities for choice and self-directed play (including time for children to make plans and anticipate what they will do), problem solving, cleaning up and taking care of individual needs (including self-help skills), group activities in which teachers introduce key concepts and skills, indoor and outdoor play, socializing with adults and peers, sharing snacks or meals, naps (depending on children's ages and the length of the program day), transitions, and consolidating and reflecting on learning. A range of learning activities allows children to learn content in different modes and make meaningful connections.

A consistent schedule means the sequence of components is predictable; but what happens within any one component should vary from day to day, depending on the children's interests and teachers' objectives. This variety is important to accommodate children's range of interests and ways of learning, so that all children can find many engaging things to do throughout the day. Also, variety, like consistency, allows children to share control with adults.

At the same time, good teachers know that too much variety can overwhelm young children. A varied routine does not mean trying to cram every possible experience into each day. Rather, the daily schedule, executed repeatedly over weeks and months, creates the structure within which content can be varied, sequenced, repeated, supported, and extended.

### 3. Use a variety of groupings

Children need opportunities to work alone, in parallel and in pairs, and in small and large groups. Some groupings happen spontaneously. Others, particularly small and large groups, should also be created by teachers to encourage different instructional opportunities. Most obviously, groups present situations in which social learning occurs as children watch, listen, play, solve problems, and share their observations with peers. Group times also provide many rich opportunities for language development. Children hear new words introduced by teachers or used by peers, and refine their own ways of speaking to more effectively communicate their needs and intentions to others. Groupings of various size are also another way that young children become aware of quantity—one of me, two of us, a few children in a small group, lots of children in a large group.

Effective teachers attend to individual and group dynamics. From observing children's comfort levels and preferences with various groupings, they can plan strategies to ensure each child feels secure and supported in trying out new or uncomfortable situations. For example, a teacher might put quiet children in the same small group, where they might be more likely to speak up knowing they won't be talked over by louder, more verbal children. Such strategies give each child the opportunity for a rewarding and positive experience during each segment of the day.

### 4. Allow just enough time for each type of activity

The time allotted to each activity should not be so short that children are frustrated in achieving their objectives (exploration as well as production), nor so long that they become impatient or bored. Children's individual preferences and developmental levels will naturally vary. For example, toddlers cannot sustain free choice time as long as preschoolers can. Another way to accommodate variations is by overlapping time frames. For example, one child might need a few extra minutes to finish a free choice art activity while the other children wash up for snack. Quick eaters could clean up and go outside with one teacher while slower eaters linger and chat with a second teacher.

This flexibility can make transitions smoother and avoid the abruptness and loss of control that can upset young children. When a classroom is beset with behavior problems, often it is the schedule that needs managing, not the children. At other times, the content, not the length of the activity, needs to be adjusted. Perhaps children are being asked to accomplish too much, or the task hasn't captured their interest.

## Interacting with children

Children's interactions with teachers and peers can determine, more than any other program feature, what they learn and how they feel about learning (National Research Council 2000a; Pianta 2003). In the early years, learning is largely a social process. Connecting with young children means recognizing that relationships are the basis of instruction and learning (NAEYC 2003, 35). Even children's encounters with materials are often mediated by others. For that reason, it is critical that teachers understand how children develop and offer them the kinds of support and encouragement that promotes growth and progress.

Below are the core strategies by which intentional teachers establish an interactive environment that is conducive to children's learning and development.

### 1. Meet basic physical needs

All children have basic physical needs regarding food and nutrition, toileting, physical and psychological comfort, and safety and health. Having one's essential needs met, beginning in infancy, forms the basis for the fundamental trust all humans need to grow and develop. Attending to children's needs for physical care also helps meet their psychological need to feel safe and secure.

Children's needs change through their early years, but the importance of adults in mediating their progress remains. Infants need feeding, changing, cuddling, and playing; toddlers venture out to explore on their own, but check back frequently to verify their trusted caregiver is still there and available. Three- and 4-year-olds can function independently or with peers for longer periods of time, if they have established this basic trust early on. The security of knowing that caring adults will meet their basic needs prepares young children to venture beyond the familiar, setting the stage for all future educational experiences.

## 2. Create a warm and caring atmosphere

Children feel secure and successful when teachers interact positively with them, both verbally (e.g., listening, conversing with interest and respect, using a calm voice to problem solve) and nonverbally (e.g., smiling, hugging, nodding, making eye contact, getting down to children's eye level).

Warm, sensitive, and nurturing interactions are more beneficial for children's development than harsh, critical, or detached adult behavior (e.g., Kontos et al. 1994; Whitebook, Howes, & Phillips 1989). Effective teachers "create a climate of mutual respect for children by being interested in their ideas, experiences, and products" and "develop individual relationships with children by providing care that is responsive, attentive, consistent, comforting, supportive, and culturally sensitive" (NAEYC 2005, Criterion 3.B.03). Such behaviors promote "positive development and learning for all children" (NAEYC 2003, 35).

## 3. Encourage and support language and communication

Teachers can support children's language development with many different strategies, including taking conversational turns with them, observing and listening while children take time to formulate and express their thoughts, and asking questions (even open-ended ones) sparingly so children can initiate as well as respond in conversation. Young children need to be exposed to a rich and varied vocabulary and the rules of discourse in order to develop the language facility that underlies the later acquisition of literacy, interpersonal problem-solving skills, and other cognitive and social abilities.

Children talk when they have something to say. Providing children with interesting materials and experiences they want to talk about, therefore, is a good way to promote language. Teachers should also establish a climate in which children feel free to talk (no sitting in place with hands folded and mouths shut!). Teachers should encourage children to talk with one another (see item 7 below), and be sure they themselves converse with all the children, including those who are quiet or whose habits or demeanor makes them harder to talk with. These strategies will increase the amount and complexity of children's language and create a classroom in which lively conversations accompany busy hands and minds.

## 4. Encourage initiative

"Initiative is the capacity for children to begin and then follow through on a task" (Hohmann & Weikart 2002, 45). From an early age, children signal and act on their intentions. An infant reaches for a bright toy; a toddler holds out a cup and asks for "more juice." Preschoolers develop and articulate more elaborate intentions, such as playing in the block area and building a house. With freedom to express choices and engage in successful undertakings, children gain the confidence to continue learning under their own power and initiative.

Teachers create the kinds of learning opportunities that encourage initiative by respecting children's interests and choices. They should be enthusiastic about what children are doing, follow their lead, and participate as partners in their play. Teachers should welcome children's ideas during group activities as well as individual choice times. They should give children opportunities to make plans and reflect on what they have learned. "When children plan, carry out, and review their own learning activities, their behavior is more purposeful and they perform better on language and other intellectual measures" (Epstein 2003, 30).

## 5. Introduce information and model skills

It would certainly be inaccurate to say that content (i.e., substantive learning in different subject areas) was absent from the early childhood curriculum

## Including Children with Special Needs in Classroom Activities

Children with special needs present specific challenges when it comes to including them in program activities. Below are some suggestions for children with different types of needs.

**Learning disabilities**—Provide extra help organizing information and performing tasks:

• Eliminate or reduce background noise and clutter as much as possible.

• Post picture and word sequences of schedules and routines in prominent places.

• Make suggestions that give children clues or choices for the next step in an activity.

• Have quiet places in the room.

• Show children how to use the tools and materials in the classroom.

• Keep transitions to a minimum.

**Cognitive impairments and developmental delays**—Accommodate a slower pace of learning. Concrete modeling and demonstration are key strategies:

• Allow lots of time for children to respond with actions or speech.

• Use lots of repetition and demonstration throughout the day.

• Give frequent feedback.

• Combine visual and verbal directions; increasingly use verbal cues alone as children become better able to interpret them.

• Sing directions for a task.

**Speech and language impairments**—Communication in any form is an important goal. Plan experiences that will motivate children to give and receive messages:

• Verbalize what children are telling you with their actions.

• Give only one verbal direction at a time.

• Reduce background noise as much as possible; avoid background music.

• Provide language experiences with repetitive sounds, phrases, and sentences, such as simple poetry, repetitive stories, and action stories and songs.

• Show pictures of what children have just been doing to encourage them to talk about it.

**Hearing impairments**—Use visual attention-getters to help orient children to what is happening:

• Avoid background noise.

• Face children whenever possible; speak using a clear voice and facial expressions.

• Use manual gestures or motions when talking, singing, or telling stories.

• Show objects to demonstrate what you are talking about.

• Sing along with song tapes to encourage children to lip read.

• Learn basic signs (for *yes, thank you, please, stop,* and so on) to communicate with children and model appropriate social behavior.

**Visual impairments**—Encourage use of hearing and touch to explore the environment:

• Keep pathways in the room wide, consistently located, and free of obstructions.

• Describe what you are doing as you do it; include your actions as well as things.

• Use large, clear, tactile labels (including Braille) to identify areas, tools, and materials.

• Use play dough and other modeling, molding, and sensory materials.

---

before now. However, the recent trend has been to both expand the content and more clearly articulate goals or educational outcomes for all domains of early learning. Some ambivalence about content remains, however; early childhood teachers are not always sure how to provide information and model skills without violating the principles of developmentally appropriate practice.

Yet, providing content by explicitly introducing information or modeling specific skills is not only permissible but essential. "Children construct their own understanding of concepts, and they benefit from instruction by more competent peers and adults" (Bredekamp & Copple 1997, 23). This book seeks to help teachers recognize that even content that can only be taught by telling and showing

- Provide many put together/take apart toys and building sets throughout the room.

- Provide many tactile-auditory experiences, and use language in conjunction with them.

- Encourage children to explore all parts of an object; discuss part-whole relationships.

- Help children feel motions; for example, put your hands on a child's shoulders while he or she is swaying to music.

- Demonstrate activities that involve spatial concepts such as on/off, up/down, and in/out.

- Encourage sighted children to be observers for visually impaired children by explaining what they are doing and how. (This is mutually beneficial.)

- Encourage other children to identify themselves and their actions as they approach their classmate.

- Record each child's voice and have children guess who it is. This helps visually impaired children match names with voices and is fun for the other children too.

**Orthopedic impairments**—Match strategies to the children's range of physical disabilities:

- Make pathways wide enough to accommodate wheelchairs, body boards, and other devices.

- Keep the classroom uncluttered, with easy-to-reach shelves, cubbies, sink, and so on.

- Use lots of nonlocomotor movement activities (i.e., anchored movement such as moving the arms with feet in place).

- Provide ample space at group time for children to maneuver.

- Modify classroom tools by adding handles or grips that are easier to grasp (e.g., add triangular grips to brushes and felt pens, rubber bicycle handles over doorknobs).

- Encourage other children to provide physical assistance when asked (picking up a crayon, closing a child's fingers around a handle).

- Plan floor activities for all the children.

- Use adapted battery or electric toys (such as remote-controlled cars) that allow children to control the toy's movement.

**Emotional disturbances**—Children who have frequent behavioral difficulties, mood swings, and problems forming relationships need predictable routines and extra interpersonal support:

- Shadow children inconspicuously, offer encouraging smiles and phrases.

- Develop mutually understood signals for when the child should stop a behavior or needs help.

- Provide for calming activities with sensory materials, water play equipment, and soothing music.

- Allow a withdrawn child to watch from a "safe" distance.

- Prevent aggressive children from hurting others; this benefits everyone.

- Provide soft lighting and cozy spaces.

- Label the feelings behind the child's actions; help children to label feelings themselves.

- Read "angry" books and discuss them individually and with the group.

- Model coping strategies for when a child feels overwhelmed.

- Be sure to give the withdrawn child as much attention as the aggressive child.

---

**Source:** K. Gerecke and P. Weatherby, "High/Scope Strategies for Specific Disabilities," in *Supporting Young Learners 3: Ideas for Child Care Providers and Teachers*, ed. N.A. Brickman, 255–66 (Ypsilanti, MI: High/Scope Press, 2001). Adapted, by permission, from pp. 255–65.

things to children (direct instruction) can be included in the early childhood curriculum by using teacher-guided strategies appropriate to young children's developmental levels and learning styles. Rather than quashing children's initiative and spirit of inquiry, such intentional teaching can give them the tools to spark further discovery and mastery.

## 6. Acknowledge children's activities and accomplishments

It is preferable for teachers to show that they value children's work through interest and encouragement rather than praise, which can have negative effects. Praise invites comparison and competition, raises anxiety about taking risks, and limits children's ability to evaluate their own work. By contrast, encouragement promotes initiative and self-confidence and develops children's ability to look at their own work objectively rather than just trying to please.

Effective teachers know many ways to recognize and encourage children's intentions and accomplishments: to comment specifically on what the child has done; ask questions to learn more about the child's plans and thoughts (not stock questions to which the adult knows the answer, but authentic queries to elicit information); repeat the child's ideas and imitate his actions; write down or tape the child's ideas; draw connections between the child's current words and actions and events or information that came up at other times or places; refer children to one another for information or assistance; display children's work; and share the child's ideas, contributions, and products with peers, other staff, and family members.

## 7. Support peer interactions

Preschoolers typically are highly motivated to establish and maintain relationships with their peers as well as adults. These relationships offer multiple benefits. Peers can become partners and collaborators in play, allow children to try out the roles of leader and follower, serve as sources of information and entertainment, help children establish a sense of identity by their growing awareness of similarities and differences, and provide emotional support, especially when adults are not available.

The primary way teachers facilitate peer relationships is by themselves building authentic, supportive, and reciprocal relationships with children. By treating children with kindness and respect and engaging in authentic conversations with them, teachers set the tone for how children interact with one another. The physical setting the teacher creates in the classroom can also contribute to positive peer relationships. Classroom materials should invite collaborative play (e.g., rocking boats, large wagons, long jump ropes, large hollow blocks and other building materials, equipment that takes two or more children to carry or operate). There should

also be enough space in each interest area for a number of children to play together.

Another strategy teachers can use to support peer relationships is maintaining stable groupings—that is, the same children meeting as a group over an extended period of time, at least several months. Children who are in sustained experiences with the same group of peers develop greater social competence than those in shifting configurations (Corsaro & Molinari 2005; Howes 1988). Teachers should also watch for peer relationships that develop at other scheduled times (choice time, outside time), and offer children who have gravitated toward each other opportunities to interact throughout the daily routine.

Finally, teachers can refer children who have questions or need help solving problems to their classmates for assistance. For example, a child having difficulty with a certain piece of equipment can be referred to a classmate who has mastered it, or two children can collaborate to figure it out. Teachers help children appreciate the contributions of their peers, for example, by giving them the task of generating a group story, rhyme, or chant. All these strategies encourage children to listen to and build on one another's ideas.

## 8. Encourage independent problem solving

Teachers who encourage children to identify problems and try out solutions on their own are helping them develop a range of cognitive, social, and physical skills. A teacher who doesn't let children struggle at all or who intervenes too quickly robs them of the chance to see themselves as competent and independent people. On the other hand, if a teacher waits too long or never offers help, children can become anxious or discouraged.

Effective teachers use several techniques to find the right balance. First, they encourage the child to acknowledge and describe the challenge he has encountered, whether with materials, peers, routines, or expectations. By waiting for the child to articulate the problem, teachers foster both cognitive and language development.

Second, effective teachers are patient, letting the child generate and try out solutions. Children get more satisfaction and learn more by figuring things out on their own. Then, as long as a child's solution satisfies her without causing problems for others, it should be accepted.

Finally, effective teachers are sensitive to instances where the child has tried but is unsuccessful after several attempts. A well-timed suggestion can help ("Have you looked for another truck in the block area?"). But sometimes teachers' direct assistance is needed to prevent frustration or harm (e.g., undoing a difficult knot, holding a toy two children are fighting over while they work out a solution). Even when the teachers intervene, though, they offer the child choices or let him follow through on his own, to support his self-image as an independent problem-solver.

# Building relationships with families

Some dimensions of best practice with families reside with the program rather than the teacher (e.g., including parents on advisory boards, linking families with community services, helping families transition to other educational settings). Teachers themselves can also do many things to encourage parents to participate actively in their children's learning. These include providing many different kinds of opportunities for parents to become involved in the program; encouraging parents to participate in program activities with their children, such as classroom volunteering; and interacting both formally and informally with parents. The **Resources** list contains sources of many helpful ideas for working with parents in all these ways.

This section focuses on two additional teacher strategies for involving families that relate most directly to intentionality. One is helping parents understand how a classroom curriculum that balances child-guided and teacher-guided experience promotes early development that is both broad and deep. The other is encouraging parents to themselves be intentional in the range of learning opportunities they provide their children at home.

## 1. Exchange information about the curriculum and how it promotes children's development

Effective teachers share curriculum information with parents in various ways, including meetings,

---

## Trusting Children to Solve Problems on Their Own

Our first reaction may be to solve children's problems for them, but they learn more when we help them define the problem and agree on a solution. In this example, the children come up with an original idea on their own.

**Teacher:** (Kneeling between two boys with an arm around each.) You look angry, Lyle; and Hank, you seem really upset. (The boys nod in agreement.) What's the problem?

**Lyle:** I want to be the dad. I said so first.

**Hank:** You're always the dad. I want to be big.

**Lyle:** I'm the biggest, so huh! You can't be the dad. You're too little.

**Teacher:** So the problem is, Lyle, you want to be the dad, and Hank, you want to be the dad too. (Both boys shake their heads yes.) What can we do to solve this problem?

**Lyle:** I could be the dad today, and then you can be the dad the next day.

**Hank:** Well, I could be the dad today.

**Teacher:** It sounds like you both want to be the dad today.

**Lyle:** We don't need two dads. Hank, you could be the ladder guy *and* wear the tool belt!

**Hank:** And the gloves?

**Lyle:** OK, the gloves. (Both boys smile.)

**Teacher:** So, Lyle, you're going to be the dad, and Hank, you're going to be the ladder guy who wears the tool belt and the gloves.

The boys nod yes and go off to play. When the teacher checks in on them later, the dad and the ladder guy have built a "swamp boat" and are giving rides to the other children.

---

newsletters, mail and email, and lending libraries of books and videotapes. They explain the curriculum and what children learn; for example, by posting signs in each area that list the kinds of learning taking place there. Good teachers also answer parents' concerns, including their anxieties about their child's school readiness. After setting goals together with parents, teachers can document and review with them how their children are progressing toward those goals.

Depending on their own experiences as schoolchildren, parents may expect teachers to use highly directive teaching strategies, as evidence that their child is being taught the information and skills he needs to enter kindergarten. When parents look for obvious signs of such instruction (such as worksheets) and don't find them, it is even more important for teachers to explain to parents how they are using a balance of child- and adult-guided experience to help children learn. Parental concerns should not be dismissed, nor should parents be seen as the "enemy" of appropriate practice. Rather, they should be respected, and teachers should emphasize the commonalities between home and school goals for children's education. Displaying and explaining the work children are doing (e.g., writing samples, charts, experiments, constructions) will further help parents recognize evidence that the learning they care about is occurring.

### 2. Provide information about how to extend learning at home

Parents need concrete and feasible suggestions about what behaviors and activities they can use with their children at home to consolidate and extend the learning taking place in the classroom. Effective teachers provide parents with simple strategies they can use during everyday interactions with their children. Parents are more likely to follow through on ideas that fit into daily home routines (e.g., during shopping, mealtimes, bedtime). If teachers find that parents don't follow through, they need to "evaluate and modify these approaches rather than assuming that families 'are just not interested'" (NAEYC 2003, 32).

For example, language is the underpinning of literacy. Teachers can offer parents many suggestions for carrying on conversations with their children as they drive them to school or wheel them down the supermarket aisles. Similarly, daily reading is essential. If bedtime is not feasible (e.g., the parent works an evening shift), teachers can problem solve with parents to identify other times of the day when they can read to their children.

Opportunities for early mathematics experiences also abound in the home setting—setting the table (one-to-one correspondence), sorting laundry (classification and seriation), and taking a walk (looking for numerals on street signs and buildings). Helping parents identify these naturally occurring learning situations will make them feel they are an active and intentional part of their children's learning. If they think of themselves as frontline teachers, parents are more likely to continue in this role when their children enter elementary school.

In addition to sending suggestions home, teachers also can help families exchange ideas and network with one another. This approach acknowledges parental expertise and can greatly expand the range of strategies and resources families can draw upon.

## Assessing children's development

Assessment, appropriately implemented and interpreted, provides valuable information to teachers, policy makers, and researchers, as well as families. "Ongoing . . . assessments enable [teachers] to appreciate children's unique qualities, to develop appropriate goals, and to plan, implement, and evaluate effective curriculum" (NAEYC 2003, 33). Best practices require teachers to demonstrate a range of competencies with respect to assessment. Among them are to objectively document children's progress on a regular and consistent basis, and to measure progress using only developmentally appropriate and validated assessment tools. Guidelines and strategies for carrying out these assessment activities are detailed in items in the **Resources** list.

This section focuses on two other aspects of assessment. One is how teachers can intentionally apply the results to understand children's development and plan appropriate ways to further their individual and group learning. The other is how, with the intention of helping children grow, teachers can use assessment results to enhance their own professional development.

## 1. Use assessment results to plan for individual children and the group as a whole

In addition to collecting objective assessment data (that is, based on reliable and verifiable observed behavior, not subjective impressions), teachers should also be able to interpret and apply it objectively. The primary way in which effective teachers use assessment is to "make sound decisions about individual and group curriculum content, teaching approaches, and personal interactions" (NAEYC 2005, Criterion 4.14). Valid assessments paint an accurate picture of what children know and can do. A teacher's objective observations also provide information about how individual children, and the group as whole, engage with new materials, other people, and ideas. Putting these pieces of knowledge together, an intentional teacher can choose the best combination of child-guided and adult-guided instructional strategies to scaffold further learning.

## 2. Use assessment results to identify areas for professional development

Teachers and their supervisors can also use the results of child assessments to identify areas where professional development might help teachers better meet children's educational needs. That is, by enhancing their own understanding and expertise—of specific content areas, in using instructional strategies, or both—teachers will be able to more effectively plan and execute activities that advance children's knowledge and understanding. For example, if a valid literacy assessment shows that children are progressing in identifying letter names and sounds but not in comprehension, a workshop

on how to encourage recall and prediction during book reading can help teachers develop these skills in children. Similarly, if objective observations indicate the class regularly loses interest at circle time, teachers can consult resources on designing and implementing large group times to improve this type of learning experience.

# Using best practices to support intentional teaching

Best practices and intentional teaching work in synergy. The mission of the intentional teacher is to ensure that young children acquire the knowledge and skills they need to succeed in school and in life. To fulfill this mission, intentional teachers conscientiously address every area of early learning—intellectual, social-emotional, physical, and creative—with sufficient range and depth. They apply the best practices summarized above in a balanced offering of child-guided and adult-guided experience. Moreover, intentional teachers attend to their own professional development. They regard themselves as lifelong learners—studying the children in their care, updating their knowledge of the latest child development theory and research, and examining the implications for practice. They are also collaborators, teaming with coworkers and families to apply their expertise and resources toward children's optimal development.

Along with a spirit of inquiry and dedication to children's well-being, intentional teachers engage in reflection and self-evaluation. They ask themselves what kinds of teachers they want to be. And to answer that question, they consider what kind of adults we want today's children to become. Only by having this vision of our society's future can we fully address the role that teachers can and should play in shaping young minds, hearts, and bodies.

It is my hope that some of the answers to these questions are contained in this book. What and how teachers teach as they interact with young children will determine the intellectual, social, physical, and creative development of next year's students and the next generation's adults. A thoughtful and well-grounded approach to resolving these questions can lead to a thoughtful and well-rounded population of tomorrow's citizens.

*       *       *

The general principles and strategies of intentional teaching discussed in this chapter can and should be applied across all the content domains of early learning. You can refer to these overall strategies as you read the next chapters, which offer specific ideas for promoting children's learning in language and literacy, mathematics and scientific inquiry, social skills and understandings, physical movement, and the visual arts. Considering and using these best practices will help administrators and teachers create an early childhood program in which adults and children are partners in the learning process.

## Questions for Further Thought

**1.** How can packaged curriculum materials help teachers provide essential content while still allowing intentionality in their application? What risks and shortcomings come with packaged curriculum, and what can teachers and programs do to address these?

**2.** How can early childhood practitioners overcome any anxiety they might have about teaching certain content areas, such as mathematics and science, or art appreciation (as a cognitive discipline)?

**3.** With so many content areas to cover, how can teachers possibly include everything in the daily schedule? Must programs be full-day to provide a comprehensive early education?

**4.** What preservice and inservice professional development opportunities are needed to train and support intentional teachers in implementing best practices?

# Language and Literacy

## 3

At large group, the teachers and children are chanting a familiar rhyme. They start off—

> Five little monkeys jumping on the bed,
> One fell off and bumped his head.
> The doctor came, and the doctor said:
> "No more monkeys jumping on the bed."

Before the next verse, the teacher asks, "How many monkeys this time?" "Four!" shout several children. "And what should they do this time?" Alana offers, "They're sitting in the tree and he breaks his knee." The group chants,

> Four little monkeys, sitting in a tree,
> One fell off and broke his knee. . . .

For the count of three, Kwan suggests "sitting on a house . . . break a mouse." When Rosie's idea for two is "chair" and "toes," Axel says, "Hey, that doesn't rhyme." Another child says, "*Hair* rhymes." The teacher turns to Rosie, who agrees to this suggestion, and the group chants,

> Two little monkeys, sitting in the chair,
> One fell off and broke his hair.

For one, Joshua says "under the table . . . cracked his drable." He giggles and everyone laughs with him. Susan says, "There's no such thing as a drable!" But the children agree it rhymes, and so they sing the verse. When they're done, they start again until everyone who wants has a turn to suggest where the monkeys are and what gets broken.

The landmark report *Preventing Reading Difficulties in Young Children* (Snow, Burns, & Griffin 1998) observes that "preschool teachers represent an important, and largely underutilized, resource in promoting literacy by supporting rich language and emergent literacy skills" (6). The best way to help children learn these skills is the subject of lively and sometimes touchy debate. The "reading wars" between the phonics and whole language approaches, which earlier divided educators in the primary grades, are now being fought on the preschool playground.

Yet there is common ground where all well-intentioned teachers can start young children on the path toward literacy. The basis of this common ground is the "consensus in the research community that reading is a *constructive* and *interactive* process aimed at meaning-making and involving the reader, the text, and the contextual setting in which the reading takes place" (Gambrell & Mazzoni 1999, 80).

In other words, learning to read is like mastering any other skill; young children do it because they want to make sense of their world, and they learn best by using real materials in real situations. Children acquire much of this learning through teacher-provided information, but children also develop knowledge and skills on their own during play as well as through their interactions with peers.

Because we now understand that younger children are interested in reading, there has been a major shift in what we call "reading readiness." Previously, children did not receive reading instruction until first grade. But in the past three decades, early education has taken up the idea of "emergent literacy." In this view, literacy is not all-or-nothing but a gradual progression that begins in infancy with learning language and looking at books. The preschool years can build on those early experiences, or fill in gaps when necessary, to prepare young children for the next steps. It continues through the formal reading and writing instruction of elementary school.

Snow, Burns, and Griffin (1998) caution against replicating in preschool the formal instruction of later grades, but do say that while providing "optimal support for cognitive, language, and social development . . . ample attention should be paid to skills that are known to predict future reading achievement, especially those for which a causal role has been demonstrated" (5).

## Young children's development in language and literacy

Recent reading research has yielded much useful information, from which the following are summarized (Ranweiler 2004):

▶ Language and literacy are connected from infancy onward. Speaking, listening, reading, and writing develop concurrently rather than sequentially.

▶ Children differ in their learning. Some pick up skills easily and quickly; others need more explicit help and time.

▶ Some language and literacy learning is "incidental." It arises naturally during play and other everyday experiences. Other learning depends on the explicit instruction that occurs during formal teaching. Thus, children actively construct their own knowledge, but they also need support from adults to further their development.

▶ Children acquire language and literacy skills as they interact with others. Young children learn to talk, read, and write because they are social beings. They want to communicate with adults and peers at home, school, and other familiar places.

▶ Children learn best when instruction is relevant and meaningful to them. When children can apply language and literacy learning to their everyday interests and activities, that learning will be genuine, deep, and lasting.

▶ Language and literacy learning happens through activities children might initiate, such as role-playing, exploring print materials, and doing inventive writing. It also happens through instruction such as book reading, letter identification practice, and performing or composing songs and poems using alliteration and rhyming.

▶ Differences among children in home language and culture can affect their language and literacy development. Any good program of support and instruction must take these differences into account.

In 1997, in response to a Congressional directive, a National Reading Panel (NRP) was convened by the National Institute of Child Health and Human Development and the U.S. Department of Education. Its report, built on the work of Snow and her colleagues (1998) as well as other research, was issued in 2000. Its recommendations were incorporated in the federal No Child Left Behind Act and Reading First and Early Reading First grant guidelines.

Particularly noteworthy for early childhood practitioners are the four abilities that the report says preschoolers must develop to become speakers, readers, and writers:

▶ **Phonological awareness**—the general ability to attend to language's sounds as distinct from its meaning. Initial awareness of speech sounds and rhythms, rhyme awareness, recognition of sound similarities, and phonemic awareness are all elements of this ability.

► **Comprehension**—understanding the meaning of spoken and written language. Comprehension is "intentional thinking during which meaning is constructed" (NRP 2000, 14).

► **Print awareness**—understanding how print is organized and used in reading and writing. Children learn that speech and written language carry messages and that words convey ideas.

► **Alphabet knowledge**—(or the "alphabetic principle") understanding that there is a systematic relationship between letters and sounds. Whole words have a structure made up of individual sounds and of sound patterns or groupings.

It also is the case that to become literate, young children must see reading and writing as not only useful but also pleasurable. Adults play a key role in promoting this positive attitude (Neuman, Copple, & Bredekamp 2000).

## Teaching and learning in language and literacy

As with all curriculum areas, a balance of child-guided and adult-guided experience is essential in early language and literacy development, and the division between the two is not cut-and-dry. "Literacy, whether oral or written language, is a social and cultural phenomenon. By definition then, the most productive child-initiated activities will still be those that involve [the child in] some kind of interaction with an adult or other children at some point during the activity" (Linda Bevilacqua, 2004, pers. comm.). In other words, even though children have language and literacy experiences and acquire many literacy skills on their own, the presence and support of thoughtful adults is critical to sustain their motivation and supply essential information.

Just as child-guided experience cannot happen as effectively without adult support, so too "even knowledge and skills acquired through intentional and explicit adult-guided instruction require child-guided exploration and practice to gain depth and extension" (Lesley Morrow, 2004, pers. comm.). So while teachers take the lead when adult-guided activities are called for, they should also encourage child choice and discovery in those areas.

The National Reading Panel (2000) says that both explicit and incidental reading instruction are necessary and can be effective. It cautions, however, that "educators must keep the *end* in mind" (10) and provide "methods appropriate to the age and ability of the reader" (14). So, for example, systematic phonics instruction cannot stop with decoding exercises (dissecting the sounds and parts of words); ultimately it must allow children to derive meaning and achieve fluency in their everyday reading and writing activities.

Similarly, the main purpose of vocabulary instruction is not to build random word knowledge but to produce gains in children's comprehension of spoken and written language. For young children "a primary motivation for acquiring vocabulary and developing rules of syntax [is] a desire to communicate with others"; further, research consistently shows that children who have made the most progress in literacy "had teachers who stressed vocabulary learning *in context*, that is, in all content areas" (Genishi & Fassler 1999, 62).

NAEYC's professional standards for initial licensure (NAEYC 2003) apply research findings to create a list of expectations for teachers. These standards say that to help young children become readers and writers, practitioners need to plan experiences that help children develop the ability to converse, use, and understand a wide vocabulary, enjoy reading and writing and see the usefulness of both, understand stories and texts, and develop basic print concepts and understanding of sounds, letters, and letter-sound relationships.

The joint position statement of the International Reading Association and NAEYC (1998) also provides context and practical examples for helping children develop specific language and literacy knowledge and skills. "The ability to read and write does not develop naturally, without careful planning and instruction" (3). Fortunately, the literature is rich with practical suggestions on how to accomplish these ends.

# Fitting the learning experience to the learning objective

The following discussion—grouped according to skills in **language** (listening and speaking), **reading**, and **writing**—should help practitioners sort out "what" and "how to" in early literacy instruction and learning. Within each, the sample teaching strategies are grouped according to knowledge and skills that seem to be gained primarily in child-guided versus adult-guided experience, but this is not a rigid division. Careful attention to children's emerging abilities will help teachers decide which approach works best for each child at any given time.

## Language

Of the key knowledge and skills in the area of language, child-guided experience seems particularly important in acquiring sound awareness and production, as well as conversational skills. Adult-guided experience seems especially significant in gaining phonological awareness, vocabulary, and knowledge of narrative/comprehension.

 **Child-guided experience is especially important for learnings such as:**

### C1  Sound awareness and production

This skill area refers broadly to awareness of sounds (including non-words) and is the simplest level of phonological awareness (more on that later); it also includes being able to produce various sounds with the vocal cords. Development begins in infancy with recognizing the sounds made by people and things. This includes learning to distinguish the noises made by significant individuals (e.g., the voice qualities of different caregivers, determining mood by tone of voice); animals (sounds of family pets, zoo animals); everyday activities (cooking and cleaning noises, stroller wheels on pavement); vehicles (starting the car, a garbage truck backing up, brakes on a bus); and other noise-making items (household appliances, machines, musical instruments). Early and frequent exposure to sounds, especially the sounds of language, is crucial for a young child's development of language and literacy skills.

Young children also naturally make their own sounds. Infants babble and play with their voices. Toddlers and preschoolers enjoy experimenting to hear the variety and range of sounds their vocal cords can create. This playfulness also appears later when young children begin to produce recognizable language. For example, preschoolers enjoy making up nonsense words or combining words with sounds that vary in loudness or pitch. By interacting with children as they create and play with these sounds, adults further support and extend early language and literacy learning.

*Teaching strategies.* To ensure young children are exposed early and often to a variety of sounds, consider and elaborate on the following ideas:

■ Provide many noise-making items inside the classroom, including musical instruments; timers that tick and ring; cassette players and tapes; computers with appropriate noise-making software; tools and a workbench; things that make noise during filling and emptying such as pea gravel, bottle caps, or running water; and bean bags filled with different types of materials. Ask children to vary the sounds they make; for example, ask them to make sounds that are loud and soft, fast and slow, high and low, continuous and interrupted.

■ Expose children to a wide variety of sounds outside the classroom, including those in nature (wind, birds, waves, running streams), throughout the school (bells, buzzers, telephones, footsteps in the hall), and in the neighborhood (cars, construction vehicles, sirens, barking dogs).

■ Call children's attention to sounds throughout the day (a falling block tower, doors opening and closing, footsteps, balls bouncing, water running). Comment on what you hear and encourage children to be alert to different sounds.

■ Ask children to identify the sounds they hear. At group time, have them close their eyes as you or another child makes sounds with different tools and materials, and ask them to guess the source of the sound. This game sets the stage for recognizing differences between the sounds of the letters of the alphabet. Tape-record sounds to use in this game, such as whistles, clapping, stomping of heavy boots, a baby's crying, crackers (or other crunchy food) being eaten, hammering or sawing, a cat's meowing, the blast of a car horn, a door slamming, and the scraping of roller skates on the pavement.

■ Use nursery rhymes, fingerplays, and songs that play with sounds.

■ Provide puppets and other props that encourage children to explore sounds in dramatic play.

■ Read books and tell stories that include sounds (*grrr, whoosh, whaa, mmm*). Add your own sound effects. Encourage children to imitate and make up sounds that go with the story.

## C2 Conversational skills

Conversation is the verbal exchange of information, observations, thoughts, and feelings. Having a conversation means using the give-and-take of language for social intercourse. Conversational skills comprise listening (especially active, engaged listening), initiating talk with adults and peers, and responding appropriately to the talk of others.

*Teaching strategies.* The most important thing to remember about conversation is that it requires at least two participants. Beware of the adult tendency to dominate when talking to young children. Patience and silence are virtues when we want to encourage preschoolers to express themselves. Here are some strategies:

■ Model active listening as well as talking with children. Remind yourself not to take over in conversations. Preschoolers are not always fluent in their speech. Wait patiently while they frame and express their thoughts. Get down on their level, make eye contact, pause to listen, repeat or clarify what they say, summarize their thoughts, and accept and expand on their ideas.

■ Play games that use verbal directions, such as Simon Says, to foster children's listening skills.

■ Speak clearly and intelligibly. Model standard language (vocabulary and pronunciation, grammar and syntax). Use more complex sentences as children's verbal skills increase.

■ Expand children's verbalizations. For example, if a toddler says "Me, banana," you might say "You are going to eat that banana."

■ Create natural opportunities for conversations throughout the day, such as during meals and snacks, greetings and departures. Use these times to talk with children about their interests.

■ Encourage children to talk to one another. Plan group activities that promote collaboration rather than solitary activity. Support peer conversations by redirecting children's attention to one another, restating the topic of the conversation, suggesting they share ideas. Support sociodramatic play among children by providing props for role-playing and pretending.

■ Use "information" talk to describe what children are doing when playing, and invite their comments. For example, say "Dwayne, you are putting lots of blocks on your tower. I wonder how you'll keep it from tipping over."

■ Engage children in "decontextualized" talk. Converse about objects, people, and events that, although familiar to children, are *not* immediately present or occurring. Talking about things that children cannot simply show or point to encourages them to use more language. (Think of information talk as "here and now," and decontextualized talk as "there and then.")

■ When children who can or should talk rely too much on gestures, gently encourage them to speak. Do not immediately comply with nonverbal requests if you think a child can use words instead. Although it is fine for children to communicate without words now and then (just as adults do), the more they talk, the better their language skills will become. Humor is a good way to get them to talk without forcing them to do so.

Consider this example:

## Questions and Comments That Open—or Close Down—Thought

Convergent or close-ended questions, where the adult already knows the answer, tend to shut children down. Divergent or open-ended questions and comments, when adults want to learn what children think, are more likely to open up conversations. Below are examples of questions and comments that encourage children to think, and also permit teachers to introduce new vocabulary words.

**Questions that encourage children to think and reason, and use expanded language:**

"How can you tell?"

"How do you know that?"

"What do you think made that happen?"

"Can you tell me how you made that?"

"I wonder would happen if . . . ?"

"How can you get that to stick [roll/stand up]?"

**Examples of questions that allow adults to introduce vocabulary words and concepts:**

"How can we move the truck [block/sand] *without* using our hands?" [If children respond only with motions, label the body parts and movements children suggest.]

"Kenisha says we can put the bowl [wet painting/ pieces] on top of the shelf or inside her cubby. Where else do you think we can store it so people don't bump into it?"

"Antoine says he sees a lot of monkeys in this picture. I count five of them. [Point to and count each one.] What else do you see a lot of?"

"What kinds of fruits do people in your family like to eat?"

"What things in the science area [house area/block area] are *heavy*? Which do you think is the *heaviest*? How could we find out?"

---

[Child hands adult a shoe.] **Adult:** "Oh, your shoe. What do you need?" [Child gives no response.] **Adult** [with actions]: "Hmmm, I could put it on my head . . . or on my foot." [Child giggles.] **Adult:** "Well, what should I do with this shoe?" **Child:** "My foot." Adult: "Oh, on your foot? Okay, I'll help you put the shoe on your foot." (Ranweiler 2004, 28)

In this exchange, only after speaking does the child bring about the desired result (help with the shoe). Also, the teacher uses this as an opportunity to expand the child's two words ("My foot") into two sentences easily understood by the child.

■ Use questions appropriately and not to excess. Bombarding children with questions tends to end dialogue, whereas making comments invites further talk. When you do use questions, make them open-ended questions to invite thoughtful and expanded answers. Avoid questions that have a single or brief "correct" answer.

■ Talk to parents and coworkers in the presence of children. Hearing adult conversations helps children expand their own vocabularies and syntax.

## A Adult-guided experience is especially important for learnings such as:

### A1 Phonological awareness

Phonological awareness, as described earlier, is the ability to attend to the sounds of language as distinct from its meaning. At its simplest level, it includes the awareness of speech sounds and rhythms, discussed above. It also extends to rhyme awareness (word endings, also known as *rimes*) and sound similarities (e.g., the initial sounds of words, also known as *onsets*, emphasized in alliteration).

Recall also that phonemic awareness is one type (or subset) of phonological awareness, an important skill for preschoolers to develop. A phoneme is the simplest unit of sound, such as the /c/ sound in cat. Phonemic skills involve blending—that is, combining individual sounds to make a word, such as putting together the sounds /c/ and /a/ and /t/ to make *cat*. Phonemic skills also involve segmentation—separating the sounds within a word, such as breaking cat into /c/, /a/, and /t/.

*Teaching strategies.* Phonological awareness is crucial to the development of literacy. When teachers introduce children to multiple experiences with oral language and systemically engage them in activities such as alliteration and rhyming, they help children develop the skills to become readers and writers. For example:

■ Point out language sounds that are meaningful to children. For example, say "I'm throwing the ball to Brian. *Ball* and *Brian* start with the same /b/ sound."

■ Share songs, poems, stories, nursery rhymes, and chants that feature rhyming, such as *The Cat in the Hat,* by Dr. Seuss. As you go, ask children to supply the rhyming words, especially once they are familiar with the verse or text. Substitute a different word at the end of a familiar rhyme and ask children to come up with a next line. For example, say "Hickory, dickory, door. The mouse ran up the. . . ." When children grasp the idea, ask them to make their own substitutions, as the children did with Five Little Monkeys in the opening vignette. Accept children's rhymes, even when they contain nonsense words.

■ Share songs, poems, stories, nursery rhymes, and chants that feature alliteration, such as "Baa, baa, black sheep" or "Fee, fie, fo, fum." Substitute a different sound at the beginning of a familiar song, poem, or chant—for example, "Wee, wie, woe, wum"—and ask children to do the same. When children grasp the idea, invite them to make up their own alliterative changes and songs. (See the box **Playing Alliteration Games.**)

■ Use rhymes and alliterations throughout the day. Many books and CDs contain ideas; feel free to make up your own. For example,

It's snack time, it's snack time,
Everyone gets a treat.
It's snack time, it's snack time,
I wonder what we've got to eat!

■ Use letter sounds during transitions. For example, say "Everyone whose name starts with the same sound as *book* and *box,* go to the circle."

■ Play games that encourage children to segment the sounds in words. For example, "I'm going to say some words, and I want you to say back just the first little part. Can you say the beginning of *shoe* [*shower, ship,* etc.]?" Do the same thing for the endings of words. For example, "Tell me what's left if I take off the first part of *shop* [*shine, shoulder,* etc.]?"

■ Play guessing games that encourage blending sounds in words. For example, "I'm thinking of someone whose name begins with the /k/ sound and ends with an 'arl' sound. Who do you think it is?"

■ When children ask for help spelling a word, say the sound of each letter aloud as you write it.

## A2 Vocabulary

Vocabulary is the sum of words understood or used by a person. Receptive, or listening, vocabulary is the number of words a child understands. It is generally greater than productive, or speaking, vocabulary, which is the number of words a child can say and use correctly. The size of a child's speaking vocabulary at school entry is highly predictive of success in reading.

Preschoolers' vocabulary depends on the language they have heard. By age 3, this can vary widely—especially by social class—from 10 to 30 million cumulative words addressed to them (Hart & Risley 1995). Children grow their vocabularies when adults comment on what children say and do, and answer their questions. When they talk with people who have larger vocabularies, children learn more words.

*Teaching strategies.* Children's vocabularies do not get larger by adding isolated or stand-alone words. The best way to grow vocabulary is to build on what children are talking about by adding synonyms and other words related to the topic of conversation. For children to learn new words, including their meaning and how to use them, they need repeated exposure and practice (once is not enough!) in one or more "communities of speakers." The preschool classroom is one such community. For example:

■ Talk with children—a lot! Talk to them during caregiving routines and during play. Make sure the

## Playing Alliteration Games

Alliteration is the repetition of the initial or beginning sound of words. Because alliteration highlights phonemes that start words, it helps young children develop phonemic awareness. Here are some alliteration games you can use in the classroom to have fun and promote learning at the same time.

**Who Is It?**—Ask children to guess who in the group has a name beginning with a certain phoneme. You can also play this game with the names of characters in a book familiar to the children.

"There are two people in this circle whose names begin with the /b/ sound. Who are they?"

"I'm thinking of a person in this room whose name starts with /sh/. Guess who."

"I remember someone in [book title] whose name begins with an /r/ sound. Who do you think it is?"

**Doing the Names**—Combine the initial sound of children's names with the initial sound of actions for them to perform.

"If your name begins with a /c/ sound, clap. Yes, Carl and Carol are clapping."

"Anyone whose name starts with the sound /w/, let's see you wave. Wendy and Walter are waving. Everybody wave with Wendy and Walter. Now let's see everyone wiggle."

**Word Starters**—Ask children to think of words that begin with the same sound.

"Let's think of words that start like *car, cat, call* . . ."

"What words begin with /d/ like *daddy*?"

"How many words can you think of that start with a /p/ sound?"

**Letter Substitution**—Pick a sound and substitute it at the beginning of words during an activity such as snack time or a transition. This game is especially good to make clean-up time silly and fun. When children get the idea, let them pick the sound.

"It's gircle time. Everyone go to the gug. Let's all glap our gands!"

"Let's begin flean-up time by putting away the flocks. Now we can do the faints and frushes. Who wants to stack the fuzzles?"

"Miguel, it's your turn to pick a sound to help us get ready for outside time." [Miguel replies he wants /m/, like in his name.] "Okay, let's put on our moats and wait by the moor until everyone is ready to go moutside." [Act out or point to some of the objects and wait to see whether children can fill in the words on their own. For example, pretend to put on a coat. Look at or gesture toward the door.]

---

conversation is reciprocal. Listen as well as talk. Be patient while children find the words to express their thoughts. Show that you value what they have to say.

■ Use words that build on children's interests. Children like to talk about what they are doing. For example, many children are interested in pets. When one child asked, "Why is Sniffy [a guinea pig] eating the tube?" the teacher replied, "He gnaws on cardboard and wood fibers to wear down his teeth. Otherwise they would grow too big for his mouth." After another child commented, "We got a new puppy last night," the teacher introduced new words by sharing: "When my dog was a puppy, she curled up beside me on the couch while I read the newspaper. She would push her nose into the pages and wrinkle them."

■ Read children books that are rich in vocabulary words and interesting ideas that will spark their questions and engage them in conversation.

■ When you use words or phrases that are new to children, provide familiar synonyms and definitions—using words already in the children's vocabulary. This helps help them grasp the meaning of the new word in context, so they can understand and use it themselves.

"We had a *debate* about where to display our rocks. When people have a debate, they talk about all the reasons they want to do something or not do something."

"We *discussed* our ideas about where to put our rocks so everyone can see them."

"We *exchanged* ideas about good places to store our rocks." (Hohmann 2005, 250)

■ Vary experiences to introduce new and unusual words. Field trips are good sources. Dramatic play helps to illustrate a variety of words. Humor is another way to encourage exploring and having fun with language. Young children like jokes and silly names and rhymes.

■ Create learning experiences in which children organize and relate concepts by using vocabulary words in classification (sorting and matching), seriation (ordering objects and making patterns), and spatial and temporal (space and time) phenomena. Doing these activities in small groups not only helps children use their own vocabulary but also allows them to hear and learn the words used by their peers. For example, give children items to sort and ask them to describe to one another the traits by which they did the sorting (see **Chapter 4** for more examples).

■ In group endeavors or games, engage children in using words to give one another directions.

■ Announce your motivations and intentions: "I'm going to the house area to see what Bessie and Vinod are cooking. It smells like they're making something spicy for lunch."

## A3 Knowledge of narrative/comprehension

Comprehension (as in "reading comprehension") involves understanding ideas and their connections in a spoken or written narrative. Children comprehend things by linking what they are learning to what they already know. Comprehension in preschool has four parts: *Understanding* is a child's ability to demonstrate through a variety of means what he knows; for example, to talk about what he sees (illustrations) and hears (oral narrative or written text read aloud). *Connection* is the ability to relate elements of the story to his own life; link new words and phrases to concepts and experiences he knows; and discover new relationships, ideas, and knowledge. *Prediction* is the capacity to imagine what will happen next. *Retelling* is recounting the story in sequence and with an increasing level of detail.

*Teaching strategies.* Think of comprehension as the steps between what goes in and what comes out when children encounter a story. As young children develop, their brains are increasingly able to construct the mental structures necessary to process this material, but they need explicit guidance from adults to build connections and make sense of the narratives they hear and read. Reading comprehension improves when oral language in general is better. That is why it is so important to talk to children from the moment of birth. The more they hear, the more they learn. Many of these strategies are also helpful in supporting and extending the comprehension of English language learners.

■ Read stories again and again. Repetition enhances children's awareness of character and narrative sequence.

■ Examine and discuss the pictures in books. Encourage children to tell or "read" the story in familiar books by looking at the pictures. Ask them to describe what they see. Converse about how the characters and situations depicted relate to objects, people, events, and ideas in children's own lives, both at home and in the classroom. For example, you might look together at the picture on the cover of a book like this:

Sit with a child or a small group of children in a comfortable spot where everyone can see the book being read. Say something like "Today we're going to read the book [read the title aloud]. Let's look at the cover. I wonder what the book is about." Show them the cover. Listen to and comment on their ideas. For example, say "Jerry sees a cow, so he thinks the book is about a farm" or "Sharon sees some corn, so maybe the story is about what a family eats for dinner." After talking about the children's ideas, say "Let's open the book and find out."

■ Discuss the text in books. Talk about what happens. Help children connect a story's characters and situations to objects, people, events, and ideas in their own lives.

■ Engage children in reviewing and predicting as you read. Stop occasionally to encourage children to recall what has happened so far. Rather than asking closed-ended questions, invite comments by saying "Let's see what we can remember so far" or "Can you help me remember what happened at the very beginning?" Ask children what they think the picture or words on the next page will be, or how a character will solve a problem. Encourage them to look and listen for clues that suggest what might happen next. Relate the picture and text at the end of the book to the title and first page. Recall what happened at the beginning, middle, and end of the story.

■ Encourage children to represent stories in various ways during art, dramatic play, movement, and other activities. Provide materials such as art supplies, props, and music to facilitate their representations. Suggest ideas such as moving to the next activity like a character in a book moves, or drawing a series of pictures to show the sequence of events in a story.

■ Recall and talk about stories at times other than when the stories are being read or told; for example, during snacks or related field trips. Listen for children's comments that can lead naturally into discussions of familiar and favorite narratives.

■ Use ideas from favorite and familiar books to plan group times and transitions. For example, plan field trips to the settings depicted in books (farm, supermarket, pet store, museum). If characters move a certain way (snakes slither along the ground), ask the children to imitate that movement while going from reading to the next activity.

■ Provide opportunities for children to talk among themselves and look at books together. Pair English language learners with fluent English speakers for some activities.

# Reading

Of the key knowledge and skills in the area of reading, child-guided experience seems particularly important in acquiring visual discrimination skills, environmental print knowledge, print awareness, and motivation to interact with printed materials. Adult-guided experience seems especially significant in understanding the relationship between spoken and written language, as well as gaining alphabet knowledge.

## C Child-guided experience is especially important for learnings such as:

### C1 Visual discrimination skills

Reading depends on the ability to visually distinguish the structural features of letters and punctuation, and how they form words, sentences, and paragraphs. Children must recognize the types of marks that make up print, such as lines, dots, and closed shapes. They have to further distinguish between types of lines—straight and curved, vertical and horizontal. Finally, children have to perceive how printed marks are arranged on a page and in relation to one another.

*Teaching strategies.* Children's visual discrimination comes with physical maturation, but there are specific teaching strategies to help them acquire the particular visual skills needed for reading. Some of these ideas will seem obvious, others may inspire your creativity. For example:

■ Provide a visually rich environment that includes not only many examples of print but also nonprint materials with diverse features. Most teachers know that having lots of printed materials in the classroom is important for early reading (see **Print awareness** below, for more on this topic). However, there are many things without letters that can also help young children become aware of the lines, marks, and contrasts they will find in print. Examples include artwork and reproductions of artwork (two- and three-dimensional, in different media); maps and diagrams; plants with flowers and variegated leaves; shells and stones; patterned fabrics; wood with distinctive grains; magnifying lenses; and different types of lighting (natural and artificial) positioned to create light and shadow.

■ Use vocabulary words related to print's visual features, such as *straight, curved, circle, long, tall, short, blank* or *empty space,* and *line.* Call attention to visual features of objects indoors and outdoors such as size, shape and form, color, and foreground and background.

■ Encourage children to describe the visual attributes of materials, tools, artwork, and so on, in their environment. Talk about the features that make things look the same or different.

■ Play games and plan art activities that focus on visual characteristics. For example, partially hide objects and encourage children to find them; ask what features helped them find the object. Make imprints and rubbings (sneaker soles, bark, keys, hands and feet); ask children to match these to the actual objects, discussing how they did so.

## C2 Environmental print knowledge

Environmental print is print encountered in the context of everyday life. Examples include company names, logos, and advertising copy that appears in stores and on television, Web pages, and vehicles; product labels; menus; street names and traffic signs; storefronts; billboards; text and captions in magazines, newspapers, and catalogs; junk mail; invitations; letterhead; etc.

*Teaching strategies.* Because environmental print is everywhere, children already encounter it all the time on their own. However, teachers play a significant role in calling it to children's attention. They can draw an explicit connection between logos or other symbols and printed words, and between the shared properties of environmental print and books. Try strategies such as these:

■ Create a print-rich classroom environment that includes environmental print materials: photo albums, magazines (for children and adults), catalogs, newspapers, brochures, fliers, telephone books, junk mail, instruction manuals, address books (especially with the letters of the alphabet written in large type) calendars, greeting cards, ticket stubs, business cards, empty seed packets.

■ Set up play centers that incorporate reading and writing materials. For example, the housekeeping area can include empty food boxes and cans with labels (cleaned and with any sharp edges smoothed), store coupons, play money, cookbooks, a telephone directory, message pads, and pencils. A restaurant center could be equipped with menus, wall signs, and notepads for taking food orders.

> ## Children Creating Environmental Print During Play
>
> Children use and make their own printed materials in the course of play, the same way they use and create other types of props. In the following example, a group of preschoolers makes tickets and signs for a pretend train trip.
>
> > Several 4-year-olds agree to take a make-believe train trip to France. They use an elevated loft as their train and move chairs up the stairs for passenger seats. Two of them go to an adjacent center and make tickets for the journey, using scribbles to represent writing. Once the tickets are ready, they are distributed to every child and collected by the "engineer" as "passengers" enter the train. While the children wait for their teacher to pack his bag and join them, they lean over the loft railing and read signs he helped them make earlier, including "Train," "No Smoking," and "No Ghosts." They have difficulty reading a sign with an arrow that says "This way to the train" and ask, "What does that say?" The teacher reads it out loud and then climbs on board.
>
> **Source:** Jim Christie, 2004, personal communication. Used with permission.

■ Ask families to contribute materials.

■ Affix labels and captions on interest centers and materials throughout the classroom. Post signs and lists such as weekly snack menus, the daily routine, or the names of children in each small group.

■ Put printed materials at children's eye level and make them accessible.

■ Include printed materials that reflect children's home languages and cultures.

■ Introduce letters and words in ways that are personally meaningful to children. For example, "letter links" (DeBruin-Parecki & Hohmann 2003) pair a child's printed nametag with a letter-linked picture of an object that starts with the same letter and sound. A letter link for Alice might be *ant* and one for Pedro could be *paintbrush*. Letter links can appear on children's cubbies, the bottom of their pictures, chore charts, and other places throughout the room.

■ Visit places in the community that feature print (library, sign shop, bookstore, supermarket). Look for large print at the children's eye level. For example, product signs on shelves are easier for children to see than aisle signs hanging near the ceiling.

### C3 Print awareness

Print awareness, or concepts of print, includes general knowledge about the conventions of print and how books work. For example, preschool children learn that books have distinctive parts (cover and pages, beginning and end), an author or illustrator or both, and a written message separate from (though related to) the pictures. Through repeated experiences, they master directionality—that is, knowing that books are held right-side up (orientation) and in this culture read from front to back (turning pages in order), and each text page is scanned top to bottom and left to right.

*Teaching strategies.* The logical structure of books is so well known to adults that we take it for granted. We sometimes forget that young children are not born knowing how books work. Repeated exposure to print helps bring about such awareness on its own. Still, adults can help by pointing out the main features of books with strategies such as these:

■ Provide a variety of print for children to hold, carry, look at, and talk about to aid their understanding and application of the general rules of print. Provide many different types of books such as illustrated storybooks, controlled vocabulary books (with word sets such as *cat, mat, bat* that encourage sight reading), picture dictionaries, and informational (nonfiction) books on topics of interest to the children. Make the books easily accessible to children. Change the selection periodically to maintain their interest.

■ Provide lots of other printed products children can interact with, such as the environmental print materials discussed earlier, dictated stories, and stories children have written (and illustrated) themselves.

■ Ask children to hand you a book "so I can read it." Accept or reorient the book as needed. Occasionally pick up or hold a book the wrong way and see how children react. Make a visual and verbal point of turning the book right-side up.

■ Point out book and print features while looking at books with children. For example, say "This is the front cover and this [turning it over] is the back cover. This is called the 'title page' because it has the name, or title, of the book." Encourage children to talk about what they see on the front and back covers. Explain the idea of author and illustrator. Before reading, say "I'm going to read the book [read the title aloud]. It was written by [author's name], and [illustrator's name] drew the pictures." Encourage children to turn the pages as you read. When you're done, you might say "That's the end of the story." Look for books that say "The End" on the last page. After finishing the book, go back and point out page numbers in sequence. (Once you begin reading, don't interrupt the story to point out book features. It can destroy the pleasure of reading. Also, children need narrative continuity to build comprehension skills. You can mention print attributes occasionally, but for the most part, point these out before and after reading the book.)

■ Make books with children that include all the parts (front and back covers, title page with their name as author and illustrator, drawings with words). Leave commercially produced books on the table that children can refer to while they make their own books. Display the children's finished books; put them in the reading area so they can look at their own and their classmates' books. Invite them to "read" their books aloud at small group and to talk about how they made each part.

### C4 Motivation to interact with printed materials

This area refers to children's interest in—or "disposition" toward—engaging with printed materials and the things that are represented in print such as stories and information. For example, it includes being positively disposed toward looking at books as well as listening to books on audiocassette.

*Teaching strategies.* Interest in reading cannot be forced on children. Fortunately, if they have positive experiences reading with adults, children will naturally be motivated to want to read. To foster positive attitudes toward reading:

■ Read to children frequently, both individually and in small groups.

■ Create cozy and comfortable places where you can read with children and they can look at books by themselves. Provide stuffed animals and dolls for children to "read" to.

■ Display books on open shelves, with attractive and colorful covers facing outward.

■ Encourage children to select which book(s) to read.

■ Choose books that interest children. Because they are curious, virtually any subject well presented for their age can intrigue them. This includes nonfiction as well as storybooks.

■ Provide books that children will have success "reading" themselves; for example, wordless books and easy-to-read books (with predictable word sets).

■ Let children see you reading for enjoyment and information.

■ Let children know you expect them to succeed at reading.

■ Encourage parents to read to children at home. Start a lending library in the classroom. Make book backpacks for each child so they can choose books to take home and return.

##  Adult-guided experience is especially important for learnings such as:

### A1  The relationship between spoken and written language

This domain involves connecting what people say with the same words as written. It requires children to understand the one-to-one correspondence between the two modes of expression.

*Teaching strategies.* The relationship between spoken and written words may seem self-evident to adults. But grasping this abstract connection is a notable achievement for young children, whose predominantly concrete minds are just beginning to form mental representations. By demonstrating visual, auditory, and tactile connections, teachers can help young children relate oral and written modes. Here are some strategies:

■ Take children's dictation and read it back to them verbatim. (When you take dictation on paper, ask children where on the page to begin writing, to reinforce that print concept.) Or type it into the computer and print it out. The power and pleasure of seeing their words in print—provided it's voluntary and not coerced—encourages children to invent additional occasions for dictation. Occasions for taking individual dictation include labels; captions on artwork; role-playing props (e.g., menus, traffic signs, party invitations); books the child creates; messages (cards, notes from the child); and original songs, rhymes, and chants. Opportunities for group dictation include original stories, songs, rhymes, and chants; rules for a game children have invented; lists (e.g., favorite foods, toys, colors; places to go on a field trip); shared experiences ("Our trip to the pet shop"), with comments from each child; plans for a group experience ("What I want to do at the park"); and small group problem-solving discussions ("How can we stop fighting over the red wagon?").

■ When reading to children, run a finger along the lines of print occasionally, point out and enunciate individual words, and model intonation.

■ Engage children in speaking and acting out written stories from their own books as well as commercial books.

■ Make picture cards, then write appropriate words (nouns, verbs, short sentences) underneath. These can be about individual items and actions, or use related word sets (buildings, planting a garden). Point to the pictures and words as you read the text aloud. Encourage children to look at the cards on their own, as well as with partners, and to say the written words aloud.

## A2 Alphabet knowledge: Letter identification and letter-sound knowledge

Alphabet knowledge means knowing the names of letters and letter-sound matches (alphabetic principle). Although knowing letter names (visual discrimination) and sounds (auditory discrimination) are distinct abilities, they usually develop in tandem because children are given both pieces of information together: "That's the letter M, and it makes the /m/ sound."

With informed guesses, as well as continued explicit instruction, children come to understand that other words they are interested in saying and writing begin with the same letter; for example, that *mom, me, mud,* and *motor* all begin with the /m/ sound. Children find it easier to identify letters at the beginning of words, especially if the letters are capitalized. For example, the initial letter B in the name Barbara is easier to find than the embedded b in the middle of the name.

*Teaching strategies.* Like phonological awareness, alphabet knowledge is critical in early literacy. The alphabet is an arbitrary "code" of letters and sounds unique to one or more related languages. Children must be taught the rules and conventions of their language(s); they cannot make them up. Adults therefore play an explicit role transmitting this body of information. At the same time, children need ample opportunity to experiment and practice the alphabet on their own.

■ Display alphabet letters where children can see them, not posted far above their heads. Provide alphabet letters and blocks children can hold, copy, trace, and rearrange. These might include cut-out letters and letter stencils made of wood, plastic, and heavy cardboard; magnetic letters; letter-shaped cookie cutters that children can press into sand and play dough; and alphabet puzzles.

■ Say the names of letters and sound them out in words children read, write, and dictate. For example, say "That's a B, and it sounds like /b/." Sound out letters, letter strings, and letter combinations in the words children dictate. For example, if they dictate a party menu, write and enunciate

"/p/ /i/ /z/ /z/ /a/. That makes the word *pizza.* I like pepperoni on my pizza!" Include the letter strings and combinations at the beginning and end of words; later, also those in the middle. For example, when Simone said to her teacher, "Write the word *Daddy* for me," her teacher wrote the letters and said, "It starts with the sound /da/ and I write it D-A. And it ends with the sound /dee/, D-D-Y. D-A-D-D-Y. That makes the word *Daddy.*"

■ Connect sounds to the letters children write to stand for whole words. For example, if a child writes "HB" and reads "Happy Birthday," say "You wrote 'Happy Birthday.' I see the H for the /h/ sound in *Happy* and a B for the /b/ sound at the beginning of *Birthday.*" Sound out the invented "words" children spell. If they ask "What word is this?" or "What does this spell?" pronounce the word as it is written or arranged. For example, if a child arranges the letters KRGMS, say "This word sounds like /k/ /r/ /g/ /m/ /s/, krgms. You wrote the word *krgms.*"

■ Involve children in searching for letters by their sounds. For example,

On a class walk, the teacher said, "I'm looking for a letter that makes the sound /s/. Can you find one?" Children pointed to signs for "gas station" and "South Street Market" and the license plate RS0371.

■ Provide alphabet knowledge in context. Call attention to letter names and sounds when it is relevant to children's playing, reading, and writing. This strategy is more effective than offering such information in isolation from children's ongoing and meaningful activities.

■ Identify initial letter sounds in children's names and other familiar words. Often the first letter and letter sound that children learn is the one that begins their own name; or it's a word they use often and find important, such as *Mom,* their dog's name, or a favorite food. Pair a child's written name and the sound made by its first letter; transitions are a good time for this:

**Teacher** (holding up Darren's nametag): Here's Darren's name. It starts with the sound /d/. I wonder what letter makes the /d/ sound at the beginning of your name, Darren?

**Darren:** D makes the /d/ sound for *Darren.*

**Teacher:** The D makes the /d/ sound at the beginning of *Darren.* You can get your coat, Darren.

**Teacher** (holding up Lydia's nametag): Lydia, your name starts with the /l/ sound. I wonder what letter makes that /l/ sound?

**Lydia:** *Lydia* makes the /l/ sound!

**Teacher:** Yes, *Lydia* starts with the /l/ sound. I'm wondering what letter makes that sound?

**Max:** I know. L makes the /l/ sound.

**Teacher:** The L at the beginning of *Lydia* makes the /l/ sound. Lydia, you can get your coat. (Holds up Max's nametag.) Now Max, what letter makes the /m/ sound at the beginning of *Max*? . . . (adapted from High/Scope Educational Research Foundation 2004)

■ Link the sounds of a word to the first letters in children's names. For example, while writing and spelling *box,* you might say "It begins with B like the /b/ sound in *Brian*. It ends with X like the /x/ in *Xavier*. In the middle is an O just like the /o/ in *Olive*."

# Writing

Of the key knowledge and skills in the area of writing, child-guided experience seems particularly important in acquiring fine motor skills, as well as awareness of the purposes and functions of written words. Adult-guided experience seems especially significant in building letter and word writing, as well as awareness of the conventions of spelling, grammar, syntax, and punctuation.

 **Child-guided experience is especially important for learnings such as:**

### C1 **Fine motor skills**

Writing, like reading, is dependent on children having certain perceptual-motor skills. Prerequisite fine motor skills for writing include being able to grasp writing materials and the eye-hand coordination to make certain types of marks in specific locations on the writing surface. (See Bredekamp & Copple 1997, p. 105, for a developmental progression of fine motor skills for ages 3–5 years.)

*Teaching strategies.* The development of the fine motor skills needed for writing is to a great degree maturational. However, like pre-reading visual acuity skills, they are also dependent on adults to provide the necessary materials and opportunities for practice. For example:

■ Provide manipulatives in all areas of the classroom to develop children's manual dexterity and eye-hand coordination. Examples include things to assemble and take apart (nuts and bolts, shoes and laces); things to copy and trace; jigsaw puzzles; small blocks and sets of small toys; dress-up and doll clothes with various types of fasteners; moldable art materials such as clay and dough; drawing and painting tools (crayons, brushes, pencils of graduated thickness); paper for children to manipulate and transform; scissors; hole punches; staplers; tape of various kinds; cooking utensils; safety knives for cutting snacks; carpentry tools and materials such as nails and wood (use appropriate safety precautions including safety goggles); and appropriate computer programs.

■ Provide writing materials of all kinds throughout the room (see suggestions in the next section).

■ Encourage children to play simple games of hand-eye coordination such as aiming at a target with a beanbag or ball. (Note: Preschoolers need a large target and short throwing distance.)

■ Model how to hold writing tools, scissors, and so on, especially for children who are having difficulty mastering these techniques on their own. Be sensitive to children's frustration levels. If you wait too long to intervene, children may simply become averse to writing.

■ Refer children to one another for help. Children often learn dexterity and coordination skills better by watching and imitating peers than from direct instruction by adults.

### C2 **Awareness of the purposes and functions of written words**

This area refers to knowing all the ways and reasons people write. Like reading, writing is done for functional reasons (to communicate an idea, remember to do something, give directions) and for pleasure (to extend an invitation, express appreciation, preserve a memory).

*Teaching strategies.* Young children want to do things for themselves and share their ideas and accomplishments with others. Writing helps them achieve these personal objectives. Strategies such as these build on children's inherent motivation:

■ Provide a wide variety of writing tools and materials throughout the classroom. Include not only materials for making written marks (such as pens and pencils, paper) but also those that record ideas (writing software) and transmit them to others (email software, envelopes and stamps). Include regular and color pencils, pens, and markers; crayons; chalk (white, color) and chalkboards; unlined paper, color construction paper, stationery; ruled notebooks; note pads; sticky notes and labels; used gift wrap; wallpaper samples; grocery bags; checkbook registers; inkpads and stamps; order forms; stickers; age-appropriate drawing software; and tape, staplers, yarn, and hole punch (so children can make their own books).

■ Provide contextualized examples of print that serves a "here and now" purpose. Examples include labels on centers and materials, rules created by children, a daily schedule, cookbooks in the house area, instructions for equipment in the woodworking or science area, lists of children's names and book titles checked out of the lending library.

■ Model the use of written language for different purposes and call it to children's attention. Point out when you write things; for example, a "to do" list, parent newsletter, or a story dictated by the children. Similarly, make children aware when you use existing writing; for example, to follow directions or look up information in a book or on the computer.

■ Encourage journal writing. Have children make their own journals with decorated front and back covers and blank pages in between. Make a class journal that individual children can add entries to. With children's permission, read from their previous day's entries at morning greeting.

■ Display children's writing where children and parents can see it.

 **Adult-guided experience is especially important for learnings such as:**

**A1 Letter and word writing**

Literacy includes the ability to write individual letters and combine strings of letters into words. As children develop, they make letter-like forms before they write conventional letters. Letter writing usually begins with one's own name, starting with writing its initial letter. Children are highly motivated to master this feat because of the personal value they attach to their name.

Between ages 3 and 6, children's name writing progresses from continuous horizontal scribbles to separate and recognizable letters arranged in the correct order (Hildreth 1936). This ability appears to develop without a great deal of direct instruction, but it does so only when adults continually make the connection explicit. Teachers need to call attention to environmental print that uses the initial letter in a child's name, or they can write the letter: "That's a P, just like in your name, Pedro."

*Teaching strategies.* Like alphabet knowledge, letter and word writing are highly dependent on explicit instruction; but to be effective, it must be provided in relevant and developmentally appropriate ways. For example:

■ Call attention to how letters are formed, particularly the lines and shapes that compose them.

■ Engage children in writing and "reading" their writing. Write down children's dictation; then read the words back yourself, and ask children to read back the words you have written for them. Have them write for a purpose; for example, encourage children to write messages to one another, family members, and teachers.

■ Engage them in name writing each day; for example, writing their name on a sign-in chart, task list, bookmark, or art project. Comment positively however children write their names, from up-and-down strokes, to continuous linear scribbles, to discrete letter-like units, partial and inverted letters, and conventional letters. For example,

## Introducing the Idea of Punctuation in Context

The idea of punctuation is too abstract for young children to learn and apply its rules. However, they are often interested in punctuation marks and how they are used when the topic comes up in meaningful contexts. In the following anecdote, some children are impressed when their teacher uses an exclamation point to convey her feelings; later, she overhears the children imitating and discussing this punctuation mark in their own play.

A teacher is sitting in the writing center with a small group of children. She writes a get-well card to a sick colleague:

"Dear Carol, We hope you get well SOON!!!" (she describes and explains to the children as she writes) "... exclamation mark, exclamation mark, exclamation mark. Because I want her to get well *soon*."

Moments later, Kira and Hana talk about exclamation marks.

**Kira:** And this is (pause) extamotion [sic] mark.

**Hana:** Three cause it's big letters.

Later still, Hana and another child, Christina, include exclamation marks in their own writing. Christina writes the letters COI over and over inside one band of a rainbow and exclamation marks inside another band. Hana writes her name and fills the bottom of the page with upside down exclamation marks.

**Source:** D. Rowe, *Preschoolers as Authors: Literacy Learning in the Social World* (Cresskill, NJ: Hampton Press, 1994). Adapted, by permission, from pp. 168-69.

---

"Zarius, you wrote your name using dots and lines."

"Anna, there's your name with two A's and two n's — Anna."

"Lee, I see you've written the L at the beginning of your name and two up-and-down lines with lots of lines crossing them, E's, afterwards. That's your name, Lee."

"Myles, I see you've written your name, M-y-l-e-s." (High/Scope Educational Research Foundation 2004)

■ Draw attention to similarities between written examples of children's names (e.g., on nametags and class lists) and their own signatures. Point out similarities between the letters in children's names and other names and words in the classroom that use some of the same letters.

■ Act as a writer as well as a teacher. When children see adults write, they want to write too. Label what you are doing as "writing" and explain to children both its purpose and what actual letters, words, and sentences you are writing.

### A2  Awareness of the conventions of spelling, grammar, syntax, and punctuation

The conventions of print include a culture's correct or accepted rules of written expression. As children become literate, they often construct unconventional rules first, then gradually move toward conventional ones. For example, they might invent spellings using the most salient sounds in words, such as "DG" for *dog*. Or they might understand the ideas of "past tense" and of adding *-ed*, but misapply those ideas to an irregular verb ("I goed to the store"). Young children cannot be expected to follow all the conventions initially; as we raise children's awareness, they will begin to use the rules as they are ready. Our task is to build on what children know; that is, young children's understanding is more important than whether *goed* is "correct."

*Teaching strategies.* Children's spontaneous and joyful writing should not be stifled by teachers repeatedly correcting them or insisting that rules must be followed. Strategies such as these help make children aware of the conventions and their application without discouraging their impulse to write:

■ When taking dictation from children, spell out the words as you write them. Emphasize middle letters and especially vowels. Children tend to notice initial letters and consonants first, so linger on other letter types to help children fill in the "blanks" in their spelling.

■ Respond to children's requests for help to spell words correctly. Once they realize that letters represent sounds, help them write the sounds they hear in words. As they get better at sounding out words, help them make the transition to conventional spellings. Here's an example:

**Child:** "Did I spell *today* right?"

**Teacher:** "T-O-D-A, you have all the sounds. Just add a *y* at the end and you'll have it. *Day, say, hay*, all those words have the ay." (Neuman, Copple, & Bredekamp 2000, 91)

■ With older preschoolers, provide word banks, word walls, and books with words that share spelling features. Post lists of "hard-to-spell words." Ask children to suggest words. Encourage children to add more words throughout the year.

■ As you read or write with children, make comments to highlight conventions, such as "This is a new sentence, so it begins with a capital letter."

■ Use punctuation while writing with children. As they observe what you write, explain the marks and their significance. For example, "We're making a list of questions to ask the lady at the museum tomorrow, so I'm writing a question mark at the end of each one."

■ When children make spoken errors in grammar and syntax, repeat back their ideas using conventional language, rather than correcting them. For example, if a child says "I goed to the barbershop yesterday. He cutted my hair," you might say "You went to the barbershop yesterday and the barber cut your hair."

\*　　　\*　　　\*

"Learning is enhanced when the classroom environment reflects a community of literacy learners" (Gambrell & Mazzoni 1999, 87). Teachers play a critical role in establishing this community through their interactions with individual children and the collaborations they foster among peers. Intentional teachers use their knowledge of child development and literacy learning to supply materials, provide well-timed information, guide discussions, make thoughtful comments, ask meaningful questions, and pose calibrated challenges that advance children's learning.

Young children's motivation to learn to read and write comes from an intrinsic desire to communicate. But they need adult guidance and support to begin the journey toward full literacy with competence and enthusiasm.

## Questions for Further Thought

**1.** What minimal language and literacy skills do teachers need to teach young children, especially children whose backgrounds place them at risk for reading difficulties? Who determines minimal requirements, and how should they be assessed?

**2.** What is the difference between "learning to read" and "reading to learn"? How do we help children make the transition? For example, why do some children—including those who appear to have learned decoding skills—fail to comprehend what they are reading?

**3.** Is there a point (age) beyond which children cannot fully recover if their early language experiences—especially their exposure to varied vocabulary—are limited?

**4.** Can/does systematic reading instruction take away from—or add to—the joy of reading?

# Mathematics
## and Scientific Inquiry

4

"Misha is only 3. You have to be 4 to join our club."

"I'm squooshing one raisin into every marshmallow. They're beanbag chairs for bugs."

"Add more water to the other glass to make them even."

"First I did the napkins. Then I put spoons on top. Last the plates with pop-up pebble pies."

"I won't be 5 until after José. But then it will be my turn to be the oldest."

"My new shoes cost my mom eleventy-eight-one dollars."

"I'm running faster. I bet I get to the top of the hill before you!"

"When the big hand points down at the 6, I'm going to clap my hands for clean-up."

"Big yellow rings in this box and small ones there. Same for the big and little green squares."

"You be the daddy kitty because you're the tallest. She's the baby because she's the littlest. And I'll be the mommy so I can sit in the middle."

Quite naturally, and without recognizing them as such, young children develop ideas about mathematics in the course of their day-to-day lives. These children's remarks, for example, overheard in a preschool classroom, reflect an interest in "mathematical" subjects that matter to them—age, speed, time, size, order. Summarizing the early mathematics knowledge base, Baroody (2000) notes:

> Researchers have accumulated a wealth of evidence that children between the ages of 3 and 5 years of age actively construct a variety of fundamentally important informal mathematical concepts and strategies from their everyday experiences. Indeed, this evidence indicates that they are predisposed, perhaps innately, to attend to numerical situations and problems. (61)

Thus, in the past 25 years, studies of the development of early mathematics have switched from looking at what children *cannot* do to what they *can* do. Observations of children during free play, for example, show them engaged in mathematical explorations and applications, and sometimes these are surprisingly advanced (Ginsburg, Inoue, & Seo 1999).

The typical early childhood curriculum, however, incorporates little in the way of thoughtful and sustained early mathematics experiences (Copley 2004). If mathematics is included, it tends to be limited to number, particularly counting. Yet young children also spontaneously explore topics such as patterns, shapes, and the transformations brought about by processes such as adding and subtracting (Ginsburg, Inoue, & Seo 1999), and there are foundational mathematical understandings children need to develop in these areas.

Along with changing our ideas about *what* children can understand has come rethinking of *how* to foster early mathematical development.

> Because young children's experiences fundamentally shape their attitude toward mathematics, an engaging and encouraging climate for children's early encounters with mathematics is important. It is vital for young children to develop confidence in their ability to understand and use mathematics—in other words, to see mathematics as within their reach. (NAEYC & NCTM 2002)

Researchers and practitioners have developed different systems for categorizing the mathematical areas in which young children demonstrate interest and ability (e.g., Campbell 1999; Greenes 1999). In 2000 the National Council of Teachers of Mathematics (NCTM) published *Principles and Standards in School Mathematics*, which includes standards for grades preK–2. And in 2002 NAEYC published a joint position paper with NCTM supporting its standards and offering recommendations for early mathematics education. The NCTM standards are now widely cited in the field and used by many state departments of education and local school districts to develop comprehensive early mathematics curricula in preschool programs and the primary grades.

The NCTM standards define five *content* areas: Number & Operations, Geometry, Measurement, Algebra, and Data Analysis & Probability. The standards are described in this chapter, along with their application in the preschool years. NCTM also defines five *process* standards, consistent with the strategies suggested here: Problem Solving, Reasoning and Proof, Connections, Communication, and Representation. Problem solving and reasoning, as the position statement phrases it, are the "heart" of mathematics:

> While content represents the what of early childhood mathematics education, the processes . . . make it possible for children to acquire content knowledge. These processes develop over time and when supported by well-designed opportunities to learn. Children's development and use of these processes are among the most long-lasting and important achievements of mathematics education. Experiences and intuitive ideas become truly mathematical as the children reflect on them, represent them in various ways, and connect them to other ideas. (NAEYC & NCTM 2002)

For further explanations of NCTM's process standards and examples, see the work of Clements (2004) and Copley (2004), as well as the National Council of Teachers of Mathematics Web site (www.nctm.org).

## Scientific inquiry and its relationship to mathematics

Young children are doing math when they measure and graph the daily growth of bean seedlings, when they notice the changing patterns of shadows on a wall, or when they predict how many more cups of sand it will take to fill a hole and then check by counting. But they are also doing science. Gelman and Brenneman point out that "to do science is to predict, test, measure, count, record, date one's work, collaborate and communicate" (2004, 156). Because of this close connection between mathematics and science, I have chosen to include "the doing of science"—*scientific inquiry*—in this chapter.

> Science inquiry refers to the diverse ways in which scientists study the natural world and propose explanations based on the evidence derived from their work. Inquiry also refers to the activities of students in which they develop knowledge and understanding of scientific ideas, as well as an understanding of how scientists study the natural world. (NCSESA 1996, 23)

Within science, scientific inquiry is perhaps the area that has been most investigated because of young children's evident interest in observing and thinking about the world (Eshach & Fried 2005). Inquiry skills are in evidence when preschoolers are:

▶ raising questions about objects and events around them;

▶ exploring objects, materials, and events by acting upon them and noticing what happens;

▶ making careful observation of objects, organisms, and events using all of their senses;

▶ describing, comparing, sorting, classifying, and ordering in terms of observable characteristics and properties;

▶ using a variety of simple tools to extend their observations;

▶ engaging in simple investigations in which they make predictions, gather and interpret data, recognize simple patterns, and draw conclusions;

▶ recording observations, explanations, and ideas through multiple forms of representation including drawings, simple graphs, writing, and movement;

▶ working collaboratively with others; and

▶ sharing and discussing ideas and listening to new perspectives. (Worth & Grollman 2003, 18)

Doing inquiry and learning about inquiry are "critical content areas" of science. Like any skills, they need to be learned and practiced—and this is where the other content areas of science make their appearance. Teachers doing inquiry-based science choose meaningful subject matter from the life, physical, earth, and space sciences for young children to practice on. In other words,

> Inquiry and subject matter are both important and cannot be separated. Children may need direct instruction for some specific skills, such as learning to use a magnifier. And they can practice some skills on their own, such as categorization. But children develop their inquiry skills as they investigate interesting subject matter, and children build theories about interesting subject matter through the use of inquiry skills. (Worth & Grollman 2003, 156)

The connections between early mathematics and science are reflected in NAEYC's own program accreditation criteria for science (NAEYC 2005, Criterion 2.G) and technology (Criterion 2.H). The NAEYC criteria note that children should have opportunities to collect and represent data, make

inferences about what they observe, and have access to technology. These opportunities and the associated learning are also explicit in the guidelines for early mathematics education (Criterion 2.F).

# Young children's development in mathematics and scientific inquiry

Young children, like those quoted at the beginning of the chapter, start with only an intuitive or experiential understanding of mathematics. They don't yet have the concepts or vocabulary they need to *use* what they intuitively know or to *connect* their knowledge to school mathematics. The preschool teacher's task is "to find out what young children already understand and help them begin to understand these things mathematically From ages 3 through 6, children need many experiences that call on them to relate their knowledge to the vocabulary and conceptual frameworks of mathematics—in other words, to 'mathematize' what they intuitively grasp" (NAEYC & NCTM 2002).

The goal of early mathematics education, then, is to build "mathematical power" in young children (Baroody 2000). This power has three components: a positive disposition to learning and using mathematics; understanding and appreciating the importance of mathematics; and engaging in the process of mathematical inquiry. Turning children's early and spontaneous mathematics play (child-guided experience) into an awareness of mathematical concepts and skills is at the heart of intentional teaching in this area.

Similarly, in science we want to capitalize on children's "natural inclination to learn about their world" (Landry & Forman 1999, 133), expose them to the uses and benefits of scientific processes in everyday life, and involve them in scientific inquiry as they figure out how the world works. Here, too, children are naturally inclined to explore their surroundings. But they depend on us to give them a rich environment for inquiry and to develop their child-guided discoveries into a growing understanding of how science works.

To promote children's science inquiry, the intentional teacher takes care to design the physical setting, plan the areas of science children will focus on, and establish overall goals for learning. Once children begin exploring, however, "what actually happens emerges from a dynamic interaction among the children's interests and questions, the materials, and the teacher's goals" (Worth & Grollman 2003, 158).

In early mathematics and science, free exploration is important—but by itself it is not enough. There are concepts, principles, and vocabulary that children will not construct on their own. Even for those areas in which their investigations are key,

---

## Materials That Promote Mathematical and Scientific Exploration

Children can manipulate, count, measure, and ask questions about almost any object or kind of material. Yet there are some things teachers should make sure to have in their classrooms to promote exploration and thinking about the components of mathematics and scientific inquiry.

### Number and operations

• Printed items containing numbers and mathematical or scientific symbols—e.g., signs, labels, brochures, advertisements with charts and graphs

• Things with numbers on them—e.g., calculators, playing cards, thermometers, simple board games with dice or spinners

• Numbers made of wood, plastic, or cardboard (make sure they are sturdy so children can hold, sort, copy, and trace them)

• Discrete items children can easily count—e.g., beads, blocks, shells, poker chips, bottle caps

• Paired items to create one-to-one correspondence—e.g., pegs and pegboards, colored markers and tops, egg cartons and plastic eggs

### Geometry and spatial sense

• Materials and tools for filling and emptying—water, sand; scoops, shovels

• Everyday things to fit together and take apart—e.g., Legos, Tinkertoys, puzzles, boxes and lids, clothing with different types of fasteners

• Attribute blocks that vary in shape, size, color, thickness

• Tangram pieces

• Wooden and sturdy cardboard blocks in conventional and unconventional shapes

• Containers and covers in different shapes and sizes

• Materials to create two-dimensional shapes—e.g., string, pipe cleaners, yarn

• Moldable materials to create three-dimensional shapes—e.g., clay, dough, sand, beeswax

• Things with moving parts—e.g., kitchen utensils, musical instruments, cameras

• Books that feature shapes and locations, with illustrations from different perspectives

• Photos of classroom materials and activities from different viewpoints

• Materials that change with manipulation or time—e.g., clay, play dough, computer drawing programs, sand, water, plants, animals

• Materials to explore spatial concepts (over/under, up/down) and to view things from different heights and position—e.g., climbing equipment, empty boxes (large cartons from appliances and furniture), boards

• Maps and diagrams

children do not always construct mathematical or scientific meanings from them. Clements (2001) suggests teachers consider whether children's thinking is developing or stalled. "When it is developing, they can continue observing. When it is stalled, it is important to intervene" (Seo 2003, 31). In this way, adult-guided experience supplements child-guided exploration.

# Teaching and learning in mathematics and scientific inquiry

Young children need many opportunities to represent, reinvent, quantify, generalize, and refine their experiential and intuitive understandings that might be called "premathematical" or emerging

---

## Measurement

- Ordered sets of materials in different sizes—e.g., nesting blocks, measuring spoons, pillows, paintbrushes, drums

- Ordered labels so children can find materials and return them to their storage place—e.g., tracings of measuring spoons in four sizes on the pegboard in the house center

- Storage containers in graduated sizes

- Materials that signal stopping and starting—e.g., timers, musical instruments, tape recorders

- Materials that can be set to move at different rates of speed—e.g., metronomes, wind-up toys

- Things in nature that move or change at different rates—e.g., slow- and fast-germinating seeds, insects that creep and scurry

- Unconventional measuring tools—e.g., yarn, ribbon, blocks, cubes, timers, ice cubes, containers of all shapes and sizes

- Conventional measuring tools—e.g., tape measures, scales, clocks, grid paper, thermometers, measuring spoons, graduated cylinders

## Patterns, functions, and algebra

- Materials with visual patterns—e.g., toys in bright colors and black-and-white, dress-up clothes, curtains, upholstery

- Materials to copy and create series and patterns—e.g., beads, sticks, small blocks, pegs and peg boards, writing and collage materials

- Shells and other patterned items from nature

- Original artwork and reproductions featuring patterns—e.g., weavings, baskets

- Pattern blocks

- Routines that follow patterns

- Stories, poems, and chants with repeated words and rhythms

- Songs with repetitions in melody, rhythm, and words

- Computer programs that allow children to recognize and create series and patterns

## Data analysis

- Tools for recording data—e.g., clipboards, paper, pencils, crayons, markers, chalk

- Materials for diagramming or graphing data—e.g., newsprint pads and easels, graph paper with large grids, posterboard

- Small objects to represent counted quantities—e.g., buttons, acorns, pebbles

- Boxes and string for sorting and tying materials into groups

- Sticky notes and masking tape for labeling

---

mathematics. To do this effectively, intentional teachers design programs so that children encounter concepts in depth and in a logical sequence:

> Because curriculum depth and coherence are important, unplanned experiences with mathematics are clearly not enough. Effective programs also include intentionally organized learning experiences that build children's understanding over time. Thus, early childhood educators need to plan for children's in-depth involvement with mathematical ideas. . . . Depth is best achieved when the program focuses on a number of key content areas rather than trying to cover every topic or skill with equal weight. (NAEYC & NCTM 2002)

This need to focus on a limited number of key concepts and skills at each level is further highlighted in NCTM's amendment of its own standards, *Curriculum Focal Points for Prekindergarten through Grade 8 Mathematics* (NCTM 2006). Intentional teachers use a variety of approaches and strategies to achieve this focused emphasis. They integrate mathematics into daily routines and across other domains in the curriculum, but always in a coherent, planful manner. This means that the mathematics experiences they include "follow logical sequences, allow depth and focus, and help children move forward in knowledge and skills"; it does not mean "a grab bag of experiences that seem to relate to a theme or project" (NAEYC & NCTM 2002).

In addition to integrating mathematics in children's play, classroom routines, and learning experiences in otherwise nonmathematic parts of the curriculum, intentional teachers also provide carefully planned experiences that focus children's attention on a particular mathematical idea:

> Helping children name such ideas as horizontal or even and odd as they find and create many examples of these categories provides children with a means to connect and refer to their just-emerging ideas. Such concepts can be introduced and explored in large and small group activities and learning centers. Small groups are particularly well suited to focusing children's attention on an idea. Moreover, in this setting the teacher is able to observe what each child does and does not understand and engage each child

# Computer Technology

Computers can also play a role in early mathematics and science education, if the technology is used appropriately (Hyson 2003). For young children, this involves becoming competent with the mechanics of the hardware and learning different software programs. Software should be open-ended and promote discovery. Good programs pose a problem, ask children to solve it, and provide feedback (Clements 2002). Programs that pose problems that have "correct" answers can be productive if the feedback causes children to reflect on where their reasoning was off and solve the problem differently. If the program does not do this, then an adult working alongside the children can.

Technology has the added advantage of increasing children's flexibility with manipulatives, that is, they can often move onscreen objects more easily than real objects. Onscreen objects don't pose the problems of size or awkwardness of handling that real ones might, and most children work well with the keyboard and mouse. This is *not* to say computers should replace real objects, which also provide other sensory feedback and foster motor skills. Rather, computers can extend the range of materials children use and their possibilities for transformation.

Finally, "contrary to initial fears, computers do not isolate children. Rather they serve as potential catalysts for social interaction" (Clements 1999, 122). Children working at the computer solve problems together, talk about what they are doing, help and teach friends, and create rules for cooperation. In fact, they prefer working on the computer with a friend to doing it alone.

Adults play a critical role in mediating children's exposure to and use of computers in learning about mathematics and science. Below are the responsibilities teachers must fulfill, and

in the learning experience at his own level. (NAEYC & NCTM 2002)

Research points us to the materials and activities that foster the development of mathematical and scientific concepts. Young children are concrete, hands-on learners. They need to manipulate materi-

the opportunities they can create, while using technology with young children.

▶ Choose child-friendly hardware such as oversized keyboards, colored keyboard keys, a small mouse, and touch screens. Help children acquire basic keyboard and mouse skills through modeling and guided instruction. Arrange the environment so children are able to work together and thus learn from their peers.

▶ Select software that emphasizes open-ended, discovery learning, rather than drill and practice. Introduce the software to a few children at a time. For example, demonstrate what you can do with a program at small group or at the beginning of choice time. Let every child who wants have an opportunity to try it. Then make the program available in the computer area throughout the day.

▶ Locate computers to facilitate social exchange. Allow enough space for more than one chair; an ideal setup is two in front for children and one to the side for an adult. If resources permit, have more than one computer in the area so children can share ideas. Place computers where they are visible from other areas in the room so children can wander over and join in. Encourage children to work together at the computer. Be available to help to mediate social disputes (see **Chapter 5** for more on this).

▶ Encourage children to verbalize their thinking and reasoning as they solve problems with the technology itself or with problems and puzzles posed by the program. Encourage them to reflect on their solutions if the program's feedback says their answer is wrong. It is especially important for adults to be present at these times so children do not get discouraged and walk away. Turn error messages into learning opportunities.

▶ Balance computer activities with lots of opportunities to manipulate real objects and solve comparable real-life situations.

## Teachers Overheard in the Computer Area

The interactions children and their teachers have around computers can enhance or diminish children's experience of technology. These comments were recorded during computer time. Characterizations of the adult's behavior are in parentheses.

Inappropriate/ineffective

"You can use the computer yourself, but I or Mrs. G. must help you." (*hovering*)

"Your four minutes at the computer is up. It's Alex's turn now." (*overscheduling*)

"Don't touch anything but the number keys and the spacebar." (*discouraging experimentation*)

"When you get stuck this way, you should hit the spacebar like this. Then hit the arrow key like this. Then hit the other arrow key like this. There. It's all fixed." (*doing it for them*)

Effective

"Why don't you see what happens when you press this key." (*letting the child do it*)

"I see. You're pressing the spacebar to move the cursor." (*labeling a child's actions*)

"Erin, can you tell Josh how you got your picture out of the printer?" (*referring one child's problem to another child*)

"The program we used to draw with at small group time today will be on the computer tomorrow for anyone who wants to play with it." (*encouraging choices and exploration*)

**Source:** W. Buckleitner & C. Hohmann, "Blocks, Sand, Paint . . . and Computers," in *Supporting Young Learners: Ideas for Preschool and Day Care Providers*, eds. N.A. Brickman & L.S. Taylor, 174–83 (Ypsilanti, MI: High/Scope Press, 1991). Excerpted, by permission, from p. 179.

als to construct ideas about the physical properties of objects and their transformation. Spontaneous investigations are most common with discrete play objects such as Legos, blocks, or puzzles and continuous materials such as sand, water, or clay (Ginsburg, Inoue, & Seo 1999). Children tend to use mathematical and scientific inquiry most frequently during construction or pattern-making activities. Computers can also play a role in early mathematics and science education, if the technology is used appropriately (Hyson 2003). (See the box **Computer Technology**.)

Perhaps less expected is the finding that mathematical and scientific thinking is fostered by social interaction. When students share hypotheses and interpretations, question one another, and are challenged to justify their conclusions, they are more likely to correct their own thinking (Campbell 1999). In fact, agreements and disagreements during peer-to-peer dialogue more often prompt reflection and reconsideration than does adult-delivered instruction (Baroody 2000), perhaps because many teachers underestimate children's early grasp of mathematical principles (Kamii 2000).

For that reason, understanding how children learn in the areas of early mathematics and scientific thinking is essential to meaningful teaching in this area. Research points to the effectiveness of the following general support strategies:

▶ **Encourage exploration and manipulation**— Provide materials with diverse sensory attributes and allow children sufficient time and space to discover their properties. At the same time, "the ways children use objects are often very different from those that we intend or define" (Seo 2003, 30). Teachers might not see art materials or dramatic play props as mathematical manipulatives, but children do, as they count the Velcro strips on a smock or the rooms in a dollhouse. Indeed, there is nothing they do not count! It's the same for science: The classroom pet may be there mostly for the purpose of promoting social responsibility, but children are also observing Sniffy the guinea pig's habits and life cycle.

▶ **Observe and listen**—Attend to the questions children ask. The problems they pose for themselves or to adults offer a window into their mathematical and scientific thinking.

▶ **Model, challenge, and coach**—Demonstrate hands-on activities that children can imitate and modify. Provide experiences that stretch their thinking. Discuss what does (not) work, pose questions, and suggest alternative approaches to finding a solution.

▶ **Encourage reflection and self-correction**—When children are stuck or arrive at an incorrect mathematical solution or scientific explanation, do not jump in to solve the problem or correct their reasoning. Instead, provide hints to help children recon-

sider their answers and figure out solutions or alternative explanations on their own.

▶ **Provide the language for mathematic and scientific properties, processes, and relationships**— Introduce the language for children to label their observations, describe transformations, and share the reasoning behind their conclusions.

▶ **Play games with mathematical elements**— Games invented for or by children offer many opportunities, for example, to address issues of (non)equivalence, spatial and temporal relations, and measurement.

▶ **Introduce mathematical and scientific content**— Children enjoy good books about counting, especially when these invite participation. Storybooks and nonfiction texts are also a wonderful way to introduce real-life problems whose solutions depend on mathematical reasoning. (See **Resources** for a Web site that suggests books for young children related to early mathematics and science, as well as other early learning topics.) Similarly, children are fascinated by observing the natural world —things that float or sink, shifting cloud patterns, plant and animal habits. Thus "science should be considered content for mathematics and literacy experiences" (Gelman & Brenneman 2004, 156).

▶ **Encourage peer interaction**—As noted above, children can sometimes explain mathematical and scientific ideas to their peers more effectively than adults can. Sharing ideas, particularly conflicting ones, prompts children to articulate and, where necessary, modify their understanding.

In general, an investigative approach works better than a purely didactic one. Begin with a "worthwhile task, one that is interesting, often complex, and creates a real need to learn or practice. Experiencing mathematics in context is not only more interesting to children but more meaningful" (Baroody 2000, 64). It also makes learning in both mathematics and science more likely and more lasting. As Ginsburg and his colleagues note,

[Rote instruction that does not emphasize understanding] does little to inculcate the spirit of mathematics— learning to reason, detect patterns, make conjectures, and perceive the beauty in irregularities—and may instead result in teaching children to dislike mathematics at an earlier age than usual. Clearly the early childhood education community should not implement at the preschool and kindergarten levels the kinds of activities that the National Council of Teachers of Mathematics is trying to eliminate in elementary school! (Ginsburg, Inoue, & Seo 1999, 88)

# Fitting the learning experience to the learning objective

The rest of this chapter describes what preschoolers learn as they begin to acquire mathematical literacy across NCTM's five content areas: Number & Operations, Geometry, Measurement, Algebra, and Data Analysis & Probability. Some of NCTM's standards, however, have labels that seem too sophisticated for what happens in preschool mathematics. That is, are young children doing what older children and adults know as "geometry," "algebra," or "probability" in preschool? In writing its standards document, NCTM opted to use one label for each area across the entire age range, from preK to grade 12, for a purpose. It wanted to emphasize that for each content standard, children at *every* age are learning aspects of math that relate to that standard. In this chapter, we have modified the labels slightly to be more descriptive of the preschool learnings: hence, "Geometry and spatial sense" and "Patterns, functions, and algebra" and simply "Data analysis."

Of those five areas, **number and operations, geometry and spatial sense,** and **measurement** are areas particularly important for 3- to 6-year olds, because they help build young children's "foundation" for mathematics learning:

> For this reason, researchers recommend that algebraic thinking and data analysis/probability receive somewhat less emphasis in the early years. The beginnings of ideas in these two areas, however, should be woven into the curriculum where they fit most naturally and seem most likely to promote understanding of the other topic areas. Within this second tier of content areas, patterning (a component of algebra) merits special mention because it is acces-

sible and interesting to young children, grows to undergird all algebraic thinking, and supports the development of number, spatial sense, and other conceptual areas. (NAEYC & NCTM 2002)

This chapter describes concepts and skills in the three key areas, as well as in **patterns, functions, and algebra** and **data analysis.** Each section is divided into those concepts and skills that seem most likely to be learned, or best learned, through children's own explorations and discoveries (child-guided experience) versus those concepts and skills in which adult-guided experience seems to be important in going beyond, as well as contributing to, what children learn through their independent efforts. As with every other domain, of course, this division is not rigid.

# Number and operations

This is the first of three areas that NCTM (2000; 2006) has identified as being particularly important for preschoolers. In the preschool years, number and operations focuses on six elements, or goals for early learning. (For further explanations and examples, see Clements 2004 and Copley 2004.) *Counting* involves learning the sequence of number words, identifying the quantity of items in a collection (knowing that the last counting word tells "how many"), and recognizing counting patterns (such as 21-22, 31-32, 41-42 . . .). *Comparing and ordering* is determining which of two groups has more or less of some attribute (comparing them according to which has the greater or lesser quantity, size, age, or sweetness, for example), and seriating, or ordering, objects according to some attribute (length, color intensity, loudness). *Composing and decomposing* are complementary: Composing is mentally or physically putting small groups of objects together (e.g., two plus three blocks makes five blocks), while decomposing is breaking a group into two or more parts (e.g., five spoons is two spoons plus two spoons plus one spoon).

*Adding to and taking away* is knowing that adding to a collection makes it larger and subtracting makes it smaller. When this understanding is combined with counting and (de)composing, children can solve simple problems with increasing efficiency. *Grouping and place value* are related: Creating sets of objects so each set has the same quantity creates "groups." Grouping in sets of 10 is the basis for understanding place value later (i.e., making groups of 10 and then counting the "leftovers"). *Equal partitioning* is dividing a collection into equal parts, a prerequisite to children's understanding of division and fractions.

To develop the mathematical understanding and skills encompassed in these six areas, preschoolers need an optimal blend of child-guided and adult-guided experiences. Because early mathematical development depends so much on manipulating objects, it is important that young children have ample opportunities to work with materials that lend themselves to ordering, grouping and regrouping, and so on. Children "intuit" certain properties and processes from their spontaneous explorations, while adults help them explore these ideas and provide the mathematical vocabulary to describe the numerical properties and transformations they observe. Adults also challenge children to try additional transformations and to reflect on the results. These experiences and the role of the intentional teacher are described below.

Of the key knowledge and skills in the area of number and operations, intuiting number and its properties, as well as performing informal arithmetic seem to develop best with child-guided experience. On the other hand, adult-guided experience seems to prove helpful for counting and numeration, as well as for performing simple arithmetic.

## C Child-guided experience is especially important for learnings such as:

### C1 Intuiting number and its properties

Even before they learn how to count, young children come to an informal understanding of quantity and equivalence. For example, they can identify small quantities (up to four or five) by eyeballing them. They use one-to-one correspondence to establish equivalence (e.g., matching each blue bead with a yellow one to see that there are equal quantities of each). And they can make equal sets (i.e., make

groups) by putting one in each pile, then another in each pile, and so on (e.g., to distribute an equal number of pretzels to each person at the table). Although lacking a formal knowledge of "sets" in a strict mathematical sense (defined as a collection of distinct elements, such as a set of squares versus triangles), young children can create groups and recognize when items share all or some attributes with other items in a group.

Mathematicians, researchers, and practitioners agree that a central objective of early mathematics education is developing children's "number sense" —an intuition about numbers and their magnitude, their relationship to real quantities, and the kinds of operations that can be performed on them. Early number sense includes this eyeballing ability, called "subitizing" (recognizing quantities by sight alone, usually for quantities of four or fewer) and establishing one-to-one correspondence, which is the foundation of counting (i.e., linking a single number name with one, and *only one*, object).

An ability to identify equivalence is also fundamental to understanding number. Most 3-year-olds can recognize equivalence between collections of one to four objects (e.g., two hearts and two squares) without actually counting items. They can also recognize equal collections in different arrangements as being the same (e.g., three squares on the top and two on the bottom has the same number as one square on top and four on the bottom). Most 4-year-olds can make auditory-visual matches, such as equating the sound of three dings with the sight of three dots. These findings suggest that by age 3, children have already developed a nonverbal representation of number, although it's unclear what this mental representation is like or how accurate it is. Regardless, they can clearly represent and compare objects even before they can count them (Baroody 2000).

The part-part-whole concept is the understanding that a whole number (e.g., 7) can be represented as being made up of parts (e.g., 4 and 3, or 5 and 2, or 6 and 1). Part-part-whole representation is a precursor to number operations, helping children understand addition and subtraction; most 3- and 4-year-olds can describe the parts of whole numbers up to 5, with understanding of larger numbers developing around age 6 (Copley 2000, 58–59).

*Teaching strategies.* Intuition develops with experience. Teachers help young children develop their number sense by surrounding them with a number-rich environment offering many opportunities to work with materials and processes that rely on numbers and their operations, as shown in the following examples:

■ Display materials around the classroom printed with numerals and mathematical or scientific symbols. Make sure the numerals are large enough for children to see and are placed at their eye level. Include manipulatives in the shape of numerals made of wood or cardboard, as well as toys and other items with numerals on them.

■ Offer materials and games that convey the concept of number, such as dominoes and dice. Encourage children to explore them and to find matches; for example, "Can you find another domino with the same number of dots?"

■ Label and describe number phenomena that occur naturally in the children's play; for example, "There are four wheels on Katie's truck and two more, or six, on Donald's" and "You found the second mitten for your other hand."

■ Provide materials that allow children to explore one-to-one correspondence, such as nuts/bolts and cups/saucers. Children will also make one-to-one correspondences with any sets of materials they are playing with; for example, giving each bear a plate or ball.

■ Include materials that can be broken down and divided into smaller parts, such as a lump of clay that can be divided into smaller balls or a piece of fruit that can be sliced or separated into sections. Unit blocks, Legos, and other toys with equal-size parts that children can build up and then break down into components also work well.

■ Offer materials that are the same in some ways but different in others; for example, blocks of the same shape in different colors. When children use these materials, make observations that highlight their attributes; for example, "All the blocks in your tower are square, but only some blocks are red."

## C2 Performing informal arithmetic

"Informal" arithmetic is something similar to adding and subtracting nonquantitatively—that is, without using numbers or other written symbols. Even before receiving formal instruction, preschoolers often are able to solve simple nonverbal addition and subtraction problems (e.g., two children are drawing at the table when a third child sits down; one child fetches "another" piece of paper for her). Children begin by acting out problems with objects (setting out two blocks, and then "adding on" one more). Later they can substitute representations (e.g., tally marks on paper) for the physical objects and form mental representations (visualizing two blocks, then adding one more). Teachers can be helpful in encouraging representation (NCTM 2000).

Forming mental representations is significant: "They understand the most basic concept of addition—it is a transformation that makes a collection larger. Similarly, they understand the most basic concept of subtraction—it is a transformation that makes a collection smaller" (Baroody 2000, 63). Preschoolers can attain this basic understanding of operations on their own, especially when adults support its development. The understanding is fundamental to later success in school mathematics.

In kindergarten, children sometimes solve simple multiplication (grouping) and division (partitioning) problems by direct modeling with objects. For example, in the problem, "Jane has 10 pennies and wants to give 2 to each friend. How many friends can she give pennies to?" the child would make piles with 2 pennies each and count the number of piles to arrive at "five friends." If the problem were stated as "Jane has 10 pennies and wants to give the same number to each of five friends. How many pennies will each friend get?" the child would put a penny in each of five piles and repeat the process until the pennies ran out, then count the number in each pile to arrive at "2 pennies per friend." With adult guidance, these informal strategies are replaced by formal number knowledge and counting strategies (Campbell 1999).

*Teaching strategies.* Because preschoolers tend to think concretely, handling objects and working with visual representations help them carry out and understand operations. Below are examples of strategies teachers can use to promote this learning:

■ Provide many small items that children can group and regroup, adding and subtracting units.

■ Pose simple addition and subtraction problems in the course of everyday experiences. For example, after a child sets the table, say "Remember that Thomas is out sick today" or "Mrs. King is going to join us for snack" and see whether they subtract or add a place setting. Or during block time, say "Jane wants to make her wall one row higher. How many more blocks will she need?"

■ Pose simple multiplication or division problems that children can solve using concrete objects. For example, give a child a collection of objects at small group and say "Give the same number to everyone." Or say, "There are five children and everyone wants two scarves to wave in the wind. How many scarves will we need to bring outside?"

## A Adult-guided experience is especially important for learnings such as:

### A1 Counting and numeration

For young children, counting and numeration (reading, writing, and naming numbers) involves understanding numbers, which is knowing the number names and the position of each one in the sequence, ordinal numbers (e.g., first, second, . . .), and cardinal numbers (one, two, . . .); notation, which is reading and writing numerals and recognizing the simple mathematical symbols +, –, and = ; counting, which is determining quantity and equivalence; and sets, which involves creating and labeling collections and understanding "all" and "some." These are each elaborated below.

As with learning letter names and shapes, children cannot acquire knowledge of number names and numerals unless adults give them this information. At times, children will ask, "How do you write *three*?" or "What comes after 10?" but the intentional teacher also is proactive in introducing the vocabulary and symbols children need to understand and represent mathematical ideas (Campbell 1999). With adult guidance, children can then apply this knowledge to solve problems, including those of measurement and data analysis.

Early counting is finding out "how many," which is a powerful problem-solver and essential to comparing quantities. Research (Gelman & Gallistel 1978) has identified five principles of counting: (1) stable order (2 always follows 1); (2) one-to-one correspondence (each object is assigned a unique counting name); (3) cardinality (the last counting name identifies "how many"); (4) order irrelevance (objects can be counted in any order without changing the quantity); and (5) abstraction (any set of objects can be counted). Adult-guided experience helps preschoolers develop these understandings.

Older preschoolers use counting to determine that two sets of objects are equivalent. Between the ages of 3 and 4, as they acquire verbal counting skills, children gain a tool more powerful than their earlier subitizing for representing and comparing numbers, including collections larger than four items. They recognize the "same number name" principle (two collections are equal if they share the same number name, despite any differences in physical appearance). Children generalize this principle to any size collection they can count. Similarly, by counting and comparing two unequal collections, preschoolers can discover the "larger number" principle (the later a number word appears in the sequence, the larger it is). By age 4, many preschool children can name and count numbers up to 10 and compare numbers up to 5. When they have ample opportunities to learn the counting sequence, children often learn to name and count to 20 by age 5 (Clements 2004). They are also fascinated by large numbers, such as 100 or "a gazillion," even if they only know them as number names without a true sense of their value.

Equal partitioning builds on and is related to the concept of equivalence. Equal partitioning is the process of dividing something (e.g., a plate of eight cookies) into equal-size parts (e.g., to serve four children). Children as young as 4 or 5 begin to solve such problems [...] using strategies such as dividing the ob[...] [...] number of piles (four) an[...] each pile (Bar[oody...]

*Teachin[g...]*
Gardner say[s...] arena for c[...] thing" (19[9...]) or take ad[...] objects an[...] example:

■ Notice t[...] number of[...] vide mate[rials...] observatio[n...] count; for [...] on an ankl[e...]

■ Make nu[...] different m[...] classroom. [...] for children to expl[ore...] Use numerals on sign-up sheets [to] indicate not only the order but also how many [...] ns they want or for how long (two minutes, three flips of the sand-timer). Children can indicate their preferences with numerals or other marks (stars, checks, hash marks).

■ Use written numerals and encourage children to write them. For example, when they play store, encourage them to write size and price labels, orders, and the amount of the bill.

■ Use everyday activities for number learning and practice. For example, as children gather or distribute countable materials, engage them in counting at clean-up (counting items as they're collected and put away), small group (handing out one glue bottle per child), and choice time (distributing playing cards). At snack or mealtimes, ask the table setter to count children to determine how many place settings are needed. Pose simple number problems such as "Our group has six, but Celia is sick today. How many napkins will we need?" or

"How many cups of sand will it take to fill the hole?"

■ Use games as a natural yet structured way to develop counting skills. Examples include board games with dice (moving a piece the corresponding number of places) or physical movement challenges [count]ing the number of times the tossed beanbag [lands] in the bowl).

[Use th]e children's own questions as the springboard [for te]achable moments. For example, Baroody [(201]0) imagines an incident when Diane says to her [tea]cher,

"My birthday is next week, how old will I be? Will I be older than Barbara?" The teacher could simply answer, "You'll be 4, but Barbara is 5 so she's still older." Or, the teacher can respond by saying, "Class, Diane has some interesting questions with which she needs help. If she is 3 years old now, how can she figure out how old she'll be on her next birthday?" The teacher could follow up by posing a problem involving both *number-after* and *number-comparison* skills: "If Barbara is 5 years old and Diane is 4 years old, how could we figure out who is older?" (65)

■ Use children's literature. Not only are there many appealing counting books, but there are storybooks in which mathematics is used to solve a problem. For example, read books where the story is about sharing a quantity of something fairly. Before the problem is solved in the book, ask children to suggest solutions by trying them out with materials or working through simple ideas in their heads. Children can work alone or in pairs. After reading the book, encourage them to comment on the solution(s) in the text. As a follow-up, they might role-play the same or similar situations using props you supply or they make themselves.

### A2 Performing simple arithmetic

Younger preschoolers perform simple arithmetic qualitatively. Older preschoolers, however, begin to add and subtract whole numbers quantitatively—that is, using numerals to abstractly represent numbers of objects, rather than physically manipulating or visualizing the objects. They are able to do this because they can hold a representation of quantities in their minds. For example, they may say out loud, "Two and one more is three" or "If Kenny isn't here today, I only need four napkins." Although they can do this most readily with numerals up to 5, some preschoolers can handle numbers up to 10.

Research shows they may also be capable of adding and subtracting very simple fractions. For example, when researchers hid part of a circle behind a screen and then hid another fraction, children could visually identify what the total amount was. They understood that two halves made a whole, a half plus a quarter circle resulted in a three-quarters circle, and so on (Mix, Levine, & Huttenlocher 1999). Such research suggests that children can grasp the basic idea behind simple fractions if adults pose interesting challenges.

*Teaching strategies.* Arithmetic follows fixed rules or conventions. Like combining letters into words, performing operations on numbers depends on knowing these rules. With support from their teachers, preschoolers are capable of solving simple arithmetic problems that come up in play and exploration. They are also motivated to use arithmetic "like grown-ups." Teachers can therefore readily implement strategies such as the following to enhance young children's early understanding and use of arithmetic:

■ Use real objects when helping children work through arithmetic problems. For example, if a child is building a tower of three blocks, count them with the child, and ask how many blocks there would be if the child added two more to make it taller. Wonder aloud how many blocks would be left if the child made it three blocks shorter. The child can add or subtract the actual blocks and count the result to determine the answer.

■ Pose challenges that build on children's interests. For example, if a child has drawn a picture of a dog, wonder aloud whether the child can draw a dog "twice as big" or "half as big."

■ Encourage children to use arithmetic to answer their own questions. For example, if a child says, "My daddy wants to know how many cupcakes to bring for my birthday tomorrow," you could reply "Well, there are 16 children and two teachers. Plus your daddy, and your brother will be here, too.

How can we figure out how many cupcakes you'll need to bring?"

■ Encourage children to reflect on their arithmetic solutions rather than telling them if they're right or wrong. When children are stumped (though not yet frustrated) or arrive at erroneous answers, resist the temptation to give the answer or correct them. Instead, offer comments or pose questions that encourage them to rethink their solutions. Baroody (2000) gives this example:

> Kamie concluded that 5 and two more must be 6. Instead of telling the girl she was wrong and that the correct sum was 7, her teacher asked, "How much do you think 5 and one more is?" After Kamie concluded it was 6, she set about recalculating 5 and two more. Apparently, she realized that both 5 and one more and 5 and two more could not have the same answer. The teacher's question prompted her to reconsider her first answer. (66)

■ Start with one fraction at a time. For example, children are fascinated by the concept of "one half." If they learn—really learn—through repeated experiences that half means two parts are the same and together they make up a whole, then they can generalize this concept later to thirds, quarters, and so on.

# Geometry and spatial sense

This is the second of three areas NCTM (2000; 2006) has identified as being particularly important for preschoolers. In the preschool years, learning about geometry and spatial sense focuses on four elements: *Shape* refers to the outline or contour (form) of objects and comprises identifying two- and three-dimensional shapes. *Locations, directions, and coordinates* refers to understanding the relationship of objects in the environment. *Transformation and symmetry* is the process of moving (sliding, rotating, flipping) shapes to determine whether they are the same. It also involves building larger shapes from smaller shapes, a common construction activity in preschool. *Visualization and spatial reasoning* is creating mental images of geometric objects, examining them, and transforming them. At first children's mental representations are static; that is, children cannot manipulate them. Later children can move and transform images mentally; for example, deciding whether a chair will fit in a given space or imaging a puzzle piece rotated.

Spatial concepts and language are closely related; for example, where someone stands determines whether he is "in front" of or "behind" another object. "Thus, it is important that young children be given numerous opportunities to develop their spatial and language abilities in tandem" (Greenes 1999, 42). Because society has specific conventions for labeling various shapes, transformations, and especially concepts of position, location, and so on, teachers especially need to enhance children's descriptive vocabulary in this domain.

Of the key knowledge and skills in the area of geometry and spatial sense, child-guided experience seems most helpful for creating familiarity with two- and three-dimensional shapes and their attributes, as well as for orienting self and objects in space. To create, name, and transform shapes, on the other hand, as well as to articulate position, location, direction, and distance, adult-guided experience seems necessary.

# C Child-guided experience is especially important for learnings such as:

## C1 Familiarity with two- and three-dimensional shapes and their attributes

For young children, shape knowledge is a combination of visual and tactile exploration, which begins in infancy. During the preprimary years, NCTM expects children to recognize, name, build, draw, compare, and sort two- and three-dimensional shapes. Although most adults support children's recognition of two-dimensional shapes, they often overlook the need to give children experiences with three-dimensional shapes, which focus their attention on geometrical features. For example, exploring the rolling of cylinders and other shapes helps children to understand the properties of the circle versus the ellipse. These skills involve perceiving (differentiating) such attributes as lines and cubes;

circles, cylinders, and globes; sides and edges; corners, angles, and so on. Preschoolers are also engaged in investigating transformations with shapes (composing and decomposing), and they demonstrate an intuitive understanding of symmetry. (Note: Children need adult-guided experiences to learn to accurately label and describe transformations and symmetry.)

*Teaching strategies.* Communication skills are important in all areas of mathematics, but especially so in geometry. Spatial concepts and language are closely related—words facilitate an understanding of such concepts as on top of, next to, behind, and inside. For example:

■ Introduce both two- and three-dimensional shapes, giving children opportunities to explore them. Include both regular and irregular shapes. Engage children in drawing and tracing the shapes. Provide models (drawings, molds, maquettes) and tools children can use to trace or copy them. Visual and physical shapes help young children grasp the essential attributes of each.

■ Encourage children to sort shapes and provide reasons for their groupings. Encourage them to describe why objects are *not* alike.

■ Encourage children to combine (compose) and take apart (decompose) shapes to create new shapes; for example, combining two triangles to make a square or rectangle (composing), and vice versa (decomposing). Engage them in discussions about these transformations.

■ Provide materials that have vertical (i.e., left/right halves are identical) or horizontal (i.e., top/bottom halves are identical) symmetry; for example, doll clothes, a teeter-totter, and a toy airplane. For contrast, provide similar but asymmetric materials; for example, a glove, slide, and toy crane. Engage children in discussing how the two sides (or top and bottom) of objects are the same (symmetrical) or different (asymmetrical).

## C2 Orienting self and objects in space

Spatial relations—how objects are oriented in space and in relation to one another—are the foundation of geometry, which involves understanding and working with the relationships of points, lines, angles, surfaces, and solids. Compared with toddlers, preschoolers navigate their bodies and move objects with greater skill and confidence. Younger children still tend to see and describe space from their own perspective (egocentrism), but older preschoolers can begin to represent and describe things from another person's point of view (perspective taking).

*Teaching strategies.* Because mathematics is the search for relationships, early instruction should focus on physical experiences through which children construct understandings about space. Teachers do this primarily by providing materials and allowing children ample time to explore them:

■ Create different types of space in the classroom and outdoor area—small spaces for children to maneuver into and around; large open areas where children can move about freely; spaces to crawl over and under, in and out, up and down, and around and through. Ask and talk with children about their relationships with objects and with one another.

■ Provide materials, time, and ample space to build with construction toys. For example, notice all the relative dimension and position concepts Trey and his friends used when they made a "bus" with large wooden blocks and invited their classmates and the teacher to get onboard:

> The group quickly decided the bus was too *small*, so they made it *bigger* by adding many more seats. The children worked hard *fitting* the big wooden blocks *end-to-end* to make the bus *longer*. They made a "driver's seat" *up front* and made a "steering wheel" to fit *on top* of the "dashboard." They also decided to build a "refrigerator" in the *back* of the pretend bus. Trey said it needed to be "on the back wall, but in the *middle* of the aisle." (Tompkins 1996b, 221)

■ Provide other materials to move and rearrange; for example, doll house furniture or pedestals to display artwork. Provide materials children can use to organize and construct collages.

 **Adult-guided experience is especially important for learnings such as:**

### A1 Creating, naming, and transforming shapes

The ability to accurately name, describe, and compare shape, size (scale), and volume is important for children to acquire during the preschool years. With appropriate experiences and input they learn to transform shapes to achieve a desired result and describe the transformation ("I'm making this bridge longer by adding more blocks at the end and holding it up in the middle"). They can also create and label symmetry in their two- and three-dimensional creations. Language is critical in all these activities. Therefore, as vocabulary expands, so does geometric understanding.

*Teaching strategies.* Building on preschoolers' explorations of shapes, teachers should explicitly focus the children's attention on features and what the shapes will do (e.g., "Which of these shapes can roll?") and provide words for these characteristics. Children should be given opportunities to identify shapes in various transformations, including reflections and rotations and (de)compositions. For example:

■ Comment and ask children about differences in the size and scale of things that interest them; for example, their own bodies, food portions, piles of blocks. Encourage them to alter two- and three-dimensional materials and comment on the transformations, including whether their manipulations resulted in regular or irregular forms.

■ Identify and label shapes and their characteristics throughout the children's environment (classroom, school, community). Go on a shape hunt in the classroom (e.g., a "triangle search"). Use increasingly sophisticated vocabulary words; for example, say "On our walk, let's look for all the square signs" or "You used cubes and rectangular blocks to build your dollhouse." Remember to supply names of three-dimensional as well as two-dimensional shapes.

■ Encourage the exploration of shapes beyond conventional ones such as circles, squares, and triangles. Young children enjoy hearing and learning names such as *cylinder* and *trapezoid*. Even if they do not fully grasp the meaning and characteristics, they become attuned to the variety of spatial phenomena in the world. Also important is giving children diverse examples of triangles and other shapes, not just the equilateral triangle that is the only example offered in many classrooms.

■ Use printed materials to focus on shape. Cut out photographs from magazines that feature shape pictures and encourage children to sort them. Create a shape scrapbook for the book area. Encourage children to build structures like those in story and information books. Refer to the books and talk with children about their choice of materials, how they match the attributes in the illustrations, and how they are recreating or modifying the structures or both.

■ Challenge children to imagine what their structures would look like with one or more elements transformed, for example, in location or orientation. Encourage them to represent and verify their predictions. For example, in *Building Structures with Young Children*, Chalufour and Worth share this note from a preschool teacher:

> I brought a whiteboard and markers over to the block area because Abigail was having a hard time imagining what her tower would look like if it were built with the blocks placed vertically instead of horizontally, as she had done. Not only did it help her to see a drawing of a tower built with verticals, but Adam came up to the drawing and pointed to one of the blocks near the top of the drawing, declaring that he didn't think it would balance on top of the one under it. So he and Abigail proceeded to use the drawing to build a tower and, lo and behold, Adam was right! Tomorrow I'm going to invite him to tell the group about the event. We can ask Adam how he knew that the vertical wouldn't balance. (2004, 45)

## A2 Articulating position, location, direction, and distance

Expectations in this area involve concepts of position and relative position, direction and distance, and location (NCTM 2000). With appropriate adult guidance, preschoolers can use position and direction words and follow orientation directions. They also are able to begin moving beyond their egocentric perceptions to predict another's perspective. For example, with experience they can describe how someone else would see something from his perspective, and can give appropriate directions or instructions to another person.

*Teaching strategies.* Teachers need to supply vocabulary, of course. But preschoolers still master such ideas through a combination of concrete experience and mental imagery, so teachers need to provide many opportunities for them to represent these concepts in two- and three-dimensional ways:

■ Make comments and ask questions that focus on location and direction; for example, "You attached the sides by putting a long piece of string between the two shorter ones" or "Where will your road turn when it reaches the wall?" Comment on naturally occurring position situations, such as "Larry is climbing the steps to the slide, Cory's next, and last is Jessica."

■ Use various types of visual representations to focus on these concepts. Engage children with making and interpreting maps—for finding a hidden object, for example. Children can draw diagrams of the classroom, their rooms at home, and other familiar places. Ask them about the placement of the objects. Comment on the location of things in their drawings using position words; for example, "You have a big poster over your bed" or "What's poking out behind the curtain?" Ask children to draw, paint, build, or use their bodies to represent favorite books featuring characters or objects in relation to one another. For example, ask them to draw the three bears sitting around the table or to lie down next to one another like the three bears in their beds. Because society has specific conventions for labeling various concepts of position, location, and so on, teachers are especially needed to enhance children's descriptive vocabulary in this domain.

■ Create occasions for children to give directions; for example, when helping one another or leading during large group. This requires them to use position and direction words such as "Hold the top and push down hard into the dough" or "Stretch your arms over your head and then bend down to touch your toes." Encourage children to volunteer as the leader.

■ Use movement to focus on spatial concepts. Provide objects that can be thrown safely, such as beanbags and foam balls, and interact with children about distance. Use simple movement directions for games and dances at large group such as Hokey Pokey. Invent variations to games and dances by frequently modeling the adding of a new twist. Get the children engaged in making up variations of their own.

■ Talk about trips children take with their families or about walks and field trips with the class. For example, "Does your grandma live close to you or far away?" or "We took a long ride to the zoo on the bus, but after we parked, it was just a short walk to the monkey cage."

## Measurement

This is the third of three areas NCTM (2000; 2006) has identified as being particularly important for preschoolers. In the preschool years, learning about measurement focuses on two elements: *Attributes, units, and processes* refers to developing concepts about size and quantity, arranging objects to compare them, estimating differences (e.g., by eyeballing, lifting), and quantifying differences with nonstandard (e.g., footsteps) and standard (e.g., tape measure) tools. *Techniques and tools* comprises learning measuring rules such as starting at zero, aligning or equalizing beginning points, and not allowing gaps. It also includes becoming familiar with standard measuring tools such as rulers, scales, stopwatches, and thermometers. As with spatial concepts, measurement benefits from language, especially comparison words.

Of the key knowledge and skills in the area of measurement, comparing (seriating) or estimating without counting or measuring seems to develop best with child-guided experience, while adult-guided experience seems integral for counting or measuring to quantify differences.

 **Child-guided experience is especially important for learnings such as:**

### C1 Comparing (seriating) or estimating without counting or measuring

Young children are able to grasp the basic concept of one thing being bigger, longer, heavier, and the like, relative to another. Making comparisons is the beginning of measurement. According to NCTM's standards (2000), preschoolers should be engaged in comparing length, capacity, weight, area, volume, time, and temperature.

At first, children make qualitative comparisons by matching or ordering things ("Stacy is the short one, and Bonnie is tall" or "My cup holds more water than yours") rather than quantitative comparisons that use counting or measuring. To estimate, they use their various senses, such as eyeballing (visual), lifting (kinesthetic), or listening (auditory). They may compare length by aligning blocks on the bottom and seeing how much they stick out on top, or listen to instruments to compare their loudness.

*Teaching strategies.* Teachers can draw on children's interest in comparing to focus their attention on quantitative and qualitative differences. Examples abound in mathematical and scientific applications, including those suggested here:

■ Make comments and ask questions using comparison words ("Which of these is longer?" or "Does everyone have the same number of cookies now?") Ask children whether they think something is wider (softer, heavier, louder, colder) than something else.

■ Provide ordered sets of materials in different sizes, such as nesting blocks, measuring spoons, pillows, paintbrushes, and drums. Affix ordered labels that children can use to find materials and return them to their storage place; for example, four sizes of measuring spoons traced on the peg board in the house center. Provide storage containers in graduated sizes.

■ Encourage children to move at different rates throughout the day and comment on relative speed. Make transitions fun by asking children to proceed to another area or activity "as slow as a snail" or "as fast as a rocket." Acknowledge their observations about speed and what affects it. A preschool teacher shared this anecdote:

> At outside time, James was pushing two children around the playground on the toy taxi. When the adult asked if she could have a ride, he said "Sure." After going around two more times, James stopped the taxi and said, "Get off. You're too fat and I can't go fast." Acknowledging the validity (if not the kindness) of his observation, the teacher got off the taxi so he could move at a faster clip. (Graves 1996, 208).

■ Call children's attention to graduated changes in nature. Comment on seasonal fluctuations in temperature (e.g., "It feels colder now than it did when we went to the pumpkin patch. We're wearing heavier jackets."). Plant a garden and ask children how long they think it will take before the seeds germinate, the vegetables are ready to eat, and so on.

# A  Adult-guided experience is especially important for learnings such as:

## A1  Counting or measuring to quantify differences

Many older preschoolers and kindergarten children are able to understand the idea of standard units, and with well-conceived learning experiences, they can begin to determine differences in quantity by systematic measurement. They use their knowledge of number to make comparisons. At first, they use nonstandard units such as how many steps it takes to cross the schoolyard in each direction or the number of song verses to clean up different areas of the room. With teachers' assistance, they acquire the understanding that it is useful to employ conventional units and measuring devices, such as inches on a ruler or minutes on a clock.

*Teaching strategies.* There are many opportunities throughout the day for children to engage in measurement; for example, when they are building something or resolving a dispute. However, it usually does not occur to preschoolers to measure or quantify things to solve these problems. Adults can actively encourage children to use measurement in these situations. For example:

■ Provide conventional and unconventional measuring devices, and encourage children to use them to answer questions or solve problems. Conventional devices include rulers, tape measures, clocks, metronomes, kitchen timers, and spring and balance scales. Unconventional ones include string or paper towel tubes for length, sand timers for duration, grocery bags for volume (three bags of blocks were needed to make a tall tower, only one bag to make a short one), unmarked bags of clay or sand

---

## Gathering Data to Resolve a Social Conflict

Undertaking an investigation with adult help is one way to resolve disputes (for more, see **Chapter 5**). Some conflict situations lend themselves to collecting information that can be quantified and interpreted to reach a fair solution. In this example, a group of older preschoolers resolve a dispute by measuring heights and are surprised by the result!

John, Liza, and Devon argued about the order of turn-taking to drive the big truck around the playground. They decided the biggest person should go first, then the next biggest, then the smallest. They would make a list and check off each name as that person finished a turn. John chalked *J, D, L* on the blacktop and moved to get on the truck. But the conflict was not yet over:

**Devon:** Hey! I'm bigger than you. I get to go first!
**John:** No you're not. I'm the biggest one.
**Liza:** Let's measure and find out.

The children stood against the wall and asked their teacher to make a chalk mark where each of their heads touched. Then they got the tape measure and asked their teacher to write down how many inches tall each child was. She wrote 41 next to the J, 42 next to the D, and 44 next to the L.

**Liza:** It's me! I'm the biggest!
**Devon:** Yeah, and I'm next. John is last.
**John:** But I can stay on the longest because there's no one after me!

---

for weight. Children can also develop their own devices. When children ask measurement-related questions ("Which is heavier?") or have disputes ("I am too taller by a whole, big lot!"), ask them which of these tools might help them arrive at an answer or solution.

■ Pose measurement challenges that children will be motivated to solve; for example, "I wonder how many cups of sand it will take to fill all 12 muffin tins?" Ask "How many more . . . ?" questions, such as "How many more pieces of train track will you need to close the circle?" Here's an amusing challenge shared by a curriculum developer and writer who works with preschoolers:

> I was stretched out on the floor against a wall. I said, "I wonder how many me's long the wall is?" The children thought this was very funny, but they were intrigued to figure out the answer. Some estimated by simply "envisioning" the response. Others wanted to use the direct route, having me move and stretch out while they counted the number of repetitions. When I said I was too comfortable and didn't want to move, the children had to come up with another solution. They decided that two of them equaled one of me, so they stretched in a line along the wall and counted how many of them it took. With my help, they then divided the number of children in half. (Stuart Murphy, 2004, pers. comm.)

■ When resolving social conflicts with children, ask how they could measure to guarantee a fair solution; for example, to make sure everyone gets to play with a toy the same amount of time.

■ Use visual models to help children understand and quantify differences. For example, make a daily routine chart where the length of each part in inches is proportional to its duration in minutes. Give time checks ("Five minutes to clean-up") with visual and auditory cues.

■ Create opportunities for group construction projects, such as laying out a garden, making a bed for each doll within a defined space, or recreating a supermarket after a class field trip. These often lead to situations where children have different opinions and need to "measure" to find out who is right or what solution will work. Sometimes you will need to suggest this method of resolving the difference of opinion.

■ Include units of measurement when sharing information with children; for example, "I went grocery shopping for an hour last night" or "My puppy gained 5 pounds since the last time I took him to the vet."

# Patterns, functions, and algebra

In the preschool years, learning about patterns, functions, and algebra focuses on two elements: *Identifying patterns* involves recognizing and copying patterns and determining the core unit of a repeating pattern. It includes visual, auditory, and movement patterns. Deciphering patterns requires inductive reasoning, which is also a precursor to understanding probability. *Describing change* is using language to describe the state or status of something before and after a transformation. For example, "When I was a baby, I couldn't drink out of a cup" or "When we raised the ramp a little higher, my car went all the way to the book shelf."

Of the key knowledge and skills in the area of patterns, functions, and algebra, child-guided experience seems to help children recognize, copy, and create simple patterns and also recognize naturally occurring change. For children to identify and extend complex patterns and to control change, on the other hand, children seem to benefit most from adult-guided experience.

**C** Child-guided experience is especially important for learnings such as:

C1 **Recognizing, copying, and creating simple patterns**

For young children, this area encompasses an awareness of patterns in the environment (visual, auditory, temporal, movement). Preschoolers can acquire the ability to copy or create simple patterns with two elements, such as A-B-A-B or AA-BB. Even before they know the word *pattern,* children notice recurring designs or routines in their lives, whether it be on their clothing, the stripes on a kitten's back, or the order of each day's activities.

Preschoolers generally need at least three repetitions of a pattern before they can recognize or repeat it.

*Teaching strategies.* Patterns and series of objects or events are plentiful in the world. Teachers can actively help children become aware of common patterns and series. Simple observations and questions can lead them to notice and create regularity and repetition. For example:

■ Ask children to do or make things that involve series and patterns. For example, at small group, give children drawing or sculpting materials and invite them to represent their families—from the smallest to the biggest members. Other materials that lend themselves to pattern making include string and beads in different colors and shapes (e.g., to make a necklace), multi-colored blocks in graduated sizes (e.g., to make a train), and pegs and pegboards (e.g., to make a design).

■ Acknowledge the patterns children spontaneously create in art and construction projects. When they are busy building, acknowledge their work with a smile and a descriptive statement such as, "I see a pattern in your tower. First you used two rectangles, then you used a cylinder, and then you added two more rectangles and a cylinder" or "This reminds me of the Eiffel Tower. It's wide at the bottom and becomes narrow at the top" (Chalufour & Worth 2004, 38). Music also provides many opportunities for calling attention to patterns; for example, "You sounded two loud, one soft, two loud, and one soft beat with the rhythm sticks." Movement provides another source for constructing patterns; for example, a series of two or three steps repeated in sequence (side, side, hop, side, side, hop).

■ At large group, encourage children to move their bodies into graduated positions such as lying, sitting, and standing. Move through transitions at slow, medium, and fast paces.

■ Read and act out stories in which size, voice, or other graduated qualities play a role, such as The Three Bears or The Three Billy Goats Gruff. At small group, ask children to make beds for the three bears with play dough. At large group, have them choose which instrument the papa, mama, or baby bear would play, depending on variations in pitch or loudness.

## C2 Recognizing naturally occurring change

Noticing and describing changes includes identifying what variable or variables are causal. This is a mathematics concept, but it is also prominent in science in children's developing awareness of changes in the world around them and possible reasons for these. For example, children see changes in their own bodies (e.g., getting taller) or the growth of a flower. Although they are often unable to identify the causal factor accurately, young children do make tentative guesses, both right and wrong, about the changes they see. For example, "I'm 5 today. That means I'm taller" or "The flower grew up because the wind blew on it from the bottom."

*Teaching strategies.* The most important strategy teachers can follow in this area is to notice and acknowledge children's awareness of changes in their environment and initiate situations in which change can be created, observed, and investigated; for example, by discussing the growth of vegetables in the school garden or experimenting with color mixing at the easel. Repeating and extending children's comments about the changes they observe is a signal you are listening to them. Calling their attention to change and showing you are interested in their reaction, and in their explanations, is also a form of acknowledgment. For example:

■ Repeat children's comments to acknowledge their spontaneous seriation. When LaToya said, "These giants are hungrier because they have bigger teeth," her teacher agreed: "Those bigger teeth will help the monsters eat lots more food."

■ Extend children's comments. Josh was washing his hands at the sink when his teacher turned on the water in the next sink full blast. Josh said "Mine is running slow." She turned down her water and said "I made mine slow*er* like yours."

■ Call children's attention to cycles in nature with concrete examples. Point out the seasonal variations in schoolyard plants or the changing thickness of children's jackets from fall (lightweight) to winter (heavy) to spring (back to light). Document changes with photographs.

# A Adult-guided experience is especially important for learnings such as:

## A1 Identifying and extending complex patterns

Simple patterning is something young children do spontaneously. With experience and adult input, they learn to do more. For example, older preschoolers and kindergartners are able to analyze, replicate, and extend the core unit of a complex repeating pattern with three or more elements (A-B-C-A-B-C; 1-22-3-22-1), provided they see or hear it several times (Clements 2004). They can also begin to recognize what are called "growing" patterns—that is, patterns where successive elements differ (rather than repeat) but still proceed according to an underlying principle, such as counting by ones or twos (2-4-6). The same principles apply to patterns in nature. Younger children may notice past and present seasons; older preschoolers are ready to grasp the cycling of four seasons in a year.

*Teaching strategies.* Young children recognize simple patterns on their own. Complex patterns are more dependent on someone pointing them out, particularly if the viewer is not looking for them in the first place. Therefore, teachers can play an especially active role in helping young children identify and create multi-part repeating and growing patterns and sequences. For example:

■ Create complex patterns, then give children art and construction materials to copy them. Encourage them to create patterns and series on their own with three or more elements.

■ Comment on the patterns children create, identifying repeating elements. For example, Leah showed a painting of "two rainbows" to her teacher. It was actually two sequences or patterns of color that were exactly the same. "Look," her teacher commented, "this rainbow has green, red, purple, yellow, and so does this one—green, red, purple, yellow" (Hohmann & Weikart 2002, 469).

■ Introduce children to the books and catalogs with complex patterns used by ceramic tilers, landscape designers (brick and paver patterns), and fiber artists (weaving, quilting, needlepoint, basketry). Decorating stores often give away books of discontinued wallpaper and rug samples. With these, engage children in describing the patterns and finding corresponding examples that contain one or more comparable repeated elements in their own environment; for example, the walkway to the school or a knitted woolen hat.

■ Call children's attention to complex patterns and sequences in their environment; for example, seasonal cycles, markings on plants and animals, art and crafts in their community. Encourage children to duplicate and extend the patterns they see. For example, collect things with complex patterns on a nature walk and have children copy and extend the patterns (or create their own comparable one) at small group or art time.

■ Provide computer programs that allow children to recognize and create series and patterns.

■ Use music to call attention to patterns. Play instrumental music with pitch, tempo, or loudness patterns and encourage children to identify them. (This works best if the children are already familiar with the music.) Sing songs with repeating patterns (where verses and chorus alternate) or growing patterns (count-down songs such as I Know an Old Lady Who Swallowed a Fly). Comment on the patterns and encourage children to identify them.

■ Use movement to focus on pattern. Older preschoolers can sequence three movements. If children can master these, encourage them to be leaders and suggest three-step sequences.

## A2 Controlling change

Younger children spontaneously notice changes in themselves and their environment. Older preschoolers not only observe but can also begin to articulate the reasons for such changes. Moreover, they can deliberately manipulate variable(s) to produce a desired effect. For example, they may alter the choice of materials and their arrangement to better represent something in a collage, or alter the length and angle of a ramp to affect the speed of a toy car.

*Teaching strategies.* Teachers can promote awareness of and curiosity about change by fostering a spirit of inquiry in the classroom. An adult's investigative attitude is transmitted to the children. They will begin to pose the kinds of questions that scientists use when they want to know about the properties of materials and how they operate, then predict and estimate or measure the results to satisfy their curiosity. Children are eager to try different things ("manipulate variables") and see the outcomes. Here are some strategies:

■ Make "I wonder what would happen if . . ." statements; for example, "I wonder what would happen if you made this end of the ramp higher."

■ Ask "Suppose you wanted to . . ." questions; for example, "Suppose you wanted to make the car go slower. How do you think you could do that?"

■ During social problem-solving situations (see **Chapter 5**), encourage older preschoolers to anticipate the consequences of their proposed solutions. If they foresee difficulties, have them consider how to change all or part of the solution to avoid them.

# Data analysis

In the preschool years, learning about data analysis focuses on three elements: *Classifying or organizing* involves collecting and categorizing data (e.g., the favorite foods of children in the class). *Representing* is diagramming, graphing, or otherwise recording and displaying the data (e.g., a list of different foods, with check marks for every child who likes them). *Using information* involves asking questions, deciding what data is needed, and then interpreting the data gathered to answer the questions (e.g., what to have for snack).

Of the key knowledge and skills in the area of data analysis, children seem most capable of making collections and sorting/classifying by attributes

when they learn through child-guided experience and seem most capable of representing gathered information when they learn through adult-guided experience.

**C** Child-guided experience is especially important for learnings such as:

**C1** **Making collections, sorting/classifying by attributes**

Children love to collect and sort things. (Adults do too; science used to be primarily about collecting specimens and developing taxonomies to describe each group's characteristics.) Sorting involves noticing, describing, and comparing the attributes of things (animals, people, objects) and events. Young children can classify according to one attribute (e.g., color), and children slightly older can classify by two attributes (e.g., color and size). Examples of other attributes by which young children typically classify include shape, texture, temperature, loudness, type, and function.

*Teaching strategies.* Because children are natural collectors, they will eagerly initiate and respond to suggestions in this area of mathematical and scientific inquiry. By showing interest in their collecting and arranging and by asking skillful questions, teachers can extend child-guided explorations. For example:

■ Encourage children to make collections of items in the classroom, natural objects gathered on field trips, and various objects they bring from home. Provide containers (bowls, boxes, baskets) for them to sort the items. Encourage them to explain and describe their collections.

■ Encourage children to explain why things do *not* fit into the categories they have created. For example, pick up an object and say "Would this one fit here?"

■ Provide opportunities to experiment with materials whose attributes involve all the senses, such as shape, texture, size, color, pitch, loudness, taste, and aroma.

■ Acknowledge and repeat children's attribute labels, including invented ones ("This fruit feels squishy on my tongue" or "The pebbles are bumply"). Use common words to build children's vocabulary ("You used lots of blue in your painting") and introduce new language to expand their descriptive language ("This cloth feels silky" or "You used all the rectangular blocks in your tower").

## A Adult-guided experience is especially important for learnings such as:

### A1 Representing gathered information

Representing information for purposes of data analysis means documenting categories and quantities with numbers, diagrams, charts, graphs, counters (e.g., one button for each occurrence), and other symbols. These activities involve knowledge of both mathematics and scientific inquiry.

*Teaching strategies.* Children are naturally curious about their environment, but their investigations tend to be limited in scope and haphazard in procedure. Adult intervention can make children's explorations and conclusions more systematic and meaningful. Strategies such as the following help them use the "scientific method" to answer questions of interest to them:

■ Provide materials children can use to record and represent data, such as clipboards and graph paper.

■ Pose questions whose answering requires gathering and analyzing data; for example, "How many bags of gerbil food do we need to feed Pinky for one month?" Focus on things of particular interest to children, such as their bodies (height, age, hair color), animals and nature (types of pets), the dimensions of things they build, and what they and their friends like and dislike (foods, favorite story characters). For example, chart the ingredients children like best in trail mix, and use the data to make snacks in proportion to their tastes.

■ Put a "question box" in the classroom, and help children write out and submit questions. For questions that involve data collection, ask children to suggest ways to answer them.

■ Be alert to situations that lend themselves to documentation, such as construction projects that involve multiples of materials. For example, if children build a train, help them chart the number of cars or units in the track. If the cars are of different sizes, create rows or columns and encourage children to record the number of each. If train building is a recurring activity, investigate whether trains made on different days are longer or shorter, and by how many cars.

### A2 Interpreting and applying information

This component of data analysis refers to making and testing predictions, drawing conclusions, and using the results of an investigation to establish or clarify facts, make plans, or solve problems.

*Teaching strategies.* Without adult intervention, children's scientific inquiries often end with just collecting information. They may need help to analyze the data to draw one or more conclusions. Further, children's learning is less likely to end there if teachers encourage them to apply their learning to related topics and to solving problems. Try strategies such as these:

■ When disputes arise, encourage children to test out their hypotheses to resolve differences.

■ Make simple summaries of the data the children have collected or displayed. For example, "So in our class we have two children who are 5 years old, eight who are 4, and six who are 3."

■ Ask children for their ideas about what to do with the information they gather. For example, "Everyone likes pretzels, half of you like raisins, but there are only two check marks next to sesame sticks. So what does this mean we should put in the trail mix for our walk tomorrow?"

■ Encourage children to predict the outcome, record their predictions, and then compare them with the results. For example, have each child guess the length of a wall and record their estimates. Measure the wall and then discuss whose guess was too long, too short, or just right.

                    *           *           *

In her book *The Young Child and Mathematics*, Copley (2000) asks rhetorically,

Should we immediately correct young children's misconceptions about mathematics? Can we expect all children to solve problems in identical ways? Should we expect all the young children in a group to "get it" at the same time? . . . [T]he answer is *No!* As teachers, we need to remember that young children construct mathematical understanding in different ways, at different times, and with different materials. Our job is to provide an environment in which all children can learn mathematics. (8–9)

This chapter demonstrates that young children are eager to enter the worlds of mathematics and science. If adults create an atmosphere that encourages investigation and engages children in reflection, they will experience the small and large pleasures of these areas in their daily lives. In addition,

Positive experiences with using mathematics to solve problems help children to develop dispositions such as curiosity, imagination, flexibility, inventiveness, and persistence that contribute to their future success in and out of school. (NAEYC & NCTM 2002)

## Questions for Further Thought

**1.** Why do some early educators underestimate young children's mathematical and scientific abilities? What does this underestimation say about how practitioners define these subject areas and their self-perceived knowledge and skills? Are these areas considered "too hard" for children because early educators fear they are too complex for themselves?

**2.** How can early childhood educators change the public perception of early mathematics to encompass more than numbers and counting; for example, to include all five areas identified by mathematics educators (NCTM 2000)?

**3.** How can the early childhood field change the public perception of early science to include more than studying nature; for example, to include the scientific method of investigation?

**4.** What scientific knowledge should we expect preschoolers to master (comparable to the early standards NCTM has developed for mathematics)? What areas of substantive knowledge are appropriate or necessary for young children to have?

**5.** Do gender differences in mathematics and science (favoring the involvement of boys) emerge in the preschool years? If no, what lessons can we learn from early childhood practice to sustain interest in these subjects and prevent the emergence of a gender gap in later years? If yes, how can we alter our practices to instill and sustain ("fortify") lasting interest in girls?

**6.** How can (and should) we take advantage of emerging technologies to enhance early learning in mathematics and scientific inquiry? Is there such a thing as "bad" technology or do the (dis)advantages lie only in its application?

# Social Skills and Understandings

5

Kevin came over to his teacher and nestled in the crook of her arm with his head down. "You look a little sad right now," she said. Kevin replied, "I need a hug today."

When a teacher said his stuffed bear was hungry, Dante pinched a piece of play dough from his pile and told him it was a Teddy Graham for his bear.

At snack time, Dylan observed, "I'm happy because I like apples and grapes. But Ibrahim is mad because he wishes there was something else for snacks."

One day Kim saw her teacher rocking and singing to Tyler, who was upset after his grandfather dropped him off at school. The next morning, when Tyler sat by himself, Kim went over, stroked his arm, and hummed "Row, row, row your boat." Tyler began to hum with her. Then they went to the book area together and chose a book to look at until it was time for greeting circle.

Ms. Bailey decided to engage the preschoolers in a study of the adults at the center—Who are they? What work do they do? How are they connected to us? In listing the people they saw every day, the children came up with Mark the custodian, Bobby the cook, the bilingual volunteers Hun and Miranda, and the bus driver, Allison, as well as the teachers and center director. After Ms. Bailey asked the children what they wanted to know about each person, the children interviewed them and dictated to Ms. Bailey what they learned.

Social-emotional development has always been an essential—even the *primary*—domain of early childhood education. Today, however, teachers face special challenges as they prepare preschoolers to face a world in which drug use, violence and delinquency, damaging health practices, and extreme pressures to perform scholastically confront them at ever younger ages. In addition to acquiring social norms from home and school, young children are increasingly exposed to influences from the media and technology, where they face evolving and often contradictory expectations for personal and interpersonal behavior.

Thus, the importance of paying attention to children's social-emotional development is receiving renewed attention in the professional literature. The National Education Goals Panel (Kagan, Moore, & Bredekamp 1995) included what it called "approaches to learning" as one of five school readiness dimensions, along with cognitive and physical domains. These components such as curiosity, creativity, confidence, independence, initiative, and persistence can be difficult to define and measure, but they shape children's educational experiences in all other learning domains.

The significance of social-emotional development in education policy is also highlighted in major reports such as *Neurons to Neighborhoods* from the National Research Council (2000b) and *Emotions Matter: Making the Case for the Role of Young*

*Children's Emotional Development for Early School Readiness* (Raver, Izard, & Kopp 2002) from the Society for Research in Child Development. Organizations such as Fight Crime: Invest in Kids (2000) are also playing a role in raising public awareness that appropriate early intervention can help set at-risk children on a path toward better social adjustment throughout their school years and into adulthood (e.g., Reynolds et al. 2001; Schweinhart et al. 2005; Yoskikawa 1995). Ongoing projects apply the lessons from research to Head Start, child care, and other early childhood settings; an example is the Center on the Social and Emotional Foundations for Early Learning (CSEFEL), based at the University of Illinois at Urbana-Champaign, in its series *What Works Briefs* (2003).

## How social studies fits in

Often it is the early childhood setting that gives young children their first sense of community outside the home. As children learn in the classroom to get along, make friends, and participate in decision making, they are engaging in social studies learning. Typically, the curriculum also expands children's horizons beyond the school into the neighborhood and the wider world.

According to the National Council for the Social Studies (NCSS 1984), the purpose of social studies for young children (K–6) "is to enable them to understand and participate effectively in their world." Although NCSS has no social studies standards for the prekindergarten year, numerous states do. Their specifics vary, but state preschool standards address these general themes: (1) membership in a democratic classroom community; (2) location, place, relationships within places, movement, and region; (3) similarities and differences in personal and family characteristics; (4) how basic economic concepts relate to children's lives; and (5) appreciation of their own and other cultures (Gronlund 2006). A common thread is beginning to give children the skills and understandings for productive problem solving and decision making in a diverse culture. In the early childhood setting,

teachers help children to apply and integrate these skills and understandings in a framework for responsible citizen participation—in the classroom or school, and later in the larger society.

Throughout the years of school, social studies includes the knowledge from several disciplines, including history and geography. Although history and geography are fairly abstract concepts for preschoolers to cope with, young children do actively explore and develop concepts about time and space. It is therefore these subject areas, respectively, that act as the history and geography components of the preschool curriculum. For example, children between 4 and 7 years old become aware of personal time; that is, how past, present, and future are chronologically and sequentially ordered in their own lives. By age 6 or 7, they have rudimentary clock and calendar skills. Likewise, the components of geography include spatial relations; places and the people, plants, and animals that occupy them; and physical systems such as earth, sea, and sky and the cycles of nature (Jantz & Seefeldt 1999). These are ideas that combine social studies with mathematics and science (see **Chapter 4**).

Social studies is connected to social-emotional development, as well. As Mindes (2005) notes,

> In the preschool and primary years, social studies offer a structure for broad, theme-based content—content organized around a topic [or project] and offering multiple entry points and significant opportunities for investigation. For children, such content serves as a training ground for acquiring problem-solving skills as well as a laboratory for the development and elaboration of interpersonal coping skills and strategies. (16)

As the rest of this chapter explains, even preschoolers are developing rudimentary concepts about community, fairness, and democracy. The promotion of such concepts is also included in the NAEYC accreditation criteria for social studies (NAEYC 2005, Criterion 2.L).

For these reasons, this chapter includes beginning social studies as well as social skills and understandings. Clearly, in the early childhood years, these areas overlap considerably.

# Young children's development in social skills and understandings

Social-emotional competence has been defined as "the ability to understand, manage, and express the social and emotional aspects of one's life in ways that enable the successful management of life's tasks such as learning, forming relationships, solving everyday problems, and adapting to the complex demands of growth and development" (Elias et al. 1997, 2). Put another way, "socially competent young children are those who engage in satisfying interactions and activities with adults and peers and through such interactions further improve their own competence" (Katz & McClellan 1997, 1). Both these definitions emphasize that social development underlies and affects all other areas of learning and development, and so it is an important part of the early childhood curriculum (Hyson 2004). With minor variations, researchers and practitioners agree social-emotional competence is made up of the following four components, which clearly are closely related:

▶ **Emotional self-regulation**—responding to experiences with an appropriate range of immediate or delayed emotions. In preschool, this component is characterized by children's growing ability to focus and organize their actions; greater forethought and less impulsivity; and enhanced awareness of and ability to follow rules, rituals, and common procedures. Young children's language development and ability to hold mental images (representations) in mind enable them to defer gratification, anticipate the eventual satisfaction of their needs, and be more flexible in creating alternative goals and solutions to problems. A related aspect that is developing over the preschool years is **self-awareness,** the understanding that one exists as an individual, separate from other people, with private thoughts and feelings. Seeing oneself as independent and self-motivated is essential to understanding the ability to control one's own behavior.

▶ **Social knowledge and understanding**—knowledge of social norms and customs. Acquiring this knowledge in the early years is called "socializa-tion," or becoming a member of the "community." The classroom as a community, and the teacher's role in establishing a supportive group environment, is central in early childhood practice (as is establishing ties with families and the community beyond the school). To become a participating member of the group, children must be able to give up some individuality for the greater good, transitioning from the "me" of toddlerhood to the "us" of preschool. This shift is also the underpinning of civic competence, a key aspect of social studies (Jantz & Seefeldt 1999).

▶ **Social skills**—the range of appropriate strategies for interacting with others. Cognitive development, especially becoming able to take another's perspective and to empathize, facilitates the development of social skills. Preschoolers' emerging classification skills—understanding similarities and differences and concepts such as some/all—mean they become aware of how they are both like and not like others. Teachers can play a crucial role in helping young children respect differences they observe in gender, ethnicity, language, ability, ideas, and so on.

▶ **Social dispositions**—enduring character traits. These include socially valued ones such as curiosity, humor, and generosity, as well as unpopular ones such as closed-mindedness, argumentativeness, and selfishness. Babies are born with innate temperamental differences that manifest themselves immediately and endure into adulthood. However, environment also plays a significant role in shaping whether a difference is expressed constructively or not (e.g., as persistence or as its relative, stubbornness).

# Teaching and learning in social skills and understandings

Educators often seem conflicted about the relative importance of child- versus adult-guided experience in contributing to early social development. On the one hand, many educators would agree with Katz and McClellan (1997) that "in the preschool and early school years, children probably do not learn social competence through direct instruction—lessons, lectures, magic circles, workbook exercises, or suggestive and sometimes exhortatory approaches . . . [especially] attempted with the class as a whole" (20). Instead, children learn through the guidance they get from their interactions and behaviors, it is argued, because such guidance is "individualized." It maximizes the child's participation in constructing new knowledge and allows teachers to be warm and supportive during the interaction (Katz & McClellan 1997).

On the other hand, researchers and early childhood practitioners recognize the value of explicit adult intervention in such areas as conflict resolution and violence prevention (Levin 2003). Furthermore, young children can learn how to solve problems collaboratively and contribute to classroom policies through group strategies such as class meetings (Vance & Weaver 2002).

Drawing on work that integrates the best of both approaches, here are some general strategies for teachers to keep in mind as they deal with the class as a whole, as well as with small groups and individual children:

▶ **Modeling.** Modeling can be done at the group as well as the individual level. "Teaching by example, or *modeling,* is the most powerful technique that educators employ, intentionally or otherwise" (Elias et al. 1997, 56). So, for example, children learn positive behaviors when they see teachers being empathetic, solving problems, taking risks, admitting mistakes, and so on. And, while children can pick up knowledge and skills on their own from observing positive behaviors, their learning is enhanced if teachers occasionally make explicit what they are doing; for example, pointing out that they are listening to each child.

▶ **Coaching.** Coaching entails teachers breaking a positive behavior into its component parts, providing children with explicit instruction on how to perform and sequence the parts, creating opportunities for them to practice, and giving feedback on their efforts. Coaching social skills is thus comparable to providing instruction in domains such as literacy or physical movement. Like modeling, coaching can be done with either individual children or groups.

Coaching may be especially helpful with children who don't seem to be accepted by their peers, and whose resulting anger only increases their rejection. For example, a teacher might coach a child who is having trouble entering an ongoing play group. She might help the child to first observe from the sidelines, then use strategies such as offering help with some task that will further the group's play (e.g., fetching blocks) or accepting a role assigned by the leader. Children can also learn to notice cues (e.g., moving over to make room) that indicate the group is open to the child's entering.

▶ **Providing opportunities for practice.** As in any domain of learning, repetition and practice are vital to mastering appropriate social behavior. However, more so than in some disciplines, social-emotional learning not only "entails the learning of many new skills, it may also require the unlearning of habitual patterns of thought and behavior" (Elias et al. 1997, 55). Unlearning may be easier at the preschool age than in later years when habits are more ingrained. Nonetheless, norms in preschool and other settings can be incongruent; for example, listening to others may not be valued, or at least practiced, as much at home as in the classroom. Lack of exposure or practice at home is all the more reason for classroom teachers to give young children repeated opportunities to integrate social skills into their everyday behavior until the skills become natural and routine. Once social skills become automatic, they are more likely to generalize from the early childhood setting into kindergarten and beyond.

Above all, to help preschoolers become socially competent, we must remember that a lack of such skills does not mean children's attitudes or behaviors are "bad" or "naughty," any more than a toddler is being ignorant or willful by not reading or doing arithmetic! Young children simply do not *know* any better—yet. But through child-guided and adult-guided experience, preschoolers can acquire the social knowledge and skills that promote individual and collective well-being. As their mastery of social skills and knowledge increases, young children's positive interactions, as well as social dispositions such as curiosity, become an effective mechanism for learning in all other domains.

# Fitting the learning experience to the learning objective

The remainder of this chapter identifies the **emotional learning** and **social learning** that children typically develop around preschool age. By emotional learning, I mean the knowledge and skills related to children's recognition and self-regulation of their feelings. Social learning means the principles and strategies young children need for interacting successfully with others.

Both of these areas are further divided in this chapter into skills and knowledge that seem most likely to be learned, or best learned, through child-guided experience (including through peer interactions) versus those that seem to depend more on adult-guided instruction. As with every other curriculum area covered in this book, there is not a hard line between the two modes. Both child-guided and adult-guided experience require adult support, and both occur in an atmosphere the teacher has created. The learnings that appear in this chapter under "adult-guided experience" are those that seem to require more explicit teacher intervention.

As a general rule, dealing successfully with one's emotional state is a prerequisite to socializing effectively with others. Admittedly these dimensions often overlap. Conflict resolution, for example, involves both emotional self-regulation and social problem-solving skills. Yet the "emotional versus social" division in this chapter can help early childhood teachers think about which instructional components to emphasize in promoting learning in each area.

For both emotional and social learning, a central role of teachers in child-guided experience is to create a warm and caring program environment, as discussed in **Chapter 2.** When preschoolers first enter the program, their primary emotional attachments may still be to parents or other important caregivers elsewhere. With the help of family members, teachers play a crucial role in making a child's transition to the school setting successful. Adults need to understand the challenges young children face when they find themselves among strangers, in an unfamiliar place full of unfamiliar social and behavioral expectations. Even if the personal and social norms of a child's home and school are congruent, there is still an adjustment to the group nature of the classroom. Teachers who establish a supportive climate help young children to discover themselves and begin to form positive relationships with others. To the extent that children can navigate this territory on their own—with adults providing support only as needed—children's social and emotional confidence will be enhanced.

In addition to creating a supportive environment, teachers' role in adult-guided experience is to explicitly transmit various social-emotional skills and knowledge to young children. They can take concrete and conscious steps to promote children's positive attitudes about themselves and their abilities in a way that allows children to develop the self-control and motivation to solve problems with others and to become respectful, contributing members of the community. While these goals may sound lofty when applied to preschoolers, the early years lay the groundwork for later beliefs and behaviors as friends, family members, coworkers, and citizens.

## Emotional learning

Of the key knowledge and skills in the area of emotional learning, a positive self-identity and the ability to empathize with the feelings of others seem especially dependent on interpersonal interactions and other child-guided experience. In comparison, young children seem less likely to develop feelings of competence or to learn to recognize and label emotions without adult teaching and other intervention.

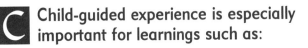 **Child-guided experience is especially important for learnings such as:**

### C1 Developing a positive self-identity

Self-identity is how one defines and feels about oneself as a person. A sense of self begins to emerge in infancy; its healthy development depends on the child establishing trusting and secure relationships with the important caregivers (parent, teacher, babysitter) in his life. Identity formation continues in preschool. When it forms "positively" it means the child recognizes and respects his own name, gender, aspects such as place in the family, physical appearance, abilities and limitations, ethnicity, and language or languages. It may include other elements such as religious group, neighborhood, and family structure (e.g., two-household family, single-parent home, foster home, grandparents or other relatives as head of the household).

*Teaching strategies.* Teachers help children develop a sense of who they are by supporting their transition from home to a school setting, providing labels for the many facets of their identity, and establishing a classroom atmosphere where every child feels valued. Children's positive self-images are fostered in an environment that uses teaching strategies such as these:

■ Support children through separations as they gradually gain in confidence that they can handle them on their own. Acknowledge and accept their feelings (e.g., anxiety, sadness) about being separated from family members. Those feelings predictably surface at drop-off time, but they also can arise at unexpected times during the day. Work with family members to help in the transition process; for example, to make it clear to their child when they will be back. Allow children to enter classroom activities at their own pace, or reenter them if children get upset and withdraw.

■ Let children know they are valued by giving them your positive, respectful attention. Focus primarily on the children throughout the day; that is, spend most of your time attending to them and what they are doing rather than in arranging materials, cleaning up, or interacting with other adults. Interact with children in calm and respectful tones; don't shout, shame, or use harsh words and actions. Address comments directly to them; don't talk about them in front of them as though they weren't there.

■ Address diversity and differences positively. Children are curious about differences, so don't shy away from naming and discussing them. Supply identity labels and use them in respectful ways. Talking with children about differences in gender, skin color, religious observances, family composition, and so on, can be affirming and instructive as long as the tone is accepting and factual, not judgmental. (See also **Valuing diversity** below.)

■ Provide children with nonstereotyped materials, activities, and role models. For example, read picture books that include women in nontraditional professions and men doing housework and nurturing children. Provide clothes and props for children of both sexes to role-play different occupations. Encourage children of both sexes to work with all types of equipment (carpentry tools, cooking utensils).

■ Encourage family members to become involved in the program. Be sure to include fathers, grandparents, and other regular caregivers, not just mothers. Provide many options for involvement so family members can choose what suits them. Examples include volunteering in the classroom (interacting with children, not just performing custodial chores), contributing materials, attending parent meetings and workshops, writing for a program newsletter, serving on advisory councils, meeting with teachers formally and informally to discuss the program and children's progress, and providing resources that can extend children's classroom learning into the home. Where feasible, provide transportation and child care as needed for families to participate in program activities.

■ Establish ties with the community. Community members may be willing and able to contribute time and caring directly to the children by serving as mentors and role models, hosting visits to their workplaces, or interacting with children in the classroom. Community members might include artists, tradespeople, business owners, senior citizens, and others involved in the community. The more diverse these community connections, the better we communicate to children that people of all backgrounds are valued and welcomed in the program.

## C2 Feeling empathy

Empathy is comprehending another person's feelings, being able to "put yourself in their shoes." Being empathetic includes traits such as caring, compassion, and altruism. Empathy has both a cognitive and an affective dimension. To be fully capable of experiencing and demonstrating empathy, the child must be developmentally capable of seeing a situation from someone else's perspective, which Piaget (1932/1965) called "decentering." This is an ability that is just emerging in the preschool years. Yet, there is evidence that even infants and toddlers have some ability to pick up on another's emotions (Hoffman 2000; Spinrad & Stifter 2006).

*Teaching strategies.* The main strategies intentional teachers use to support children's discovery of empathy are modeling, acknowledgment, and encouragement. Here are some examples:

■ Show (model) concern for children who are upset or angry. Use verbalizations, facial expressions, and body language to show you are aware of the way others feel. Describe your reactions and actions; for example, you might say "I'm giving Taryn the fuzzy monkey to cuddle. She's sad because her grandma is leaving today." Use your observations of children to provide them comfort in ways that suit their individual temperaments and preferences and so are likely to be effective. Children will follow your example, as this older toddler did:

> Devon sees his teacher give a teddy bear to Jason, who is crying when his father drops him off. The teacher holds Jason in his lap until he calms down and is ready to join others in play. The next day, Devon sees Susan crying after her mother leaves. He brings her a cuddly toy and pats her arm.

■ Allow and encourage children to express their feelings. Make them aware that others in similar situations share such emotions; for example, you could say "Claudia is mad because her dog chewed a hole in her new shoe. Tommy also felt angry the time his brother's puppy peed on his baseball hat."

■ Introduce perspective-taking activities and questions other than about feelings. For example, ask children to give directions for their classmates to follow, or wonder aloud how something looks to a person sitting on the other side of the table. Practicing the cognitive and perceptual skills required by perspective taking can generalize those skills to social-emotional situations.

■ Pair children of different ability levels or ages to sensitize them to the fact that often older or more able people can help others, while younger or less able people can learn from others. If children find themselves in either position at one time or another, they can better adopt different perspectives as the occasion warrants. Because young children are more often on the receiving end of help, it is especially empowering for them to be able to give it. They come to see the recipient of their assistance as an individual and feel good about their ability to bring about change. For example, a supervisor in an inclusion preschool recorded this anecdote:

> The children were very impatient with Michael, a learning-disabled child, who was often confused or took longer to accomplish things. Each day over a two-week period, the teacher asked a different child to help Michael with a task (e.g., cleaning up, pouring juice, putting on his coat). By the end of this period, most children became less impatient or angry. A few asked the teacher if they could continue to help; some asked Michael directly if he wanted help. The child helpers began to take pleasure in Michael's incremental but meaningful accomplishments, such as the first time he poured his own juice while a helper held the cup. They encouraged him to try more things on his own, which he did. In fact, Michael was more willing to try things with encouragement from his peers than he was with similar support from adults.

## A Adult-guided experience is especially important for learnings such as:

### A1 Developing feelings of competence

Competence is being able to do something. Feeling competent means having the self-confidence to undertake tasks with the expectation of success. For young children, it is important to judge success not according to adult standards but by what the child sets out to accomplish. Developing feelings of competence in young children is important because how children feel about themselves when they enter school has a great influence on their motivation and willingness to undertake challenging tasks.

*Teaching strategies.* Instilling self-confidence in young children is arguably the single most important task of early childhood teachers. Many of the strategies listed below were introduced in **Chapter 2** as best practices for early childhood teachers generally; they are especially pertinent here.

■ Create a classroom space and schedule that promote children's sense of efficacy and control. Establish and follow a consistent daily routine so children feel they know about and have some control over what happens in their environment. Arrange and label the classroom so children can find, use, and return materials on their own.

■ Encourage self-help skills in ways consistent with children's abilities and developmental levels. Give them time to do things on their own—getting dressed, cleaning up spills. Resist the temptation to do it easier, faster, or better yourself; don't worry if tasks are not done perfectly, because improvement will come with practice and maturation. Similarly, let them practice a task as often as they want to achieve mastery. Don't rush them or insist they do something else instead. The goal is for children to believe in their ability to take care of their own needs.

■ Introduce the next level of challenge once children have mastered the current one and are ready to move on. For example, at cleanup time, a younger child may be able to return blocks to the correct storage area but not yet be able to sort them on the shelf by size. For an older child, a teacher might ask, "Can you put this block with the others just like it?" Coach or model ways children can make everyday tasks easier or more efficient; for example, stacking dirty dishes instead of bringing them to the sink one at a time.

■ Support children's ideas and initiatives. Welcome their contributions, and encourage them to share ideas with peers. During choice time and other individual activities, encourage them to make plans and choices: for example, in what area or areas they will play; what materials they will use and how; whether to play on their own, or with others and with whom; how long they will engage in each activity. Equally important, during group activities, even during teacher-led group times, encourage

children to make choices and use materials in their own way. For example, provide just a general context (e.g., a fingerplay) but let children determine exactly how the activity unfolds.

■ Acknowledge and encourage children's efforts and accomplishments. While praise (e.g., "What a nice picture you've painted") can make them depend on the judgment of others to feel good about themselves, encouragement helps them evaluate their own competencies positively (e.g., "You really put a lot of interesting detail into your painting"). To encourage young children, watch and listen, imitate their actions and repeat their words, comment on what they are doing, and display their work to peers and parents. Involve families further by sending work home, sharing it at parent conferences and during informal contacts such as pick-up, and explaining what it shows about their children's learning.

■ Provide opportunities for children to be leaders; for example, ask them to suggest movements at large group or ways they might transition from one activity to another. Do not force or require children to lead, but give everyone the opportunity to do so. If you sense children are not listening to or do not fully understand what the leader is saying or doing, repeat the leader's ideas (making sure you have correctly understood them yourself) so the children can listen and try to carry out the ideas.

■ During large group activities, tune into the involvement level of the children. Be open to making group time longer or shorter, depending on how children respond. To allow extra time for children who are very involved, schedule something afterward that doesn't require initial participation by the entire group (e.g., outside time) so that children can join when they are ready (Perrett 1996). In this way, you communicate that task persistence is a worthwhile trait and also instill a sense of confidence that children can carry out their intentions to completion.

### A2 Recognizing and labeling emotions

Emotional awareness is understanding that one has "feelings" as distinct from thoughts, being able to identify and name those feelings, and recognizing that others have feelings that may be the same or different from one's own.

*Teaching strategies.* One's emotions arise naturally, but knowing what they are, what they mean, and how they are labeled by one's culture are things we must learn from others. Intentional teachers are ready to take advantage of events as they arise to introduce children to specific knowledge and skills in this area. Because preschoolers are capable of forming mental representations, teachers also can refer to hypothetical, past, and future situations in helping children master emotional experiences and vocabulary. Here are some strategies:

■ Attend to children's emotional states. When children express emotions in words or action, convey with your words, facial expressions, and gestures that you are paying attention. Make eye contact, get down on their level, focus on them.

■ Accept children's full range of emotions as normal. Do not judge emotions as "good" or "bad." However, do stop cruel or unsafe behavior that may result from emotions such as hurt, anger, fear, and frustration.

■ Label children's emotions and your own with simple words such as *angry, happy, sad.* Encourage children to name their own emotions; repeat the words they choose to use (e.g., "You said you feel all squiggly inside?"). Wait to introduce children to new emotions vocabulary until the heat of the moment has passed. During times of upset, children are usually too distracted by or invested in their feelings to absorb new words for them. Or introduce new words for feelings before conflicts arise; for example, while reading a book in which emotions are part of the story.

## Validating and Putting Words to Children's Feelings

Some children talk readily about their feelings. Some do not, perhaps because they are not encouraged to vocalize feelings at home. Here, a teacher helps a preschool class, and one child in particular, deal with the sadness of a friend's moving away.

Jack's family was moving to a distant city and he would be leaving preschool at the end of the week. Before Jack left, the teachers talked about his upcoming departure at greeting circle and asked the children how they felt about it. They used words like *sad* and *unhappy* and said they would miss him. After Jack was gone, they kept his name on the board for a couple of weeks with a line through it, talked about the fact that he had moved away, and shared things they remembered about him

The week after Jack left, a teacher noticed that Sean, who generally collaborated well with other children, was kicking over their blocks, grabbing away toys, and engaging in other nonsocial interactions. After solving a few immediate crises, she remembered that Sean had often played with Jack, and wondered whether he was having some unexpressed feelings about his friend's leaving. During a calm moment, she sat on the couch with Sean:

**Teacher:** I'm still sad that Jack moved away.

**Sean:** It's not fair.

**Teacher:** You think it isn't fair that he moved away.

**Sean:** Yes. Now I have no one to build big towers with.

**Teacher:** That's no fun.

**Sean:** I'm mad at Jack.

**Teacher:** You're mad because Jack moved away and now you can't play with him.

**Sean:** Yeah. He shouldn't have done that!

**Teacher:** Jack had to go because his mommy got a job in a different city. But it makes us sad and mad that he had to move away.

**Sean:** Yeah, really, really mad.

**Teacher:** It's okay to feel that way.

Just expressing his anger helped Sean to be less angry, but it didn't fully solve his problem. A few days later, the teacher had another one-on-one talk with him about what would make him feel better. Sean thought of two other children who liked to play with the blocks, and he used his existing social skills to enter their play.

Later, when Jack's mother sent a photo of him and his family, the teachers and children commented on how *happy* he looked in front of his new home. Sean told his teacher, "I still miss Jack; but I'm happy too, because now I have two new friends."

■ Especially during social problem-solving situations, point out to children that others also have feelings, but first make sure you correctly understand what each child is feeling; for example, say "Jimmy said it made him angry when you grabbed the toy from him." Refer children to the body language, facial expressions, and verbalizations of their peers ("Carla banged her fist on the table. People sometimes do that when they are angry"). Adult interpretation is especially helpful for children who are not yet adept at picking up these cues themselves or who are too overwhelmed and self-focused at a particular moment to notice others' feelings on their own.

■ Comment conversationally on the emotions you observe children expressing throughout the day. Be sure to notice and remark on both positive and negative feelings. For example: "You look sad this morning," "What a big smile! I think you're very happy," or "You sound excited about playing at Sally's house after school today."

■ Plan small group activities that focus on feelings. Preschoolers do not often talk about emotions in the abstract, but they can do so readily by reading books or creating and discussing artwork about people and events that evoke emotions (e.g., a visit from a grandparent, the arrival of a sibling, the loss of a pet).

■ In nonthreatening ways, help parents understand that children need to express and label their feelings appropriately. In workshops and informal exchanges, explain to parents that labeling and showing emotions in acceptable ways is an important part of early learning. Doing so will help their children adjust to the wide range of people and experiences they encounter in school and beyond. It can also help them deal better with situations at home, such as conflicts with siblings, limit setting by parents, or disappointments when hopes and plans do not work out.

## Social learning

Of the key knowledge and skills in the area of social learning, developing a sense of community, engaging in cooperative play, valuing diversity, and developing a framework for moral behavior all seem to typically develop in the course of child-guided interactions. But young children seem to need adult-guided experience to resolve conflicts, create and follow rules, and create and participate in democracy.

### C Child-guided experience is especially important for learnings such as:

### C1 Developing a sense of community

A community is a social group with common interests. Community members receive and give one another support for individual and group undertakings. Having a sense of community means seeing oneself as belonging to the group and sharing all or a significant number of its characteristics, beliefs, and practices. Through their interactions with peers in the classroom community, young children also deepen their understanding of social norms and conventions.

*Teaching strategies.* Intentional teachers create a sense of community in the classroom and help young children feel they belong to that community by employing strategies such as these:

■ Create an atmosphere in which children are expected to be kind to and supportive of one another. Refer to the children and adults in the classroom with phrases such as "our class," "all of us," "our group," and "all together." Express your own pleasure at being part of the classroom.

■ Arrange the room to include both open areas where large groups can assemble and enclosed areas with comfortable furniture conducive to intimate interactions.

■ Establish a consistent daily routine. When everyone is engaged in the same type of activity at the same time each day, it creates a sense of community. However, participating in the same *type* of activity does not mean everyone necessarily is doing the same thing. For example, all children can be engaged but involved with different activities during choice time; at small group, they may use the same materials but in different ways. During each activity, set an unhurried pace that lets children enjoy one another's company instead of feeling pressured to finish a task.

■ Call attention to occasions when children are working or sharing an experience together as a group. The occasions can be routine ("We got everything put away at clean-up so we can find them tomorrow at choice time") or special ("Look at all the shells we gathered at the beach. I wonder what we could do with them?"). Take photos of the group activities and put them in a class album, labeled with simple captions.

■ Organize activities that foster children's participation with others. Even those who tend toward solitary play can feel safe in groups that are noncompetitive and don't call attention to the individual. During brief whole group activities (such as greeting time or class meeting), encourage children to share problems and solutions. Or invite them to share something they are looking forward to. Or plan a special event together, and write down the children's ideas.

> [Adult-initiated] group times offer special social opportunities. During the child-initiated parts of the routine, children can choose how solitary or social they want to be—working by themselves, with a friend or adult, or with a group. Since some children will choose not to play with others during these times, the group times offer additional opportunities for them to participate in a social experience. At small group time, for example, where everyone is working with the same materials, children often share and discuss what they are doing, learn from one another, and help one another. At large group time, where everyone is engaged in a common action game or song (all of which are safe, low-risk social experiences), children have opportunities to contribute and demonstrate their ideas to the group as well as imitate and learn from their peers. (Hohmann & Weikart 2002, 246)

■ Involve children in the larger community. For example, involve children in projects around school, such as picking up playground trash or recycling classroom materials. Use stories, poems, songs, and chants ("narratives") to illustrate classroom and community activities. Welcome community guests to the classroom; make them comfortable, by children giving them a tour of the learning

centers, for example. Walk around the neighborhood and draw children's attention to how residents decorate their windows and yards and to what shopkeepers put in storefront displays. Visit local places (e.g., public library, farmers market) and take part in community activities (e.g., street fairs). Clip newspaper photos of familiar people, places, and events; write simple captions; and post them near the door so children and families can see and discuss them at drop-off and pick-up times.

## C2 Engaging in cooperative play

Cooperation is acting together toward a common goal. Cooperative play and collaboration in the early childhood classroom means playing and working with others. It includes sharing toys, space, friends, conversations, resources, skills, and ideas.

*Teaching strategies.* Learning to play with others happens through young children watching and imitating, and by trial and error. Because humans are social beings, we are intrinsically motivated to master techniques for human interchange. Nevertheless, it would be a mistake to assume children therefore engage in role-playing and collaborative behavior without any adult intervention. In fact, teachers perform a vital function helping children elaborate their roles in interactive play. Here are some strategies:

■ Promote interaction through your use of space and materials in the classroom. Examples include providing dress-up clothes that inspire group role-play and playground equipment that requires two or more children to operate. Don't arbitrarily limit the number of children who can play at one time in a given area, because it models exclusionary behavior. Whenever possible, provide enough of the same type of materials so children are not preoccupied with having access to them. If space or supplies are limited (e.g., the classroom has only one couch or only two computers), problem solve with the children on how to accommodate everyone who wants to use them. (See **Engaging in conflict resolution** below for individual and group problem-solving ideas.)

## Referring Children to Each Other for Assistance

Child-guided experience does not happen only when children play on their own. It often occurs when they interact with other children, and teachers can facilitate this interaction. Not only does the "recipient" benefit from the learning, but the "provider" also gets a sense of confidence in being able to help a peer.

At small group, the children are exploring play dough. Their teacher notices that Kyle is having trouble and refers him to Gabriella for help:

**Teacher:** Kyle, you look frustrated. What do you want to do with your play dough?

**Kyle:** I'm trying to make it go down, but it won't.

**Teacher:** You want your play dough to go down. You want to make it lie flat on the table?

**Kyle:** Yes, but it's not staying.

**Teacher:** Show me how you are using your hands to make it stay flat.

He shows how he presses down on the play dough.

**Teacher:** Gabriella, I see your play dough is lying down flat. Can you show Kyle how you did it?

**Gabriella:** Look Kyle, I used this roller to push it. I think there's another roller in the bucket. (She gets a roller and gives it to Kyle.)

Kyle tries the roller, but still does not get the effect he wants.

**Gabriella:** You have to push down really, really hard. (She puts her hands over Kyle's and pushes down with him.)

**Kyle:** Hey, it's working. Let me try. (He does, and the play dough stays flat.)

**Gabriella:** There. You got it to go way down.

**Kyle:** I did it! I made it flat like a pizza. Here, Gabriella, I'll slice you a piece.

---

■ Create opportunities for collaborative interaction. Allow sufficient time for children to elaborate on their play ideas and incorporate peers into their role-playing. Encourage collaboration by pairs in some activities by suggesting children work with a partner *if* they choose. Plan small and large group activities that naturally involve working in dyads or triads. These can include movement and music activities where children move or dance as partners; construction activities where two children hold something steady while a third builds on it; conversations where children alternate asking and answering questions; and data-gathering activities where one child collects information and the other records it. Refer children to peers when they need assistance.

■ Help aggressive or withdrawn children to join their peers. For example, coach children who enter a group too forcefully by suggesting noninvasive strategies; you might say something like "Maybe if you help carry blocks, they'll let you build the tower with them." At the other end of the social continuum, reticent children may benefit from a tool such as a "talking stick" (only the person hold-ing it may talk; everyone else must listen). Here's an example:

> At greeting circle, the teacher invites children to tell the group about something they saw on their way to school. She gives the first child the talking stick, and each child passes it to the next one who wants to speak. Those who do not want to speak are not pressured to do so. However, the teacher notices that even children who are often shy or reserved feel "empowered" when they hold the talking stick and take a turn speaking before passing it to a peer. (Emily Vance, pers. comm., 2004)

■ Allow children to discover the consequences of their actions—provided no one is being hurt or endangered. They will adjust their own behavior accordingly, especially if they are rejected by their peers. Here's an example recorded by a preschool teacher:

> Jim brings his new fire truck to school and announces that no one is allowed to touch it. When he brings the truck over to where Zack and Maggie are playing with toy cars and ramps, they tell him he cannot join their game. This continues for two days. On the third day, Jim puts his truck on the ramp and says to Maggie, "You can push it if you want." She does and then gives

it to Zack. Maggie asks Jim, "Do you want to play racing cars with us?" Jim says yes and joins their play, letting his friends take turns with his truck.

This teacher didn't jump in to give social directions, offer opinions or interpretations, or solve problems for the children. If the teacher had insisted Maggie and Zack let Jim play with them, Jim might not have figured out how to alter his behavior to achieve his social goal of inclusion. Teachers also can point out the beneficial consequences of cooperative behavior, to encourage children to continue or increase it. The focus should be on how the behavior makes the child feel, rather than how it pleases the adult. For example, you could say "You're having fun building that tower together," rather than "It makes me happy to see you sharing."

■ Model cooperative play by partnering with children. Get down on their level, imitate their use of materials, and follow their ideas and play leads. Act out the roles and attributes they assign ("You're the dog, and you chase me"). Be careful not to take over and direct the play.

■ When possible, share control in the classroom in other ways, too. For example, solicit ideas for a rotation system to pass out snacks or let children choose a song or lead an action at large group. Give children conversational control by listening to and commenting on what they say, not overloading them with questions.

## C3 Valuing diversity

Diversity can take many forms, including gender, ethnicity, age, religion, family structure, ability levels, body shape, hair/eye color, culture, language, ideas, aesthetic preferences, and so on. Valuing diversity means accepting and appreciating the differences of ourselves and of others as normal and positive. It means treating people as individuals and not as stereotypes, and recognizing that preferences are not always value judgments.

*Teaching strategies.* We all may be uneasy with differences we encounter for the first time. If children's experiences with variety are positive, they may develop an appreciation for diversity on their own. Nevertheless, preschoolers are old enough to have encountered and possibly internalized harmful stereotypes from the culture that surrounds them. Intentional teachers can help them accept and even embrace diversity in the classroom and community in ways such as these:

■ Model respecting others by the way you listen to and accept children's ideas and feelings. Let them see you treat everyone equally and fairly, including children, families, and your coworkers.

■ Avoid judgmental comparisons. Instead, comment on specific attributes and accomplishments without labeling one as better than the other. For example, if you say to Yolanda, "I like red hair," Nicole may infer there is something wrong with her brown hair. A better observation would be, "Yolanda has short, red hair, and Nicole has her brown hair in braids."

■ Include diversity in every classroom area and activity. For example, in the dress-up area, provide a range of clothes and costumes representing the cultures and activities of the children and their families. The house area might contain work clothes and tools used in different types of jobs and equipment used by people with various disabilities, such as crutches and magnifiers. Serve food from various cultures (e.g., African, American Southern, Kosher) on a regular basis at snack time, as well as special treats brought in by parents at holiday times. Put empty containers and the cooking utensils used to prepare a range of ethnic foods in the house center. In the reading area, feature books, magazines, and catalogs with illustrations and photographs of people performing nonstereotypical jobs, families of varying structures, and people of different ages and appearances.

■ Diversity isn't only about differences in people. Hang reproductions of artwork in diverse media at eye level throughout the room. At large group, explore music and dance of different styles. Grow seeds of different vegetables and flowers in the school garden. Go to places and events in the community that showcase local diversity; for example, different kinds of shops, festivals and concerts, cars, animals, buildings, and the like.

■ Ensure that bias and prejudice are not part of your program. For example, preview materials and field trip sites before sharing them with children. Anticipate questions children might have about the individuals and groups portrayed; answer questions with simple and honest responses. For example, a child might ask "Why is this man dark?" You don't need to give a complex answer about the science of skin color; you can simply say "He has dark skin because his mother or father has dark skin. You have freckles just like your mother."

■ Ensure that bias and prejudice are not part of your school or center. Work with program administrators to enact nondiscriminatory recruitment and admissions policies; for example, make sure informational brochures or translators are available in the languages spoken by the children's parents. Where and how the program is promoted (e.g., only in English, picturing only black families), as well as office furnishings, staff behavior, and the way staff address family members, will make families and visitors from different backgrounds feel either welcomed or unwanted. For example, displaying posters on the office wall from a local multiethnic fair, avoiding cultural taboos, and addressing parents formally or informally according to their preference are all signs of recognition and respect that can enhance feelings of acceptance.

## C4 Developing a framework for moral behavior

Morality is a system for evaluating human conduct. Conscience is an internal sense of right and wrong that is not dependent on external censure or punishment. Moral development is a long process that extends well into adolescence and even early adulthood. Preschoolers, especially older ones, are beginning to wrestle with questions of moral behavior, particularly with regard to the treatment of others. They are interested in, and capable of, reflecting on their own and others' deeds and misdeeds.

*Teaching strategies.* Our moral sense develops to a great extent through our following (or sometimes explicitly rejecting) the examples set by significant others in our lives, particularly in our home setting. Nevertheless, behavioral models in the classroom and the ways teachers articulate moral principles help lay the groundwork from which children build their own value systems. To support children as they begin to construct a moral framework, teachers can employ several strategies, including these:

■ Be consistent and fair-minded. Provide clear expectations about behavior, but emphasize problem solving rather than blame or punishment.

■ Verbalize in simple terms the reasons for your actions and decisions that involve moral matters such as fairness. For example, "I'm making sure every child who wants a piece of birthday cake has one before giving out seconds. It isn't fair if someone gets two pieces before every child has one."

■ Work with children's families to achieve as much congruence between home and school values as possible. When you find that a child's home beliefs about right and wrong diverge from your classroom's moral principles, explain clearly and simply to children and families why this is so. Try not to put a negative value judgment on beliefs families may hold that conflict with yours; rather, problem solve conflicts between how situations are handled in the two settings. (For more on problem solving, see **Resources.**) For example, "messiness" is an area of potential difference. In some cultures, parents may see it as a sign of disrespect if a teacher covers a child's new outfit with a spattered smock, and they may become quite upset if some paint nevertheless gets on the child's clothes. In this case, while acknowledging the parent's discomfort, you should also do your best to explain why being able to explore messy materials helps children learn important concepts in math, science, and other areas. If the parent accepts this explanation, you might talk about having a spare set of the child's "old" clothes on hand or ask whether the parent would prefer a different or more effective cover-up.

## A Adult-guided experience is especially important for learnings such as:

### A1 Engaging in conflict resolution

Conflict resolution refers to using appropriate, nonaggressive strategies to settle interpersonal

## One Approach to Conflict Resolution

Recommended approaches to conflict resolution vary somewhat, but they all contain the same basic elements. Here is one 6-step procedure. Applying steps 1 and 2 sets the tone for the rest of the process, as shown in the example that follows.

### Mediating conflict

**1.** Approach calmly, stopping any hurtful actions. Place yourself between the children, on their level. Use a calm voice and gentle touch. Remain neutral, rather than taking sides.

**2.** Acknowledge children's feelings. If the conflict is over an object, let the children know you need to hold the object ("neutralize" it) until the conflict is resolved.

"You look really upset."

**3.** Gather information.

"What's the problem?"

**4.** Restate the problem.

"So the problem is . . . "

**5.** Ask the children to think of possible solutions, and choose one together.

"What can we do to solve this problem?"

**6.** Be prepared to give follow-up support. Stay near the children.

"You solved the problem!"

### An example

Shari is feeding her doll a bottle. Daniella grabs it away and says "I need that." When Shari takes the bottle back, Daniella punches her in the arm and says "I hate you, you stupid baby!" Their teacher comes over and kneels down between the two girls.

**Teacher (to Daniella):** You're angry because you want to feed the bottle to your doll. But you cannot punch Shari or call her stupid.

**Teacher (to Shari):** Let me hold the bottle while we talk about this. (He takes the bottle.)

**Shari:** I had it first.

**Teacher (to Shari):** You're upset because you were using the bottle and Daniella grabbed it away from you.

**Shari:** (Nods yes.)

**Teacher (to Shari and Daniella):** So you both want to feed this bottle to your dolls. How can we solve this problem?

As the children calm down, the teacher takes them through the rest of the problem-solving steps. Each child says in her own words what happened, the teacher repeats and verifies their statements, then asks them to suggest solutions. The girls decide to make another bottle. Shari holds a block while Daniella tapes on a red Lego "nipple." Shari uses the original bottle; Daniella uses the one they made together, happy because "My bottle is bigger." When the teacher checks back later, the dolls are taking a nap in the carriage, and Shari and Daniella are building a cradle out of blocks.

---

**Source:** B. Evans, *You Can't Come to My Birthday Party! Conflict Resolution with Young Children* (Ypsilanti, MI: High/Scope Press, 2002). Adapted, by permission, from pp. 117–18.

---

differences. This domain also goes by other names such as social problem solving, behavior management, anger management, and classroom discipline. Resolving conflicts when needs and emotions are running high is a challenge; sometimes even adults cannot or choose not to use the skills at such times.

*Teaching strategies.* Because preschool-age children developmentally still are quite egocentric, and thus focused on their own needs, they often get into conflicts with others. Typically they do not intend harm or mean to act selfishly; they are simply goal-oriented ("I want that truck; I'll grab it"). Intentional teachers, therefore, explicitly model, coach, and teach children the behaviors necessary to resolve conflicts. Understanding that children are not misbehaving but rather making mistakes as they learn how to behave appropriately, we avoid using value-laden or negative terms with them.

As in many early childhood areas, young children need *concrete* experience with conflicts to learn how to resolve them. Once conflicts arise, as they inevitably will, teachers can use the occasions to begin teaching children conflict-resolution skills, and proactively help them learn how to avoid future conflicts. To become skilled at conflict resolution takes a great deal of repetition, but preschoolers can begin to implement problem-solving strategies on their own, with sufficient modeling and support from their teachers. For example, consider the following strategies:

■ Establish a safe classroom. Let children know they will not be physically or verbally hurt. Stop children's hurtful or dangerous behaviors immediately, including aggression and rejection. Set clear limits ("No hitting") and expectations ("Everyone gets a turn"), and inform children about them verbally and in writing. Be consistent in implementing rules and following through on expectations.

■ During a conflict, stay calm in voice, body language, and facial expression. Show concern, but not alarm. Be aware of your own emotional triggers beforehand to help prevent your overreacting during a conflict situation. When you are in control of yourself, you help children regain or maintain control of themselves and you communicate that having feelings (even negative ones) need not be scary. Your remaining calm, rather than being upset with or critical of the children involved, also focuses attention on solving the problem.

■ Children's emotions can run high during a conflict. Soothe children who are upset, relying on your previous observations of them to choose individual strategies you know will be effective. Acknowledge

## Making Up Rules to Govern Play

When play becomes too rough or dangerous, we often need to step in to set limits. Sometimes, however, children themselves can be involved in creating rules to ensure their own comfort or safety.

After Khalid went to a wrestling match, he got several classmates in his preschool interested in playing "wrestling" during choice time. They used an area rug as their mat, pushed up their sleeves, and thoroughly enjoyed the rough-and-tumble play. The game went on for several weeks, becoming progressively more elaborate; for example, they gave themselves wrestlers' names and developed a scoring system.

In the second week, however, a few children clearly felt the play was *too* rough. The teachers did not want to stop a game that many children clearly enjoyed and that promoted learning in many areas. So at the beginning of the next choice time, when the wrestlers were setting up their game, a teacher gathered them and voiced her concern, "What rules can we make up so no one will get hurt?" She wrote down their ideas and posted the rules on the wall above the mat. Here are the rules the children came up with:

1. Take off your shoes (but not your socks).

2. No hitting.

3. No punching. (The children debated whether punching was the same as hitting, but decided it deserved its own rule.)

4. No pinching.

5. You can't call someone a bad name.

6. No spitting.

7. No head butts.

8. ~~Only boys can play~~. (Several girls protested this rule and it was dropped.)

9. At least three people have to play, so one can be the referee and make sure the match is fair.

10. The referee has to be able to count to 10. (After a count of 10, the match is declared over.)

11. You can't wrestle if you don't have a wrestler name.

12. You can't have the same wrestler name as someone else.

13. Everyone who wants to wrestle gets a turn. The referee decides who goes next.

14. People who want to watch have to stand behind the line. (After some debate, they decided the edge of the block shelf would mark the "watching line.")

The children referred to the rules in subsequent weeks as their interest in wrestling continued. If one of them broke a rule, the other children—rather than the teacher—were always quick to point out the infraction.

and respect children's feelings. Encourage children to name their own emotions, and use the words they use. Help children to become aware of one another's feelings by calling attention to body language, facial expressions, and statements. (See **Recognizing and labeling emotions** above.) Act and speak sincerely; for example, make eye contact with all the children involved, and reflect your warmth and concern in your voice. In nonthreatening ways (no grabbing or jerking), touch or hold children to reassure them and help them regain self-control.

■ In mediating the conflict, observe children's behavior and collect information to arrive at an insightful interpretation. Remain neutral; don't assign blame or take sides. For example, take time to assess whether a child has knocked down another's block tower in a misguided attempt to enter the play or because the child is angry with the builder. Involve children in describing problems and proposing solutions. Listen actively. Repeat accurately what children say, or paraphrase their words for clarity. Check with children to confirm the accuracy of what you are restating.

■ Develop solutions together with children by soliciting their ideas and deciding which one(s) to try. If the children are having difficulty coming up with problem-solving solutions on their own, coach them by offering one or two suggestions. Sometimes, if the children involved cannot generate ideas or agree on a solution, they may agree to ask one or two other children for help or even bring the problem before a class meeting. (See **Creating and following rules** below.) Respect children's definition of "fairness." Their definition may differ from yours, but as long as all the parties involved agree on the solution, accept it and help them carry it out. Follow up to see whether the solution is working. If conflicts reemerge, repeat the problem-solving steps until all the children appear settled and reengaged in play.

■ Help children reflect on the problem-solving strategies they are learning at times other than during actual conflicts. It may be easier for children to absorb information when they are not emotionally involved. For example, read books and sing and listen to songs about characters coping with anger and other conflict-producing feelings. Role-play conflict resolution scenarios with puppets, dolls, or other props. Pose simple and familiar "what if" situations for small group discussion. To elicit their ideas on how to solve problems, suggest situations you know the children will find unacceptable; for example, "What if I decided that only teachers could mix the paints?" Review with children successfully resolved episodes from their past; for example, do this at snack time or when reading a book that contains a comparable situation.

## A2 Creating and following rules

A rule is an authoritative direction for how to act or what to do. Just as licensed programs must follow health and safety rules, programs and teachers have rules that children must concern themselves with, such as who will pass out snacks, feed Sniffy the guinea pig, sit next to the teacher, choose the song for circle time, use the computer, and so on. Children may create rules for games they invent, such as the start and finish line in a race or what constitutes "in bounds" in a bean bag toss. Sometimes the class feels the need to establish policies for preserving quiet areas, respecting block structures built by others, or protecting "work in progress" overnight. Setting rules also can be a way to deal with interpersonal conflicts, especially if they affect groups of children or the whole class.

*Teaching strategies.* Young children need explicit information and guidance from teachers to understand, establish, and follow rules governing classroom behavior. They also need help sorting out when rules may be fluid (e.g., players agree to change the rules mid game) and when they must remain fixed (e.g., they deal with health or safety). Like a personal code of morality, competence in making and respecting rules begins in childhood and continues to develop into adolescence and early adulthood. Teachers can be instrumental in laying the foundation by carrying out practices such as those listed below:

■ Make children aware of basic health and safety rules that have everyday meaning to them. Be

## Preschool Democracy in Action

Here is an example in which the children helped to solve a classroom safety problem. Some experienced the satisfaction of seeing their ideas adopted, one had to deal with the disappointment of "majority rule." All ended up feeling good about contributing to the well-being and enjoyment of the group.

Many of the children enjoyed carrying water from the sink to various areas in the classroom, such as the house area when they were "cooking spaghetti." The teachers supported the idea, but were concerned by the large amounts of water being spilled on the floor. Because virtually everyone was affected by the situation, the teachers decided to bring up their concerns at a class meeting and asked the children for ideas to solve the problem. They wrote down the children's suggestions; and after the group discussed each, they took a vote on which one to adopt.

**Tamika:** Make a rule that no one can carry water any more.

**Teacher:** What if someone wants to fill pots for cooking? (Several children said they liked being able to cook "just like at home.")

**Dominic:** Turn off the water. My mommy did that when we had a flood in the kitchen.

**Lisa:** We can put a towel in the house area. Whenever someone spills water, they have to go back and wipe it up.

**Leah:** We can put a towel in every area! Then we can bring water there, as long we clean up.

**Lisa:** We can put two towels, so children can wipe up together.

**Teacher:** (After reading back the list of ideas) Which idea should we try? (Dominic voted to turn off the water, but all the other children were in favor of the towels.)

**Teacher:** We have five areas in the room. If we put 2 towels in each area, we'll need 10 towels. Where can we get that many towels?

**Tamika:** We can buy them at the store.

**Teacher:** We don't have enough money for that. Any other ideas? (The children could not think of another way to get towels, so the teacher offered a suggestion.) Do you suppose if we asked parents, they could bring in some old towels their family doesn't use any more?

All the children agreed this was a good idea. The teachers posted a request on the Parent Bulletin Board, and by the following week, families had donated a dozen old towels. Water carrying (and probably some intentional spilling) actually increased for a while, because children enjoyed wiping up after themselves. They invented different wiping methods, including "skating" towels along the floor or having one child hold each end of the towel. Dominic, whose idea had been voted down, was one of the most avid spiller-wipers.

---

concrete. Children relate to the dos and don'ts of behavior (e.g., "Always wash your hands after using the bathroom"), not abstract principles of protection or well-being (e.g., "Germs make us sick"). Write out the rules using simple words and pictures, and post them at children's eye level.

■ At small group or class meeting, describe a problem that affects everyone and invite children to suggest one or more rules to solve it; typical examples include children running through the block area and knocking things down, or clean-up taking so long that it shortens outside time. (Children may also use small group or class meetings to allow the whole group to resolve problems that involve just a few children, provided those directly affected agree to using this strategy. See **Engaging in conflict resolution** above.) Encourage children to discuss the pros and cons of each suggestion. Write down and post the rules they decide to try, and refer to them when appropriate. Revisit the rules as a group in a few days to see whether they are working. Ask children to take turns announcing to the class the rules that work.

■ Encourage children to share responsibility for taking care of the classroom; for example, cleaning up, passing out snacks or meals, weeding and watering the garden, feeding the class pet. Establish rules and procedures together with the children for carrying out these responsibilities.

■ Make simple rules for yourself; for example, how to decide who gets to sit beside you at story time each day. Write down and share the rules with children, and point out when you are following them. In other words, model the use of rules by creating and following them yourself.

## A3 Creating and participating in democracy

Democracy in the early childhood classroom means conditions of equality and respect for the individual. Developing a sense of democracy grows out of experiences with rule making and social problem solving. For young children, it means learning that everyone has a voice, even those with minority opinions. Democracy entails compromise and negotiation. We do not always get our way, but the democratic process does provide the satisfaction of being heard and knowing that solutions, policies, decisions, and the like, can be reviewed and revised if needed.

*Teaching strategies.* Participating in a democratic society and in a democratic classroom require similar skills. They both call for "reflective problem solving and decision making, managing one's emotions, taking a variety of perspectives, and sustaining energy and attention toward focused goals" (Elias et al. 1997, 8). Preschoolers are not ready for abstract civics lessons; but fostering the development of skills in appropriate, concrete ways prepares them to become responsible and productive citizens. To bring about this understanding in ways that make sense to young children, teachers can use strategies such as these:

■ Ask children to consider alternative ways to reach a goal; for example, "What do you think would happen if . . . ?" or "Can you think of another way to do that?" Encourage them to plan more than one way to accomplish a task. Pose questions to help them anticipate consequences and reflect on outcomes; for example, "What will you do if the children who build ramps in the block area tomorrow don't follow the rules you came up with today?"

■ Build children's skills of perspective taking and turn taking. Remind children to listen before they add their ideas to the discussion. Ask them to repeat back what they hear and check it out with the speaker. Encourage children to use their imagination. Role-playing helps them adopt the behavior and viewpoint of another. Because preschoolers are not natural turn-takers, use a tool to help them develop this skill and not have to fight for a turn to speak and be heard. For example, you can use a timer or a talking stick. Such tools are especially effective in guaranteeing that shy or quiet children participate in group processes.

■ Express satisfaction about children working collectively, especially when everyone performs roles according to his or her interests and abilities. Observe aloud how much more can be accomplished as a team than as one or two individuals.

■ Deal evenly with bullies and those they target. First, stop hurtful behaviors immediately, whether physical or verbal, and remind children that classroom rules prohibit such behaviors. Engage children in the conflict-resolution strategies (see **Engaging in conflict resolution** above). Bullies, who sometimes act aggressively out of fear or mistrust, may need reassurance that their needs will be met and their rights respected. Explain that their goals can be achieved with nonthreatening and nonaggressive behaviors. Coach them in appropriate social behavior and call their attention to its positive consequences. The targeted children may need encouragement to defend their rights by voicing their needs and feelings or expressing themselves in other acceptable ways. Give particular attention to children who are timid or reluctant to speak up in social problem-solving situations. Validate their feelings, ask them to suggest solutions, give them ample time to respond, and repeat what they say to make sure others involved in the situation listen and hear their perspective.

■ Introduce other ideas and vocabulary words at the core of democratic principles and actions. Carry out mathematics activities to help children understand *more* versus *less/fewer*, which are foundational to the "majority rule" principle. For example, ask children to indicate their preferences (for a color or food) by a show of hands. Count and record the results on chart paper, using the appropriate vocabulary words. Many other terms we associate with early mathematics or scientific investigation also apply to social processes. For example: *is/is not, same/different, all/some, other/else, before/after, now/later,* and *when/where/with whom.* Apply them to people and actions as well as concrete objects. Help children develop an overall sense of the patterns in human interaction and the principles governing behavior.

■ Expand conversations children may initiate about their parents' voting at election time. If your location is a polling place, ask permission to visit the voting booths with children during off hours. Keep your explanation of the voting process simple; for example, "Everyone gets to say who they think will do the job best. Whoever is picked by the most people wins the job."

*    *    *

Acquiring social skills and understandings is an essential developmental domain for young chil-dren. They need to develop social competence to experience satisfying interpersonal relationships. Such learnings are also the mechanisms through which learning in other domains occurs, via observation and imitation, requests for assistance, direct interactions, collaborative exchanges, and the like.

We help young children construct and master emotional and social skills by bolstering their sense of competence and initiative and by creating a classroom environment in which their independent problem-solving abilities can thrive. Teachers also provide explicit guidance in the complex rules of social intercourse, by informing children about classroom and societal norms and offering suggestions when children's own resources prove insufficient to achieve their goals.

Between their intrinsic motivation to be social beings and our desire to socialize them, young children can and will develop the skills they need to be ready for interpersonal and civic relationships inside and outside of school.

## Questions for Further Thought

**1.** How can early childhood education promote emotionally positive self-images for all children in the face of conflicting messages portrayed in the media?

**2.** What role can early education play in counteracting the intolerance young children observe and learn at home, in their communities, and in the media?

**3.** As the population becomes more diverse, what is the potential for conflicting social values and beliefs between home and school? How can early childhood professionals anticipate and address this gap?

**4.** Is "consumer education" a necessary and appropriate new content area in early social studies? If so, what constitutes an appropriate consumer education curriculum and pedagogy?

**5.** What strategies can teachers employ when children refuse to participate in conflict resolution, rule setting, or other social processes in the classroom?

**6.** Given that young children vary in emotional and social development, can we develop reliable indicators for teachers to use to identify children with potential problems? What are the trade-offs in the benefits of early detection and intervention versus the dangers of false and premature labeling?

# Physical Movement

Carol, a preschooler, was on the swing set, pushing herself to go higher. Her teacher came by and began to chant, "Higher, higher, see Carol swing higher." Carol picked up the chant and then Nathan, swinging next to her, crooned, "Higher, higher, see me swing higher." Soon the other children gathered around and started chanting encouragement too.

The teacher said, "I wonder what else you could do *higher*?" Some children began to jump and chanted "Higher, higher, I can jump higher." Others bounced, leaped, or kicked a leg in the air. The teacher posed the same challenge for doing something *lower*, and the children crawled and rolled on the ground. When she asked what they could do *in the middle*, some children draped their bellies over the swing seats and dragged their feet on the ground so they couldn't go too high. Others bent their legs and waddled like ducks, saying they weren't walking "too tall or too short."

The idea that children need to be "taught" physical movement skills and concepts may seem odd. We assume children develop physically on their own, provided they receive adequate nutrition and have safe opportunities to move around in the environment. Certainly there is a typical progression in what children are capable of in terms of their gross motor and fine motor development (see Bredekamp & Copple 1997, 102, 105). However, it is a mistake to view the development of children's physical skills as being purely maturational or opportunistic in the early childhood years.

Research confirms that young children do not learn fundamental physical skills simply through play (Manross 2000). Left on their own to respond to music, for example, preschool children tend not to make use of all the movement possibilities. A 3-year-old typically remains stationary; a 4- or 5-year-old tends to move around more (Stellaccio & McCarthy 1999). But whatever they do, young children tend to limit their movement to repetition of a few patterns.

To ensure that children gain the basic physical skills they need, adults must plan movement experiences and structure physical activities that introduce a range of movement options. They must also provide children with time, space, and equipment to practice those skills. "Play provides children with the opportunity to practice movement skills in a variety of contexts. [However], some structuring of physical activity is necessary to help children maximize their movement experiences" (Sanders 2002, 31).

Movement education has received increasing national attention because of its potential health benefits. This country has seen an unprecedented rise in childhood obesity, which is in turn associated with increased risk for diabetes, heart disease, high blood pressure, colon cancer, and other health problems in adulthood. The percentage of children identified as overweight has more than doubled in the past 30 years. Along with poor diet, "physical inactivity has contributed to the 100 percent increase in the prevalence of childhood obesity in the United States since 1980" (Sanders 2002, xiii). By contrast, children who develop basic motor skills (such as throwing, catching, skipping, galloping) and are physically active are more likely as adults to be healthy and be participating in daily physical activity (National Center for Health Statistics 2004).

Developing and exercising basic physical abilities are also important in their own right. Gross and fine motor skills serve multiple functions. Physical coordination is essential to accomplishing many, if not most, everyday tasks. In addition, movement is, or should be, inherently pleasurable. There is joy in moving the body, whether one is feeling the freedom of using different muscles or expressing creativity through music and dance.

Physical development can also promote growth in other domains.

> Not only does movement stimulate learning physiologically, but it also helps young children to experience concepts so they can process them cognitively. Teachers must offer children opportunities to solve movement problems, invent their own solutions to challenges, and make abstract concepts (like high and low) concrete by physically experiencing them. (Pica 1997, 4)

For example, patterning, an underlying phenomenon in brain development, is echoed in the body's physical rhythms. Preschoolers often respond to music with physical movement or gestures, suggesting they may need to "replicate the musical stimuli to get at the substance" of music's underlying pattern (Scott-Kassner 1992, 636). Many areas of intellectual development are linked to physical abilities. When children act out stories, they enhance two essential components of early literacy development—comprehension and representation. Writing requires physical coordination and dexterity. As the opening vignette illustrates, movement is also intrinsically tied to forming concepts about space, which is in turn the foundation for understanding geometry. Other mathematical concepts are reflected in movement vocabulary terms such as *up* and *down, straight* and *curved,* or *flat* and *angled.* Bending, crawling, stretching and other flexible movements are vital in scientific investigations of the natural world, and they help children construct basic principles about physics.

Movement also offers many opportunities for developing and expressing creativity. Children move to music in dance-like ways, and experiment with direction and speed as they maneuver objects through space. Such freedom of expression can boost self-esteem and social confidence.

Conversely, being less physically adept is somewhat associated with having mental health problems (Sanders 2002). The source of this relationship is unclear; more research needs to be done to determine whether the connection between low physical competence and mental health problems (where that relationship exists) reflects nature, nurture, or some combination of the two. Maybe children who lack movement competence are ostracized by peers and lack the play opportunities in which young children develop many social skills. Maybe peer ridicule or rejection adversely affects their self-esteem, with troubling implications for their willingness to take on other interpersonal or cognitive challenges. As a result, the overall school performance and social adjustment of children with undeveloped physical skills can suffer.

# Young children's development in physical movement

Implementing appropriate teaching strategies depends on understanding how young children develop physically. Learning new movement skills is a process, in which children move through four "generic levels of skill proficiency" (Graham, Holt/Hale, & Parker 2004). Preschoolers are generally somewhere in the first two levels, depending on the skill and the child:

**1. Precontrol level** (beginner)—Children cannot consciously control or intentionally replicate a movement. At this stage, they need many opportunities to explore and discover movement.

**2. Control level** (advanced beginner)—Children's movements are less haphazard, as their bodies begin to respond to their intentions. Exploration and practice are still central at this stage.

**3. Utilization level** (intermediate)—Children's movements are increasingly automatic. They are able to join one movement skill with another in a game-like situation.

**4. Proficiency level** (advanced)—Children's movements are mostly automatic and begin to seem effortless. They are now ready to participate in a formal game situation. (Sanders 2002, 48)

Children who do not get opportunities to learn and practice a particular skill may grow up unable to perform that skill. Perhaps they just never had an occasion to throw or dribble, for example. Or they may not have had sufficient time or motivation to practice. Research suggests that children are not motivated to practice a new skill unless they experience success close to 80 percent of the time—that is, the task can't be too hard or too easy, because the child will lose interest (Sanders 2002, 45).

Several documents provide administrators and practitioners with summary statements about early physical development, as well as guidance on how to apply it in program settings. The Council on Physical Education for Children (COPEC) developed *Appropriate Practices in Movement Programs for Young Children Ages 3–5,* a position statement of the National Association for Sport and Physical Education (NASPE 2000). NASPE issued its early childhood standards in a publication titled *Active Start: A Statement of Physical Activity Guidelines for Children Birth to Five Years* (2002).

Both publications, as well as other contemporary writings in the field of movement education, share appropriate child-centered practices with other developmental domains. In addition, they all emphasize two points specific to early physical education. First is that the development of any motor skill is sequential. "No matter what the activity, one cannot take part successfully if the essential fundamental movement skills contained within that activity have not been mastered" (Gallahue 1995, 125). So, for example, a child who doesn't achieve basic competency in running, stopping, kicking, and dodging can never become competent at soccer and is unlikely to enjoy or participate in it as an older child or adult. Consequently, there has also been a shift away from discrete "units" focused on one instructional area at a time (for example, three weeks of throwing followed by three weeks of skipping), toward a variety of motor experiences throughout the year for practice and cumulative mastery. Like other content areas then, the movement curriculum should be designed so that later learning builds on earlier experiences and skills.

A second principle is that movement programs and youth sports are different. Sports programs are only appropriate for older children who have matured to the "proficiency" level and have refined the basic physical skills necessary to compete. Most children do not attain this readiness until age 6 or 7, and for quite a few it is even later. By contrast, movement programs for young children are meant for everyone. They emphasize self-improvement, participation, and cooperation instead of competition. Following this principle would mean the early childhood physical education curriculum should shift toward a focus on building basic skills and away from games and sports—that is, activities should focus on large muscles instead of large group games. "Inclusion of [adult-oriented activities such as sports] in early childhood or preschool movement programs has little support among educators because these activities are considered developmentally inappropriate. . . . Simply stated, group games and gymnastics, traditional dance, or fitness experiences have no place in preschool movement programs" (Sanders 2002, 40).

An effective physical education curriculum, following the above principles, should provide appropriate opportunities for young children to develop in two separate but related areas: movement skills and movement concepts. Children learn about the concepts as they practice the skills, so teachers need to incorporate both in preschoolers' physical activities (Sanders 2006, 130).

### Movement skills

This first curriculum area is the actual physical/motor movement skills (also called *skill themes*) that young children need to develop and refine. There are three categories of movement skills (Gallahue 1995; Sanders 2002):

▸ **Locomotor**—The body is transported in a horizontal or vertical direction from one point in space to another. Children's locomotor skills are the first to develop; these include walking, running, hopping, skipping, galloping, sliding, leaping, climbing, crawling, chasing, and fleeing.

▸ **Stability**—The body remains in place but moves around its horizontal or vertical axis; or it balances against the force of gravity. These skills develop next; they include turning, twisting, bending, stopping, rolling, balancing, transferring weight, jumping/landing, stretching/extending, curling, swinging, swaying, and dodging.

▸ **Manipulative**—The body moves to apply force to or receive force from objects. These skills develop last and are throwing, catching/collecting, kicking, punting, dribbling, volleying, striking with a racket, and striking with a long-handled instrument. Manipulative skills are important in many games and sports such as kickball and catch. The fine motor skills needed for tasks such as writing and drawing are also manipulative skills, although less vigorous than the gross motor ones.

### Movement concepts

The movement concepts are the knowledge component of the curriculum. If movement skills relate to *what* the body can do, movement concepts relate to *where, how, and in relationship to what* the body moves. Put another way: If movement skills are "body verbs," then movement concepts are "body adjectives and adverbs." Learning these movement concepts helps to modify or enrich the range of movement skills and the effectiveness of children's use of skills (Graham, Holt/Hale, & Parker 2004). There are three categories of movement concepts (Sanders 2002, 91):

▸ **Space (or spatial) awareness**—Where the body moves in space. Space awareness concepts are *space, directions, levels,* and *pathways.*

▸ **Effort awareness**—How the body moves in space. These are awareness of the components of time *(speeds, rhythms),* force *(degree, creation, absorption),* and control/flow *(dimensions).*

▸ **Body (or relational) awareness**—Relationships that the body creates. These are relationships with the self *(body parts, body shapes, roles)* and relationships with others and the environment *(locations).*

## Teaching and learning in physical movement

NASPE (2000) offers the following specific recommendations for preschool physical activities. Preschoolers should:

1. Accumulate at least one hour of daily structured physical activity.

2. Engage in unstructured physical activity whenever possible and should not be sedentary for more than one hour at a time.

3. Develop competence in movement skills that are building blocks for more complex movement tasks.

4. Have indoor and outdoor areas that meet or exceed recommended safety standards for performing large-muscle activities.

5. Be under the care of teachers who are aware of the importance of physical activity and facilitate each child's movement skills.

Developmental and educational wisdom supports the use of both child- and adult-guided experience in physical education.

> Teachers should employ both direct and indirect teaching methods. Direct methods provide instructional models for children to replicate. Indirect teaching methods encourage children to explore and discover a range of movement possibilities. Teachers provide opportunities for children to make choices within and between tasks, while actively exploring their environment. Teachers serve as facilitators, preparing a stimulating environment with challenging activities. (Sanders 2002, 13)

In other words, physical education, like any other content area, requires that adults take an active and deliberate instructional role.

Intentional teachers fulfill these recommendations by creating an appropriate learning environment and using effective interaction strategies with young children. Providing an appropriate learning environment is essential regardless of who guides the learning. Needs such as time, space, and equipment to practice are universal for children's learning. Similarly, each interaction strategy can be used with child-guided and adult-guided experience, but their frequency and intensity should vary depending on the skill in question. For example, the strategies of modeling and providing cues may be useful to support child-guided experience, but they are more often necessary in adult-guided experience. Likewise, challenges make learning fun in both instances but become more salient in adult-guided instruction to raise movement possibilities that children are unlikely to think of on their own.

## Physical education learning environment

NASPE (2000) defines the movement environment as comprising these components: scheduled activity, class size, equipment, play, facilities, allowance for repetition and success, participation for every child, and integration of movement into other subject areas. While several of these have been touched on above, a few points are worth emphasizing and expanding here.

First, movement education (I use the terms *physical education* and *movement education* interchangeably) should be a **scheduled activity,** like small group, snack, or any other part of the daily routine.

Regarding **class size,** "large classes are accidents waiting to happen" (Sanders 2002, 24). The number of children in large group physical activities should not exceed class size, which is another way of saying that two or more classes should not share a gym or playground at the same time. Best practice says maximum group size with two teachers for 3-year-olds is 18 children; for 4-year-olds, it is no more than 20 children (NAEYC 2005, Table 2).

Third, **space to play and practice** is particularly important in the development of gross motor skills. Because the amount of space required is more than the dimensions of a typical classroom, physical education is often moved elsewhere, such as a gym, multi-purpose room, large hallway, or outdoors. Wherever movement learning takes place, safety is a primary concern. Environments should be free of obstacles (tables, chairs, shelves, sand and water tables, easels, computers). Equipment specific to large-muscle activity (hoops, balls, mats) should be located around the perimeter or stored nearby with easy access. Having to haul gear long distances is a disincentive to its frequent and spontaneous use by both children and teachers.

**Equipment** is another key component. "Learning to move is like learning to read, write, or understand principles of math and science in that each requires a manipulative of some type to best develop skills and knowledge in a content area" (Sanders 2002, 25). In acquiring movement resources, consider scale and quantity. Equipment should be child size; for example, many preschoolers cannot kick a soccer ball or catch a softball that is regulation size. Have sufficient equipment so every child can participate without waiting. That means if the activity is throwing and there are 12 children in the class, have 12 items to throw (balls, beanbags). Every child does not need to have the same item, as long as there is something

# Basic Equipment and Materials for Early Childhood Movement Programs

Some items are only available commercially but are worth the basic investment. Others can be made or collected at minimal cost, especially with contributions from children's families and local businesses. Materials should be varied and plentiful. It is not always necessary to have one of each for every child.

**Balancing equipment**—beams 4" to 6" wide and no more than 30" off the ground; boards or platforms raised off the ground with a narrow base of support; railroad ties, bricks, blocks, or rocks arranged in various configurations

**Balls of many types**—lightweight foam, rubber, and plastic balls; old tennis balls; yarn and cloth balls; smooth and textured balls; whiffle balls; beach, tennis, and soccer balls; in different diameters up to 10 inches

**Balloons in different sizes and weights**—sometimes recommended for indoor use only, to avoid potential environmental hazards

**Baskets, bowls, and boxes**—various heights and widths, to throw things into

**Basketball hoop**—child size; or other types of anchored nets

**Bats**—plastic and foam, rather than wood; 2" to 4" in diameter and 28" in length; foam bats have a larger head and make connecting with the ball easier

**Beanbags**—square and cubed, about 5" per side, filled with dried beans, rice, sand, birdseed, or plastic pellets

**Bowling pins**—foam, 3" to 4" in diameter

**Carpet squares**—good to practice jumping; many carpet businesses will donate old samples

**Climbing equipment**—jungle gym, ladder, tree stumps, boulders, snow piles

**Crawl-through shapes and tunnels**—of heavy duty foam, or cut your own out of cardboard in different geometrical shapes and colors, approximately 3' by 2'

**Disks**—Frisbees, paper plates, plastic paint can lids, clean pizza cardboard

**Hockey sticks**—foam; 24" handles are good for young children

**Hoops**—plastic, in 24", 30", and 36" diameters; smaller diameters are better for young children

**Jump ropes**—7', preferably weighted along length with plastic beads

**Launch boards**—child steps on one end and beanbag at other end flies up for child to catch

**Mats**—don't teach rolling without them!

**Music tapes, CDs, and simple instruments**—percussion, string, wind

**Paddles**—foam, with different length handles

**Parachute**—6' to 12' in diameter

**Pull and push toys**—wagons, toy lawnmowers, shopping carts, doll strollers, vacuum cleaners, wheelbarrows

**Rhythm sticks**—wood or plastic; about 5/8" in diameter and 1' long

**Ribbons, ribbon wands**

**Ribbon sticks**—to perform expressive rhythmic movements; sticks are 18" long and ribbons 6' to 12' long; use shorter ribbons with younger children

**Ring toss**

**Rocking toys**—wooden or plastic horse, boats

**Scarves**—for throwing, catching, and rhythm activities; lightweight scarves fall slowly, so they are ideal for catching; 11" to 16" square

**Scoops**—plastic, make homemade ones from empty milk jugs; act as extensions of arm to assist in catching

**Sleds**—length should be shorter than the child

**Sliding equipment**—commercial slide, fireman's pole, water slide

**Stilts**—foam, 8" off the floor

**Swings**—commercial swings, tire swing, rope swing

**Target board**—can be constructed of plywood or other sturdy material, with targets painted on them; to practice overhand and underhand throwing

**Traffic cones**—good to mark boundaries or serve as base to practice knocking something off

**Wedges**—foam

**Wheeled vehicles**—tricycles, toy cars and buses, scooters; always wear helmets

**Compiled from:** R. Clements & S. Schneider, personal communication, 2004. V. Harris, "The Playground: An Outdoor Setting for Learning," in *Supporting Young Learners: Ideas for Preschool and Day Care Providers,* eds. N.A. Brickman & L.S. Taylor, 167–73 (Ypsilanti, MI: High/Scope Press, 1991), 172. M. Hohmann & D.P. Weikart, *Educating Young Children: Active Learning Practices for Preschool and Child Care Programs,* 2d ed. (Ypsilanti, MI: High/Scope Press, 2002), 141. S.W. Sanders, *Designing Preschool Movement Programs* (Champaign, IL: Human Kinetics, 1992), 116–18. P.S. Weikart, *Round the Circle: Key Experiences in Movement for Young Children,* 2d ed. (Ypsilanti, MI: High/Scope Press, 2000), 94–107.

appropriate for each child. Another option is to create multiple activity stations for children to visit, so fewer items of each kind are needed.

Finally, the principle of **active involvement** is crucial and a distinguishing difference between a movement program and sports. Rather than winning, a movement program's goals are to have children "experience the joy and satisfaction inherent in movement . . . [as well as to] foster a positive attitude toward physical activity, self and body images, and physical skill competency" (Sanders 2006, 127). So elimination games such as Duck, Duck, Goose; Musical Chairs; and Simon Says are poor choices, as players spend most of their time sitting or standing, and they exclude some children altogether. And races can promote feelings of inadequacy and discouragement for all except the winner. Instead, teachers should select activities and attend to issues of scheduling, space, and equipment to ensure every child is an active participant and experiences that 80 percent level of success.

## Physical education interaction strategies

"Providing appropriate adult encouragement and support not only enables young children to learn about movement but also ensures the success of their many movement ideas and experiences" (Weikart 2000, 28). The following interaction strategies promote movement learning of all types in young children:

**Facilitate access and exploration** by providing materials, space, and time for young children to explore movement. Feedback from the sensations of moving will help them discover and adjust what their bodies can do.

Teachers can **model a skill** to demonstrate for children how to use their bodies or equipment to accomplish a physical objective. This demonstration technique is especially useful for children who cannot easily process verbal instruction or have limited vocabulary. The goal is not for children to copy exactly what the teacher or more skilled peer is doing, but rather to help them get the idea and then practice it on their own. Teachers should also use modeling to prevent and correct children's errors, describing and modeling the correct way to

hop, skip, and so on. Teachers should "know what common errors to watch for, even with simple skills like walking (pronated feet that roll in with [the outermost] toes lifting off the floor) and jumping (landing with knees straight and on balls of feet only). Motor skill errors and delays do not go away on their own" (Rae Pica, 2004, pers. comm.). Teachers or other professionals (e.g., physical education specialists, occupational therapists, etc.) need to intervene.

**Add descriptive language.** Describing movement serves a dual purpose. It makes children more aware of what they are doing, so they pay attention to their bodies and the feedback they receive from their nerves and muscles. It also increases their vocabulary. Once they hear movement words from teachers, children can begin to use labels such as *over* and *under, fast* and *slow, straight* and *bent*—not just in physical education but also to convey concepts in literacy, mathematics, and other content areas. Movement awareness and verbal skill serve children later, too, as they combine skills to master new challenges. For example, when the teacher says (pausing between directions), "Put your foot *in front of* you and lean your body *forward* with your arms out to the *side . . .*" a child who has learned these physical skills and verbal labels can accomplish a throwing or balancing act.

While children are practicing and refining a new skill, teachers can **provide small bits of key information *(cues)*** about that skill to help them learn it more quickly and correctly. A well-timed cue can also prevent the formation of bad habits (a point that movement educators say should be applied to other curriculum areas, as well). Cues can take three forms (Weikart 2000): verbal, visual (demonstration), and hands-on guidance. A *verbal cue* might be, for example, telling a child "Hold your hands in front of your body to catch the ball." *Visual cues* can replace or supplement verbal cues; for example, pointing to your eyes as a reminder to the child to look at the target when throwing a beanbag. For *hands-on cues,* the teacher, with the child's permission, gently moves the child's body into a more efficient position; for example, centering his body over a balance beam. Good teachers are sensitive to which type works best for each child, skill, and situation, and they individualize the cues they provide.

**Create skill challenges.** Challenges are "tasks or activities made measurable (or more fun) by the teacher. In making a task measurable, the teacher motivates a child to try it in a different way" (Sanders 2002, 55). For example, the teacher might say "I wonder how many different ways you can bounce the ball?" or "Can you hop from here to the wall and back?" Challenges can increase children's interest and enjoyment and encourage them to stay with a task longer. Challenges also can extend the physical learning and help children apply a skill to other situations.

**Invite children to lead the movement activity.** As leader, the child would make verbal suggestions or demonstrate an action to be copied by the class. Being leaders develops children's confidence and independence, as well as makes them more aware of verbal labels and motions because they have to communicate them to others. Most children will want to be leaders, but never require them to be; let them volunteer. You may find that children who typically don't speak up in a group will feel comfortable leading. Even children who are pre- or nonverbal can lead physical activities.

# Fitting the learning experience to the learning objective

The rest of this chapter examines aspects of physical movement learning, looking first at the **movement skills** (locomotor, stability, manipulative) and then at the **movement concepts** (awareness of space, effort, body). Each section is in turn divided into those skills or concepts that seem to be acquired primarily through child- versus adult-guided experience. As with all areas of development, this division is not rigid, but various elements of this content do tend toward one mode or the other.

Along with gross motor skills such as running and throwing, fine motor skills also develop in the preschool years. Activities to promote the development of fine motor skills, such as stringing beads, putting together puzzles, cutting, sorting cards, drawing, writing, and copying, are typically part of the daily classroom routine. Because large motor development is frequently taken for granted and not promoted as explicitly and intentionally in early childhood programs, I focus on it in this chapter. For discussion of fine motor skill learning in the context of writing, see **Chapter 3.**

# Movement skills

Movement learning, more than the other content areas in this book, can be difficult to attribute to child- or adult-guided experience. Because many movement skills appear spontaneously, at least in rudimentary form, the assumption (as noted at the beginning of the chapter) is that adult intervention is unnecessary. Yet movements that are more difficult or complex and involve greater coordination of muscles, senses, and feedback loops require a certain amount of direction and refinement, much as a team with a coach executes the same moves but at a higher level than a group in a sandlot or pickup game. As well, children are more likely to learn the "correct" version (performed safely; not stressing the body; for maximum efficiency/accuracy) of any movement skill through direct adult intervention, but children are more prone to mistakes (and therefore more likely to need or benefit from adult assistance) in the more complex adult-guided skills listed in this chapter. It is the relative importance of independent versus assisted learning that underlies the assignment of movement skills to either the child-guided or adult-guided category.

Locomotor skills, for example, often mature on their own, and children spontaneously practice and improve them as long as teachers give them opportunities to explore and discover. Similarly, children are likely to learn many stability skills independently. However, there are some locomotor and stability skills that require adult intervention before children can come to a more mature form and eventually combine and apply them in games and sports. On the other hand, only a couple of manipulative skills seem to be acquired primarily through child-guided experience, and only if the appropriate equipment and support are there. Otherwise, manipulative skills depend more on adult-guided experience than do skills in the other two movement areas.

Whether a skill fits in one category or the other is an empirical issue currently; that is, it is based on the observations and systematic research of those who work in the field of movement education. As the concept of the intentional teacher takes hold with respect to physical development and more work is done to generate theories and research, a higher-order explanation for what constitutes each type of skill should emerge.

 **Child-guided experience is especially important for learnings such as:**

### C1 Locomotor skills: crawling, walking, running, climbing

These four locomotor skills seem to be primarily learned by children through exploration and discovery. Although adults typically take walking for granted, it actually requires considerable balance and strength (Weikart 2000). Running, because it is faster and contact with the ground is not continuous, requires even more strength and balance than walking. Children typically begin walking at about age 1, but running doesn't begin until around 2. Climbing, which combines crawling and walking skills, involves both arm and leg strength—and often strength of mind, as the parent or teacher of a determined toddler can attest!

*Teaching strategies.* Young children bring a high level of motivation to mastering basic locomotor skills. Quite simply, they enjoy moving. Nevertheless, teachers play a critical role in creating a physical environment that supports movement exploration. Their attitudes are also important in helping children overcome their fears and in sharing their joy of discovery. To provide this wide-ranging support, teachers can implement a variety of strategies, including these:

■ Provide ample space and time. Buy or construct appropriate equipment, including ramps, bridges, and playground climbers, as well as large blocks you and the children can use to construct similar structures.

■ Promote children's free exploration and practice of locomotor skills. Accept and respect children's originality and creativity. To encourage children to create movements, make interesting or novel suggestions; for example, say "Imagine you are a squirrel scampering along the ground" or "Pretend to be. . . ." Or select a favorite action storybook (or make up an action story) at group time and suggest children mimic the actions of the characters while you read or tell the story. Pause as the action in the story progresses to allow time for the children's movements, then recap the story to that point before proceeding with the narrative.

■ Model locomotor movements and encourage children to imitate them (but don't insist on exact duplication). For example, demonstrate a crawling movement using your knees and forearms (instead of hands) and say "Let's all crawl around the table."

■ Provide specific cues as needed to help children improve the quality of their movements. For example, walking cues include: keep your head up; look where you want to go; and swing your arms.

■ Challenge children to practice and extend a movement, such as "How can you walk to the sink faster?" or "How else can you . . . " or "Who has a different way to . . . ?"

■ Use these basic locomotor skills to enhance other areas of learning. For example, if children are exploring short and long strings at small group, encourage them to take short and long steps at outside time. Stopping and starting, which are time concepts, can also be combined with movement activities; for example, to stop and start moving when a piece of music starts and stops.

### C2 Stability skills: turning, twisting, bending, straightening, curling, stretching/extending, swinging, swaying, pushing, pulling, rising, falling, dodging, stopping

These stability skills seem to be primarily acquired in exploration and discovery. Children typically use these skills while standing in place. For example, turning rotates the body in a 360-degree movement; a twist is a partial rotation before returning to the starting point and rotating in the other direction. Bending is a movement around a fulcrum such as the wrist, knee, elbow, or waist (because it can stress the spine, bending at the neck is discouraged). Swinging means moving a suspended body part (e.g., a leg or arm) back and forth. Swaying means a smooth shifting of one's weight from side to side or forward and back (also called *rocking*, especially if done repetitively, rigidly). Dodging and stopping are two stability movements that can involve the child traveling (e.g., dodging behind a tree, stopping in mid run), but don't always (e.g., ducking one's head, stopping in mid twist). While any of these stability skills can be practiced by children individually, they are often done in groups; for example, swaying together to music.

*Teaching strategies.* Teachers can build on young children's spontaneous movements to suggest many games and challenges that will further develop their basic stability skills. Many of these activities can be done during large group, with each child on a carpet square or small mat or on a soft surface outdoors. Pretend play also offers opportunities for children to act out the stability movements natural to animals or illustrative of characters in stories. Try strategies such as these:

■ Buy or construct equipment to facilitate practicing stability skills; for example, ramps, beams, low risers, pull and push toys, rocking toys, swings, and wheeled vehicles.

■ Provide cues for performing specific stability skills. Cues for bending include: spread your legs; hold out your arms; and bend in stages for balance. Cues for stopping include: allow enough time; try to slow down gradually; and lean back slightly.

■ Demonstrate and practice stability skills with children. For example, bend and straighten different parts of your body, describing the movements as you do. Ask the children to do this with you. Have them suggest body parts to bend and straighten. Together practice curling and stretching/extending

fingers and toes. Explore the words *curl* and *stretch* with familiar situations. For example, ask children to pretend to be sleeping kittens that wake up. Or have them pretend to sleep all curled up, and then waken them with an "alarm clock" sound; they can take turns making the wake-up noise.

■ Challenge children to practice and extend a movement, such as "Who can stretch only one side of your body?" or "Show me how you can lie on the floor and stretch your legs."

■ Have a child lead the group in an activity exploring a stability skill such as swinging, letting him choose which body part to swing and how. Encourage the leader to describe the movement before performing it. Supply the words for body parts and motions.

## C3 Manipulative skills: throwing, kicking

These are the manipulative skills children typically seem to discover on their own. Throwing is the easier skill, and children may naturally use an underhand, overhand, or sidearm motion. Kicking develops later because children's lower-body control typically lags behind upper-body control. Initially they kick using a lateral pushing motion along the ground, often from a stationary position. Later, children approach their target with one or more steps and swing their foot upward, which gives momentum and height to the kick.

*Teaching strategies.* Children naturally throw and kick things, curious about the effects of such motions. They may also imitate the actions of older siblings or sports figures. Although their abilities are rudimentary at first, children enjoy seeing their accuracy improve with practice. For example:

■ Provide appropriate equipment and materials for children to throw and kick during choice time, group time, and outdoor time. Equipment should be child-size and accommodate children's wide range of abilities and interests, including objects to throw and kick (e.g., soft balls, beanbags, balloons, Frisbees). Children may also kick objects they find lying on the ground such as cans, sticks, and pebbles.

■ Provide cues for performing specific manipulative skills. Cues for throwing include: look at the target; hold your arm far back; and step forward with the foot opposite the throwing arm. Cues for kicking include: swing your foot back; make contact at the instep; and stop your body after you kick.

■ Encourage children to practice and explore manipulative skills. For example, they can toss a beanbag overhand and underhand, or kick a ball with their toe (in a sturdy shoe) or the side of their foot. Encourage them to use their nondominant as well as dominant leg or arm. After children master basic motions, provide targets for them to throw or kick objects at (e.g., hoops; baskets, bowls, and boxes; target boards). Begin with large/close/low targets, moving to smaller/farther/higher targets; also progress from stationary to moving actions.

■ Challenge children to extend and vary their skills; for example, say "Try to throw the ball farther" or "I wonder how you could kick it a different way?"

■ Use children's interest in throwing and kicking to explore movement concepts. For example, challenge them to throw a beanbag up or down, or to stand near or far away from the target, or to throw with a straight or curved arm. Invite them to suggest other variations. Encourage their use of position and distance words.

## A Adult-guided experience is especially important for learnings such as:

### A1 Locomotor skills: marching, plodding, hopping, galloping, sliding, slithering, leaping, chasing, fleeing, skipping

Plodding is a heavy walk with feet dragging. Hopping usually is done one-footed (two-footed it's also called jumping). Galloping is an uneven transfer of weight while traveling; the same front foot leads and takes the weight as the rear foot comes up to meet it. Sliding is like walking, but without lifting the feet. Slithering is crawling with the entire body pressed to the ground. Chasing and fleeing are purposeful running, using cognitive as well as movement strategies to anticipate or avoid the other person. Skipping is the most difficult locomotor skill, because both sides must perform equally well and in alternation.

*Teaching strategies.* Once children have mastered the basic locomotor skills learned through child-guided experience, there is an almost endless range of variations to explore. However, children may not create or chance upon more complex movements on their own. Adult interventions, such as those described below, can help open up the world of movement.

■ Provide cues for performing specific locomotor skills. Cues for skipping include: lift knees; and step, hop, and land on one foot and then the other. Cues for galloping include: put the same foot forward every time; and begin with a big step forward. You can also emphasize the beat of locomotor activities, such as chanting "DA-da, DA-da, DA-da, . . ." during galloping.

■ Issue movement challenges and encourage children to make up their own. Create opportunities to navigate difficult spaces. For example,

> In the activity "A Walk Through the Woods" (Sanders 2002, 22), children take a pretend trip through the woods, walking around foam pins, cones, and two-liter soda bottles representing trees. Children first "plant" trees, by placing the objects themselves (you may need to move some "trees" farther apart). Then they practice different locomotor skills such as walking, skipping, and hopping through the "woods."

Provide targets or goals to locomote to; for example, say "Let's gallop to the fence" or "Hop to the coat rack to get ready for outside time." Ask children to suggest targets. Provide time and number challenges for locomotor movements; for example, "How many times can you skip to the book shelf and back before the music stops?" or "Let's see how fast you can skip around the circle." Ask the children to issue time and number challenges. For activities that favor one side, such as hopping or galloping, encourage children to practice on one foot and then the other.

■ Provide space, time, and equipment for children to practice these locomotor skills. In addition to purchasing standard playground equipment (slides, swings, climbers), use furniture or recycled items (such as empty cartons or old tires) to enhance movement opportunities.

### A2 Stability skills: transferring weight, balancing, jumping/landing, rolling

Adult-guided stability skills extend those learned primarily through child-guided experience, and may build on the young child's growing muscle control and coordination. Transferring weight involves shifting one's center of gravity; it is a controlled movement that is essential in many movement activities. Balancing means evenly distributing the body's weight on each side of a vertical axis. "For young children, being in balance simply means not falling over. This is critical in developing physical skills" (Sanders 2002, 40). Rolling is traveling by transferring weight to adjacent body parts around a central axis; children can roll like a log, rock on their backs, and roll headfirst.

*Teaching strategies.* Stability—bodily control—underpins many movement tasks. For that reason, the teacher's role in helping children master these foundational skills is particularly important for lifelong physical activity. For example:

■Buy or construct equipment to practice stability skills, such as an inclined mat for rolling, a wide beam or strip of tape on the floor for balancing, string for jumping over. For example,

> Stretch two pieces of tape or string along the floor that start close together and get farther apart. Have children jump over both at once, beginning at the narrow end and progressing as far as they can toward the wide end. Children can suggest other ways to cross over, such as leaping or jumping sideways.

■Provide cues for performing specific stability skills. Cues for rolling like a log include: keep your legs together; and keep your arms at your sides or over your head. Cues for transferring weight include: keep your movements smooth; and don't lean too far in one direction. Cues for balancing include keep your head and body still; and extend your arms. Cues for jumping/landing include: crouch before jumping; and land on both feet at the same time with your legs apart. Practice at jumping/landing should start on safe places such as low steps, curbs, or boxes; if children wish, hold their hands and jump/land with them.

■Issue stability challenges and encourage children to invent their own. For example, "Roll like your legs were glued together" (demonstrate if neces-

---

## Practicing Skills with Old Tires

Recycled items provide many creative opportunities for young children to march, hop, skip, and leap. (Make sure all materials are clean and safe before using them with the children.)

Garages often give away old tires. Try to get one tire for each child or two children, but certainly enough tires to make straight and staggered lines. (If tires aren't available, all the locomotor skills can be practiced using hula hoops instead.)

   Give one tire to each child or pair of children and pose the following locomotor and stability challenges:

"Hop [march/skip/gallop/slide] around the tire." (*locomotor skill*)

"In pairs, chase each other around the tire." (*locomotor; give starting/stopping signals*)

"Jump into the middle of the tire. Now jump back outside." (*locomotor*)

"Stand on the edge of the tire." (*stability*)

"Crouch inside the tire like a frog and jump out." (*locomotor, stability*)

"Crouch like a duck and waddle around the tire." (*locomotor*)

   Arrange the tires in a straight line or zigzag path or both and pose the following locomotor challenges:

"Walk [march/hop] from the middle of one tire to another."

"Walk [march/hop/run/gallop] up one side of the row and back down the other."

"Walk [march/hop/run/gallop] around the edges of the tires in a weaving [zigzag] pattern."

"Slide [slither] over the first tire and into the next tire in the row. Go to the end this way, and come back."

*The Intentional Teacher*

sary) or "Who can roll left? Right? In a circle?" Suggest balancing challenges for the floor or a low beam; for example, varying the position of a raised leg. Ask children to suggest other positions.

■ Build on children's interests and imaginations to develop stability skills. Design a balance trail with items children are interested in standing or walking on. As they become more competent, gradually add more difficult items. For example, begin with wide planks on the floor and taped pathways; later add twisted ropes and low elevated beams. Or make up and act out group stories. For example,

> "We're searching for buried treasure. Everyone get on the boat. Uh, oh. I can feel big waves rocking the boat." Pause while children are "rocked" back and forth by the waves. Encourage children to pretend scenarios that challenge their stability; for example, maintaining balance on the rolling seas, jumping onto land or back in the boat, or rolling away from "sharks" in the water.

**A3 Manipulative skills: catching/collecting, punting, dribbling, volleying, striking with a racket, striking with a long-handled instrument**

Catching/collecting (sometimes called *fielding*) is difficult because it involves visual tracking plus motor coordination; children may be startled by the approaching object and close their eyes or freeze. Dribbling involves moving an object forward by striking it repeatedly using hands or feet while following along behind. Children can dribble, if primitively, with their feet (e.g., kicking a pebble along the path) before they have the control to dribble a ball with their hands. Volleying involves passing an object back and forth using the hands or feet.

*Teaching strategies.* The development of these fundamental manipulative skills is critical for children's later participation in sports or games. Because some involve interacting with others (throwing, catching, volleying), their mastery also opens a world of social relationships. For example:

■ Provide equipment and materials for practicing manipulative skills with the hands and feet. For example, children can use a launch board to practice catching; they place a beanbag on the low end of the board then stand at the high end and stomp on the board, making the beanbag fly into the air. They can also play this game in pairs. Items to catch, volley, and strike should be soft and slow-moving at first, such as scarves, beanbags, and oversized balls.

■ Provide cues for performing specific manipulative skills. Cues for catching a rolled or thrown ball, for example, include: watch the ball; move to where it is; and bring the ball toward your body and hug it to you. Cues for hitting with a racket include: turn the flat side of the paddle toward the object; keep your wrist stiff; and follow through on the swing.

■ Incorporate manipulative skills into different parts of the daily routine. For example, incorporate catching into transitions by saying, "I'm going to throw the beanbag to a girl in a red shirt and after she catches it, she can go to the small group table." At large group, have children choose partners to practice catching, volleying, or hitting something back and forth with a paddle or racket. Encourage their suggestions; for example, catching down low and up high; standing face-to-face or side-to-side. Collect things on a field trip that can be thrown and caught, punted, struck, and so on; for example, fallen acorns, small pebbles, shells. Children can sort the materials into baskets for use at subsequent outside times.

■ Build children's skills in sequence. For example, at first children should use their hands to strike stationary objects (e.g., a balloon placed on a table or tee), then objects suspended from a string or rope. Next is dropping the object in front of the child, and finally throwing a moving object to the child waiting to strike it. When an implement is introduced, it should first be large and flat (e.g., a paddle or racket); using long-handled instruments (e.g., a bat or golf club) comes last, since it involves estimating distances as well as physical movements.

## Movement concepts

From infancy on, children begin to differentiate the space they occupy from that filled by others. As motor skills develop, children form an initial awareness of how and at what rate their body moves. Young children also develop many aspects of body awareness, such as awareness of body parts and body shapes, through their own exploration and feedback, especially when adults supply appropriate labels (see **Orienting self and objects in space** in **Chapter 4**). Because they are interested in their own bodies, preschoolers are generally motivated to learn body vocabulary. As with any vocabulary set, learning the names for body parts, shapes, and other concepts requires direct instruction or conversation. (For more on vocabulary learning, see **Chapter 3.**)

Most movement concepts seem to be learned through adult intervention, although children's initial experiments and observations form the foundation for understanding them. For example, beating on a drum with a stick explores hard and soft (levels of effort); climbing steps is an experience with low and high (space awareness); and observing a bird flying overhead but a fish swimming in a pond below creates awareness of location (body awareness or relations). Even for such basic concepts, adult guidance is essential to help children become aware of, label, and apply what they learn.

# C Child-guided experience is especially important for learnings such as:

### C1 Space awareness: self space, shared space

Children learn primarily through self-discovery about the space they themselves occupy, versus the space they share with other people and objects. In infancy, children perceive themselves and their caregiver as one entity; but one of the earliest spatial understandings that develops is the capacity to distinguish the space they alone occupy from that shared by others. Preschoolers have long since mastered this basic concept, but they continue to explore the boundaries between themselves and others, especially when trying movements they do not yet fully control.

*Teaching strategies.* Viewing the world from their own (egocentric) perspective, young children

naturally test the boundaries of their bodies. Teachers facilitate this exploration by providing both limited and wide-open spaces for them to navigate. For large group activities, large, open spaces, where children are less likely to bump into one another or objects as they experiment with movement, are needed. Some activities are best accomplished outdoors, others will work in uncluttered indoor spaces. For example, the area used for block building might be suitable. Minimize sharp edges and provide soft surfaces (such as carpeting) so bumps, when they do happen, do not result in injuries.

To develop an awareness of personal space necessarily means paying attention to the space filled by others. Hence, this area of physical development has both individual and social aspects. Here are some strategies:

■ Introduce self and shared space activities gradually. Begin with large group activities where children stay in their own space; for example, movements such as swaying or bending. You may need to provide visual markers, such as carpet squares or tape on the floor, to help some children stay in their own area.

■ Then have children move through space. Line up half the group on each side of the room and say "Now see if you can move to the other side without touching anyone or anything else." Begin with a simple locomotor movement the children have mastered (such as crawling or walking) and progress to more advanced movements (such as plodding or skipping).

■ Provide children with opportunities to discover their personal body boundaries; for example, by their moving through narrow and wide spaces, or low and high ones. Use existing spaces and create others with furniture, cartons, sheet-draped tables and chairs, beanbag chairs, hula hoops, and the like. For example, challenge children to perform increasingly difficult motor movements while inside a hula hoop. Begin with movements that require little balance (e.g., raising the arms) and progress to ones that require more control and stability (e.g., lifting one leg). Ask the children to suggest movements.

■ After they have experimented with movement in their own hula hoop, ask each child to choose a partner and perform the motions while inside the same hula hoop together. This activity also presents a good opportunity for social problem solving, such as establishing "rules" about how to avoid actions that might hurt the other.

## C2 Effort awareness: time (speeds)

The aspect of effort awareness primarily learned in exploration and discovery is the time concept of speeds. (The other time concept is *rhythms*, discussed below under adult-guided experience.) For preschoolers, speed concepts include slow, moderate or medium, and fast, as well as accelerating and decelerating (going faster and slower). For example:

*Teaching strategies.* Children love to play with speed—the more extreme, the better. "From their point of view, 'slow' more often means 'not-quite-as-fast-as-fast'" (Hohmann & Weikart 2002, 414). However, children also enjoy experimenting with slow movements, especially if these too are "verrrry sloooow!" Teachers have many options for supporting this natural fascination with rates of movement, including these:

■ Call children's attention to moving things and comment on their rate of speed. Ask them to imitate the fast and slow movements they observe. Describe the speed of various activities; for example, say "Those are slow-cooking cookies. I'm getting hungry" or "Jamie is running the water faster than Suzie. His bucket will fill up sooner." Comment on the speed of creatures and events in nature; for example, the rate at which animals travel, clouds move, seeds germinate, leaves fall, and so on. And comment on objects in the environment; for example, a fast-moving jet or a slow-moving freight train.

■ Ask children to name things that move at slow, fast, or medium speed and demonstrate the corresponding movement. Then copy the children's movements and ask "Am I moving too fast or too slow?" Follow their suggestions for making a movement faster or slower.

■ Invent games or transitions that feature moving at different speeds. For example, suggest children move to snack "as slow as a turtle." Or say "Let's see how fast we can clean up and get ready to go outside." Scarves are wonderful for observing and experimenting with slow movement. For example,

One group of children became very interested in dropping scarves from the climber and were quite amazed at how *slowly* they drifted to the ground. "It takes a long time for them to go down," one child noted. This observation led the children to try out being "slow scarves" during large group, in which they exhibited an understanding and tolerance for moving slowly, a capacity they had not shown before.

## C3 Body/relationship awareness: with myself (body parts, body shapes)

At its most basic, body awareness is the relationship we each have with our own body. Children come to understand that their body comprises various parts—i.e., that the thing sticking out of their shoulder is their arm, at the end of that is their hand, and at the end of that is their fingers.

Those individual parts take various shapes, as does their whole body in relation to the world around them. The body shapes (or characteristics) that preschool children can create and comprehend with minimal adult intervention include round, straight, tall, long, short, little, small, and big. With a bit more guidance, they can grasp such concepts as narrow, wide, stretched, twisted, square, rectangular, triangular, diamond, thin, thick, pointed, oval, flat, angular, curved, curled, crooked, sharp, smooth, tiny, gigantic, and skinny. They also experiment with and experience the concept of like and unlike (see also **Chapters 4 and 5**).

(The other with myself body awareness concept is *roles*, discussed below under adult-guided experience.)

*Teaching strategies.* Young children's fascination with their own bodies offers many natural oportunities for teachers to support their learning of relational movement concepts, including these:

■ Refer to children's body parts by name in natural conversation. For example, "Trisha, I see you're wearing a new red hat on your head" or "Lyle, can you show Ian how you kicked the ball by turning your foot to the side?" Comment when a change in position creates a change in body shape; for example, "When I sit down on this chair, I'll make a flat lap for you to cuddle in while we read."

■ Use the arts to enhance children's awareness. Read books and tell stories that feature body parts. Sing songs and chants that use body parts, such as holding up the number of fingers when singing Ten Little Monkeys Jumping on the Bed. Encourage children to name a body part to put in and take out when you sing Hokey Pokey. Use various noise-makers, and ask children to represent the sounds with their bodies. For example, a jingly sound they might show by wiggling, a gong by standing up straight, and a ticking with head-bobbing. Describe the sounds, acknowledge children's labels, and provide additional vocabulary words.

■ Pose movement challenges and problems to enhance body awareness. This problem-solving approach is more effective than showing or telling. For example,

> Rather than demonstrating a crooked body shape, which would only inspire imitation on the part of the children, a teacher could invite them to show *her* a crooked body shape. Divergent problem solving of this nature could result in as many different crooked shapes as there are children! The teacher must then validate the variety of responses she's seeing by describing two or three. The children then get the impression that it's a good thing to find their own response, and they become more willing to take creative risks. Similarly, once the children have responded, the teacher can invite them to *find another way*. This encourages further problem solving. If the teacher were to *demonstrate* another way, she would be giving the impression that her way was the better one. (Rae Pica, 2004, pers. comm.)

## A Adult-guided experience is especially important for learnings such as:

### A1 Space awareness: levels, directions, pathways

The space awareness concepts in this category are levels, directions, and pathways. Levels refers to the position of the body or a body part in space; that is,

high, middle or medium, and low. Directions concepts include up/down, forward/backward, beside, and sideways. (They also include right/left and clockwise/counterclockwise, but preschoolers are not yet ready for these.) Pathways refers to straight, curved or circular, and zigzag movements.

*Teaching strategies.* These areas of spatial awareness have important implications not only for physical education but also for other domains. As teachers help young children move in different ways through space, they are also creating the foundation for many areas of mathematical and scientific understanding. For example:

■ Suggest ways children might use or place their body parts at different levels. For example, "Walk around the playground with your nose as high in the air as you can" or "Think of a way to move with your elbows down low." Invent activities in which children move their bodies or manipulate objects in different directions or along different pathways. For example, suggest they crawl across the room forwards and backwards. Ask them to suggest ways to move forwards and backwards, up and down, sideways, and in straight or zigzag patterns. Encourage children to invent their own activities, and follow their suggestions.

■ Play musical instruments of varying pitch and ask children to position their bodies according to the sound. For example, they might stand on tip-toe for a high pitch or crouch for a low one. Describe the sounds and label children's actions.

■ Create pathways that are circular, straight, or zigzag using chalk, tape, and other materials. Suggest ways to move in, out of, and around these paths. Follow children's ideas. Use large blocks to set up straight and zigzag pathways. Encourage children to observe and comment on their differences, and extend their language. For example, if a child says "One road is straight and the other is funny," say "Yes, this one is a straight line and that one is a zigzag." Encourage children to walk or move in other ways along the paths.

■ Set up obstacle courses involving changes of direction, different levels, and various types of pathways. Use things such as blocks, carpet squares, shelves and ramps, chairs and tables, and tape marks on the floor to create the course. Encourage children to create their own obstacle courses.

■ Incorporate into the daily routine pathways and ways of moving along them; for example, during transitions (going from the table to wash up) and cleanup (moving between areas to put away toys). Suggest movement ideas and ask children to contribute their own. For example,

> Children in High/Scope preschools make plans to indicate what they will do at work (choice) time. Part of planning is deciding what area of the room to work in. One teacher suggested this idea: "The teacher lays a 'planning path' (made from long sheets of fabric) on the floor and asks children to choose a way to move their bodies along the path (e.g., crawl, hop, go backwards, jump, walk like a crab) to an area where they plan to work." (Strubank 1991, 106)

■ Use naturally occurring situations to supply vocabulary words that describe level and direction as children move about the room and play outdoors. Encourage them to use these vocabulary words as they describe their own actions.

## A2 Effort awareness: time (rhythms), force, control/flow

The component of time in which adult intervention seem to play a salient role is rhythms; that is, beat, cadence, and pattern. Beat is the "consistent, repetitive pulse that lies within every rhyme, song, or musical selection" (Weikart 2000, 122). Cadence is the musical measure of movement; pattern is its systematic or regular repetition. The force component of effort awareness has three aspects: degree (strong, medium, light); creation, when the body is the source of a force (starting, sustained, explosive, gradual); and absorption, when the body reacts to a force (stopping, receiving, stabilizing). The control component (sometimes called *flow*) refers to the complexity of movement; that is, single movements, combinations of movements, and transitions between movements.

*Teaching strategies.* Just as space awareness concepts apply to other domains of learning, so too does effort awareness, by contributing to children's

musical development, mathematics (patterning) understanding, and ability to carry out increasingly complex directions. Try strategies such as these:

■ Incorporate different strategies to increase children's familiarity with rhythms. Use poems, chants, and songs with steady beats. Instrumental music is best, so children are not distracted by the lyrics. Emphasize beats with your gestures and words, such as clapping your hands, tapping your foot, nodding, and accenting syllables. Call children's attention to actions that involve a steady beat. For example,

> One spring day during outside time, Jessie, an adult, was pushing 4-year-old Timmy on the swing. She noticed that his legs were beginning to perform the bending and straightening motion used in pumping. She began to reinforce Timmy's natural movement with language, saying "BACK" as his legs went back and "OUT" as his legs went out. As Timmy felt the timing of the words, his movements became larger and more pronounced, and he moved to the steady beat. From that day on, Timmy was able to pump himself on the swing. (Weikart 2000, 138)

■ Provide children with different experiences that involve weight and force. As they work with objects of different weights, comment on their level of effort; for example, "Lucy carried that heavy box all the way across the room!" Ask children to pretend to carry things of different weights: "Let's imagine we're lifting a hammer over our heads. Now pretend it's a feather from a tiny bird."

■ Provide children with hard and soft materials to transform, and comment on how much effort it takes; for example, hammering nails into wood versus golf tees into foam (use safety goggles and take other appropriate precautions). Use clay or dough that varies in plasticity, and encourage children to comment on how easy or hard they are to shape.

■ Gradually increase children's ability to follow and sequence movement directions. Children often follow and respond to movement directions better if adults separate the verbal and visual components (Weikart 2000). Demonstrate the movement without talking *or* describe it in words without moving, then ask children to try it. Children may differ in which type of cue is most effective for them, so use both visual and verbal. After children master a movement, you can combine the two components when you give the direction next time.

■ When you are building a movement sequence, always begin with one motion at a time and encourage children to practice it for a while. Add a second motion only after the children appear comfortable and confident with the first one. When sequencing, keep each movement simple and familiar; for example, patting the knee and touching the shoulder. Encourage children to suggest pairs of movements.

### A3 Body/relationship awareness: with myself (roles), with other movers and objects

The concept relating to the self that requires adult intervention is roles. Roles that children create with their bodies include copying, leading/following, meeting/parting, passing, mirroring, acting in unison, alternately, solo, partner, and group. Children also use their body to create relationships with other people and objects; this concept is called locations. Locations includes above/below, near to/far from, over/under, in front of/behind, on/off, together/apart, facing/side by side, around/through, between, and into.

*Teaching strategies.* Like advanced manipulative skills such as volleying, relational awareness also has social and cognitive implications for young children's development. Thoughtful teachers support the learning of these movement concepts with those impacts in mind:

■ Give children opportunities to manipulate equipment (such as hula hoops, scarves, cartons) to help them discover relationships between themselves and objects. For example, with hula hoops,

> "Walk [march/hop/gallop/jump] around the outside of the hula hoop."
> In pairs, have one child hold the hoop on edge while the other child crawls through it.
> "Lift the hoop up around the outside of your body. Now lower the hoop down around the outside of your body."
> "Walk away from the hoop. Walk towards the hoop."

■ Create imaginative ways for children to use their bodies, and ask them to suggest other ideas. Invent games in which they change the location of their bodies relative to others and to objects; for example, jumping in and out of a large circle, facing toward and away from a partner, or stepping in front of and behind a chair.

■ Encourage children to use their bodies to express emotions such as friendly, sad, mad, frightened, brave, shy, silly, and adventurous. Say "How do you move your body when you are happy?" or "Let's move to the snack table as though we're tired and sleepy." Ask them to suggest feelings to represent with their bodies.

■ Provide vocabulary words to describe the body's position relative to people and objects. Give children simple definitions. Insert location words into conversations; for example, "Tawana is moving her finger along the shelf to find a book that begins with the letter T" or "Let's stand farther apart while we do the Hokey Pokey so everyone has room to *shake it all about!*"

■ Give children opportunities to lead and follow during movement activities. For example, ask them to suggest ideas for Hokey Pokey or other familiar songs. Repeat or clarify their ideas to make it easier for other children to listen and copy. Have children observe others and perform the same movements (they need not duplicate them exactly). For example,

> In [the game] Mirrors, children pair off and stand facing each other. While standing in place, partners trade off performing and imitating a series of simple movements. Variations include having one child stand in back of the performer and another in front or having one child lead a group. (Sanders 2002, 35)

\*     \*     \*

Children's development of physical skills during the preschool years, facilitated by informed teachers, is "fundamental and crucial to the goal of helping all children become physically active and healthy for life" (Sanders 2002, 58).

Movement experiences can also enhance learning in other domains, such as mathematics and peer interactions. But the mastery of motor skills, and their application to cognitive and social content, will not happen through maturation alone. Teachers play a vital role by arranging and equipping the learning environment, scheduling physical education activities in addition to choice time, issuing physical challenges, and offering concrete cues to help children develop physical knowledge and skills.

## Questions for Further Thought

**1.** What arguments can early childhood advocates use to preserve physical education in the face of budget allocations favoring scholastic disciplines at the expense of other content areas?

**2.** What role can and should early childhood education play in preventing obesity, inactivity, and other physical conditions that predispose children to later health and related problems?

**3.** If developmental research shows it is inappropriate for preschoolers to participate in sports, how can the early childhood field address the current trend toward involving children in organized athletics at younger and younger ages?

**4.** What political and practical roles can early childhood professionals play to promote large motor activity in neighborhoods where children do not have access to safe outdoor play areas? Can and should early childhood agencies serve as community organizers, advocates, mediators, builders?

# The Visual Arts

After reading the book *Where the Wild Things Are*, a group of preschoolers discussed what they would do if they were sent to their rooms for being bad. Most agreed they enjoyed spending time in their rooms, either alone or with family members. The next day, their teacher set out paper and drawing materials (colored pencils, markers, pastels) and asked the children to draw their rooms.

Five-year-old Marta began with a rectangle. Outside the rectangle she made small red squares for the "rest of my house cause it's brick." Inside she drew a door, a bed, two windows, and a big overhead light. Then she made small dots all over because "my rug has speckles."

Four-year-old Eric drew two beds, a small cage, and a large box in the middle. He explained, "One bed is for me and the other is for Grampa Johns. That's for the gerbil and this big box is for my toys and books and Grampa's books and extra blankets and a flashlight." After looking at his picture, Eric made another rectangle in the corner. "I almost forgot the closet," he said. "Grampa Johns keeps his squishy, smelly galoshes in there!" Then he drew a pair of big black boots. "Now it's done!" he announced.

Developing artistic knowledge and ability has been a central feature of early childhood programs since their beginning. Although this chapter's focus is on the visual arts, many of the principles and strategies discussed also apply to creating and appreciating other arts disciplines such as music, dance, and drama. Attention to the role of the arts in perceptual, cognitive, and social development spans the pioneering work of preschool educator Rhoda Kellogg (Kellogg & O'Dell 1967), the constructivist theories of Vygotsky (1978), and the current worldwide interest in Reggio Emilia's use of representation to support learning (Gandini et al. 2005). Although early art education has been supplanted somewhat by the focus recently on school readiness (Seefeldt 2003), most educators continue to believe that the arts are central to young children's development and merit a place in the early childhood curriculum.

The value of artistic learning for children is both emotional and intellectual, as illustrated in the story that opened this chapter. Art is *intrinsically rewarding*; that is, studying art is important for its own sake. The arts provide an inner sense of competence and control. Especially for children whose language skills are just developing, the arts open up new avenues for expression and communication. But the arts can be empowering for all children. The

Task Force on Children's Learning and the Arts notes that "as they engage in the artistic process, children learn they can observe, organize, and interpret their experiences. They can make decisions, take actions, and monitor the effect of those actions" (Arts Education Partnership 1998, 2). Diversity is another important, intrinsically rewarding concept expressed through the arts. Through art education "students begin to see the rich mosaic of the world from many perspectives" (Dobbs 1998, 12).

The arts are also *extrinsically valuable* in promoting other areas of development, as studies have shown. For example, the work of Eisner (2004) on the development of aesthetic intelligence applies critical thinking in the arts to educational practices across many disciplines, and Arnheim (1989) emphasizes that art is as much an intellectual activity as an intuitive one. The Arts Education Partnership (1998) also recognizes this correlation: "For all children, at all ability levels, the arts play a central role in cognitive, motor, language, and social-emotional development. The arts motivate and engage children in learning, stimulate memory and facilitate understanding, enhance symbolic communication, promote relationships, and provide an avenue for building competence" (v).

Research confirms the role of the arts in promoting development from infancy through adolescence. For example, exposure to patterns is important in early brain development (Healy 1994; see also **Chapter 4**). A 10-year national study by Shirley Brice Heath of after-school arts programs found children gained cognitive and linguistic skills that transferred to other content domains (Olszewski 1998). *Champions of Change: The Impact of the Arts on Learning* (Fiske 1999), presenting seven major arts education studies, quoted then U.S. Secretary of Education Richard Riley: "For young Americans to succeed in today's economy of ideas, they will need an education that develops imaginative, flexible, and tough-minded thinking. The arts powerfully nurture the ability to think in this manner" (vi).

In the last two decades, there has been an effort to include both self-expression and intellectual components in visual arts education. An influential movement in this regard has been discipline-based art education (DBAE), a concept introduced by Greer (1984) and field-tested with support from the Getty Center for Education in the Arts (later renamed the Getty Education Institute for the Arts, and eventually discontinued). This movement takes the position that the teaching of art should integrate art history, art criticism, aesthetics, and the creation of art. An earlier goals statement of the National Art Education Association (1982) also endorses a comprehensive approach, comparable to DBAE, that includes analyzing art as well as producing art. And the educational objectives of the National Endowment for the Arts (1988) list fostering creativity, promoting communication skills, making choices based on critical assessment, and learning about the significant achievements of the world's civilizations.

This broad focus was reflected in *National Standards for Arts Education: What Every Young American Should Know and Be Able to Do in the Arts* (U.S. Department of Education 1994). The arts were also included in the mandated reforms of the Goals 2000: Educate America Act passed by Congress (National Education Goals Panel 1994), which established the Task Force on Children's Learning and the Arts: Birth to Age Eight (Arts Education Partnership 1998). The Task Force explicitly recognized the role of the arts in promoting language and literacy and thereby concluded that they contribute to Education Goal 1 that "all children will start school ready to learn."

## Young children's development in the visual arts

Knowledge and skills in the arts, as in other areas of content, do not develop in isolation from other abilities. The connections are apparent in the questions we ask about children's artistic development:

▶ Are their muscles ready to build and mold with solid materials?

▶ Do they have the fine motor and eye-hand coordination to manipulate tools?

▶ Can they differentiate lines, colors, and shapes?

▶ Are they able to collaborate on art projects with peers?

▶ Do they have words to describe what they see and how it makes them feel?

▶ Can children say what they like or dislike and why?

Implied in these questions is not only a range of general developmental abilities but also two related art abilities—**creating visual art** and **appreciating visual art.** Most treatments of artistic development in early childhood deal only with the former. However, by encouraging children to reflect on their actions and experiences with arts media, as we do with other materials and activities, we can also lay the groundwork for them to understand and appreciate art.

## Stages in creating visual art

Stages in artistic development do not have discrete beginnings and endings (Taunton & Colbert 2000). Children tend to move back and forth within levels as they learn and grow. In some respects, this is true of adult artists too, particularly when they first encounter an unfamiliar medium or begin to explore an idea. Nevertheless, theory and research on how young children make art emphasize four general progressions over time (Epstein & Trimis 2002):

▶ **From accidental or spontaneous representation to intentional representation**—Studies show that only 30 percent of 4-year-olds, compared with 80 percent of 5-year-olds, begin to draw with an intention in mind (Thompson 1995). Younger children begin by accidentally creating a form and then deciding it looks like something. They may shape a wedge of clay into a rectangle and decide it's a car. This order reverses at a later stage in children's development, in that the older child has characteristics in mind and purposefully finds or manipulates materials to match that mental image. (At any age, however, found or accidentally made objects can inspire creativity and vice versa.)

▶ **From simple to elaborated representations**—Initially, children hold one or two distinguishing characteristics in mind and recreate them in their artwork. Later, as they are able to hold more attributes in mind and grow more adept with materials, their two- and three-dimensional representations also become more detailed.

▶ **From marks and lines to shapes and figures**—When children first explore an art medium, the sheer joy of using motion to make a mark is satisfying, even if repeated to the point of leaving a hole in the paper! With increased control comes experimentation and then deliberation. Children begin by making lines, followed by shapes and forms. Drawing an enclosed shape—making a line that changes direction at least once and returns to the starting point—requires visual-motor coordination and intentionality. In keeping with the developments described above, the process of making shapes itself moves from accidental to deliberate, and from simple to complex.

▶ **From random marks to relationships**—In addition to progressing in *what* they mark on the page, children become increasingly aware of *where* marks are in relation to one another. At first, marks are random, appearing wherever an exuberant hand lands them. Later, placement is intentional, with a deliberate consideration of other markings. This trend reflects greater interest in representational accuracy and growing spatial awareness. Aesthetic considerations also begin to enter into decisions. Children place colors or objects in proximity because they "go together" or "look nice next to each other." In this way, creating and appreciating art converge.

## Stages in appreciating visual art

Stages of art appreciation are often related to the developmental progressions of Piaget and other cognitive theorists (Kerlavage 1995). For example, Parsons (1987) posits a series of stages that begins with concrete and personal judgments and ends with abstract and socially developed views about art. Although theorists differ over the number, labels, and characteristics of particular stages, they typically note at least three general levels that characterize young children's aesthetic growth:

▶ **Sensorial**—The youngest children like abstract, nonobjective images and respond intuitively to works that please their senses. They do not yet care about or understand symbols. Therefore colors (especially bright contrasts) and patterns (the bolder the better) are the dominant influences. Because young children respond viscerally to a work of art, they may have difficulty explaining the reasons for their choices. Often, one object or event will catch their attention to the exclusion of other aspects of the work. In addition, they may not attend to the form the work takes; for example, a painting versus a sculpture or a reproduction versus a photograph. Their concern is with how something looks or affects their senses, rather than with how it is made.

▶ **Concrete**—As children develop an understanding for symbols, their preferences depend more on subject matter or theme. They like artwork that conveys ideas they can relate to, portrayed in a simple and realistic manner. Children in this middle stage also develop an initial concept of beauty, again related to the realism and qualities of the subject matter. They see the purpose of art as telling a "story" about a real person, object, or event. Children at this stage are also able to sort art by its medium; for example, differentiating a photograph from a reproduction of a painting. Time is understood, too. Generalizing from their experiences, they can tell whether the images represent a period long ago, now, or in the future. Children may also have a sense of when the artwork itself was created based on its condition or the materials used.

▶ **Expressive**—By late preschool or early kindergarten, children are less egocentric and can begin to think about works of art from the artist's point of view, speculate on the artist's intentions, and judge the success of the artwork based on their response to it as viewers (Seefeldt 1999). They may use this knowledge as a source of subject matter or technique in their own artwork, choosing a medium or image because it is best suited to convey their ideas or because they think it will appeal to viewers or the recipient (if it is meant as a gift) or both. Because they are less egocentric, children in this stage also become more aware of different artistic styles, aesthetic choices, and outside influences on artists and their work such as culture. While they still prefer realism, they become more interested in subtle colors, complicated compositions, and the

feelings behind the message. The expressive qualities of different media also enter into their evaluation of the artwork. Taking all these factors into account, children at this stage will defend their preferences in terms of artistic style, expressive qualities, and aesthetic principles.

## Teaching and learning in the visual arts

Developing knowledge and skills in art, like mastering any other content area, requires time, materials, and encouragement. Adults must value the lessons to be learned from art and make a conscious decision to feature an arts program in the curriculum. Without this commitment from administrators and teachers, young children's artistic development will not extend beyond the conventional and unsophisticated. Attitudes as well as behavior will be affected; children will have lost an early opportunity to view art as a legitimate field of study. As a result, art educators agree that the intention to teach and respect art is vital to creating a climate in which art learning can thrive, but they do hold differing views on how to establish an artistic foundation in young children.

Followers of *expressive* theories of art believe children's everyday lives provide them with inspiration, and they often support child-guided teaching strategies. These theorists conclude that the more teachers help children explore everyday experiences in-depth—through discussion, small group activities, field trips—the more elaborate the artworks expressing those experiences will be. Likewise, as long as adult direction builds on children's interests, it is acceptable for teachers to introduce materials and demonstrate specific techniques.

Whether supporting exploration or actively teaching techniques, the "expressive" teacher's place in the classroom is never disposable. "When experiential learning is at the heart of the early childhood curriculum, there is a role for teachers" (Seefeldt 1999, 212).

Theorists and practitioners who believe artistic growth is tied to *perceptual development* tend to advocate more direct, adult-guided teaching strategies (Seefeldt 1999). These involve focusing children's attention on specific attributes of any number of things in their environment to improve their visual discrimination. Research suggests such training does help children see more details in and relationships among objects. Moreover, the visual training need not be extensive. Even something as minor as pointing out the differences between three shapes can help children to draw them more accurately (Mathews 1997), perhaps because an unconscious perception is made concrete.

However, highly directive methods, such as teaching drawing by copying, are not effective. Children may advance through the stages of representation more quickly (e.g., including more details or rendering proportions more accurately), but there is no evidence their learning generalizes beyond the immediate task or leads to more sophisticated art production overall.

# Fitting the learning experience to the learning objective

Both expressive and perceptual development theories about teaching art have validity; but once again, it is best to balance child-guided and adult-guided experience in this curriculum area. Research shows children left on their own tend to use materials in stereotypical ways. Copying or following adult orders also limits children's creativity. However, when adults work next to them without directing how to use the materials, children stay in the art area longer and engage in more experimentation with materials and ideas (Kindler 1995).

# Creating visual art

Of the key knowledge and skills in the area of creating visual art, child-guided experience seems particularly important for manipulating two- and three-dimensional art materials and tools, making representations from experience, making accidental representations, and making simple representations. Adult-guided experience seems to be especially significant for naming art materials, tools, and actions; becoming adept at using two- and three-dimensional art materials and tools; making representations using imagination; making intentional representations; and making complex representations.

 **Child-guided experience is especially important for learnings such as:**

C1 **Manipulating two- and three-dimensional art materials and tools**

Handling two-dimensional media requires having the manual dexterity to draw, paint, and print with appropriate materials and tools. Manipulating three-dimensional media requires the manual dexterity and strength to mold, sculpt, or build with materials using one's hands or tools.

*Teaching strategies.* The primary role of teachers in encouraging young children to make art is providing abundant and diverse materials, along with the time and space to explore them. For example:

■ Set up a spacious, attractive, and permanent art area. A permanent art area that is labeled and inviting tells children that what happens there is important. When setting up this space, make sure there is ample room to work individually and collaboratively, and to store easily accessible materials. Locate the art area near water (an indoor sink or outdoor spigot). Make sure the floor is easy to clean (tile, linoleum, large sheets of plastic) and that clean-up materials are nearby. The art area should have both vertical and horizontal work spaces (easels, walls, tables, pavement) and provide natural as well as artificial light (incandescent is preferable to fluorescent). There should be drying areas for finished work (clotheslines, flat surfaces, cubbies) and safe areas to protect unfinished work (including "Work-in-Progress" signs). Finally, make sure there is ample display space at children's eye level, including walls, bulletin boards, shelves, pedestals and boxes, and frames.

■ Provide a wide and abundant variety of tools and materials. Children need more variety than the crayons, paints, play dough, and modeling clay typically provided in early childhood settings. Many inexpensive materials—recycled paper, carpet scraps, items gathered from nature—offer opportunities to create. Teachers should be careful not to overwhelm children with too many materials at once and to introduce new materials gradually. Give children easy access to the materials so they can retrieve and use them independently and return unused supplies where they belong. Also provide non-art materials and experiences that develop children's fine motor and eye-hand coordination, such as scissors, puzzles, and small manipulative toys.

■ Incorporate art activities throughout the daily routine. The visual arts should not be limited to choice time or small group. For example, children can move with scarves and banners during large

---

## Art Materials and Tools for the Early Childhood Classroom

Young children can use a wide variety of conventional and unconventional materials—many of them low cost or no cost—to create two- and three-dimensional art.

### Two-dimensional media

**Drawing and printing**—Colored markers and felt-tip marking pens; crayons; chalk and chalkboard; charcoal sticks; regular and colored pencils; oil pastels; ink pads and stamps; and computer drawing programs.

**Painting**—Tempera paint; watercolors; fingerpaints; liquid starch and soap flakes (used to thicken tempera paints); brushes in different widths; tools to make marks (combs, toothbrushes, sticks, feathers, leaves, cotton swabs, string, shoelaces, rubber bands, bottle caps); containers for holding paint (paper cups, muffin tins, empty food containers, plates, metal trays, buckets); plastic squeeze bottles; spray bottles; and screening with holes of various sizes.

**Paper**—White drawing paper; large roll of white butcher paper or craft paper; construction paper in various colors; lined paper; graph paper; fingerpaint paper (glossy coating); shelving paper; clear and colored cellophane; newsprint; magazines and catalogs; cardboard and mat board; paper bags (grocery bags, gift bags, shopping bags); plain wrapping paper and decorated gift wrap; tissue paper; foil paper; waxed paper; crepe paper; wallpaper samples; paper tubes; paper plates; cardboard boxes and gift boxes; and used greeting cards, postcards, and stationery.

### Three-dimensional media

**Modeling and sculpting**—Natural (earth) clay and modeling clay; dough and play dough; moist sand; beeswax; natural dyes and food color (coffee, cinnamon, cocoa, mustard, black and red pepper); tools for molding and making impressions (bowls, dowels, tongue depressors and popsicle sticks, toothpicks, kitchen utensils, natural materials such as shells or nuts, hardware, plastic letters and numbers, old toy parts, lace, buttons and beads, hair rollers and barrettes); plywood boards or heavy cardboard (to use as portable work surfaces); and heavy plastic bags or rolls of plastic (to keep clay moist and allow work to dry slowly without cracking).

**Mixed media and collage**—Boxes and cartons in all sizes and shapes; cardboard or plastic tubes; egg cartons; yarn, ribbon, string, and twine/rope; fabric of various materials, colors, and textures; pipe cleaners, shoe laces, elastic strips; buttons, sequins, beads, feathers; clothespins; wood scraps; plastic foam pieces; cotton balls; old socks and stockings; small unbreakable mirrors; materials from nature (wood, sticks, leaves, grass, bark, shells, pebbles, stones, pine cones, feathers); straws; empty thread spools; cutting devices (scissors, plastic knives, hole punch); and fastening devices (paste, liquid glue, glue sticks, staplers, paper clips, cellophane tape, masking tape, rubber bands, yarn and string, wire, tapestry needles with big eyes and thread).

**Note:** For additional ideas on two- and three-dimensional art materials and tools, see R. Althouse, M.H. Johnson, & S.T. Mitchell, *The Colors of Learning: Integrating the Visual Arts into the Early Childhood Curriculum* (New York: Teachers College Press, 2003), 25–40; and A.S. Epstein & E. Trimis, *Supporting Young Artists: The Development of the Visual Arts in Young Children* (Ypsilanti, MI: High/Scope Press), 67–69.

group, observing how color and shape are altered by light and wind. Outdoor time in general is a wonderful opportunity to explore visual variety in nature. At snack and mealtime, make comments about the color, shape, and textural appearance of food. Also take advantage of special occasions, such as holidays and birthdays, to showcase the role of art.

■ Encourage in-depth exploration. Enlist children's interest by making comments and observations about what they are doing and by manipulating the art materials yourself. Encourage them to sort and classify the materials to discover their basic properties. Let children work with their hands before introducing tools so they get a "feel" for each type of medium, its properties, and how their actions transform it. Limit what you introduce at any one time; for example, let children explore one color with black and white before they mix two or more colors.

■ Encourage collaboration. Ask children to share their discoveries about materials and tools. Their insights will inspire further innovation in their peers.

■ Stress process over product. Children need to work with the same materials over and over again. Allow time for experimentation, repetition, and reflection. Only by letting children freely explore can they eventually produce original and unique art. Unfortunately, "the use of art materials to complete designs prepared and distributed by teachers is all but universal in preschools and the primary grades" (Thompson 1995, 2). Tell parents and school administrators why product pressure is actually counterproductive to artistic development. Resist pressure to showcase "polished" work.

■ Challenge children to use materials in creative ways. For example, a group of preschoolers were cutting paper into squares and strips. Their teacher asked "I wonder what we could do with the paper so it doesn't lie flat." The children made loops, coils, and accordion folds with the paper.

## C2 Making representations from experience

This area of learning refers to young children representing familiar objects, people, places, and events through all forms of media. Children might create representations of family members, pets, home and school settings, foods, birthday parties, or anything else present in their lives.

*Teaching strategies.* Just being aware of children's experiences and interests will suggest numerous possibilities for the things they can represent in their art. An observant teacher can build on and expand these possibilities using the ideas suggested below:

■ Suggest that children represent specific objects, places, people, and experiences that are familiar to them. Drawing familiar places (such as the child's bedroom or classroom) also helps children develop map-making skills.

■ When experiences arise naturally in the course of conversation, say "I wonder if we could [draw/paint/construct] that at small group?" Ask the children to suggest materials for representing the object or idea. For example, while getting ready for outside time, a discussion of new winter clothing led one group of preschoolers to represent their jackets, mittens, and boots with fabric, carpet samples, and recycled cardboard.

■ Draw on other imagery and experiences as subjects for visual representations. For example, take photographs of the objects children play with and construct, and post them in the art area as inspiration for things children might represent in their artwork. Use the natural environment to motivate art expression. For example, take a walk in a garden or bring cut flowers to class. Hang art reproductions showing familiar experiences (e.g., a Mary Cassatt painting of a mother bathing a child). Encourage children to represent their own similar experiences. Take field trips and give children a variety of art materials to use in representing what they remember.

## C3 Making accidental representations

An accidental representation means making something that becomes recognizable *after* it is created. For example, a child exploring clay might flatten it and then declare, "Hey, look what I made. It's a pancake."

*Teaching strategies.* Because something cannot be purposely accidental, the role of the intentional teacher here is to create an environment in which such discoveries are likely to occur. For example:

■ Provide a wide variety of materials and tools children can use to represent things.

■ Accept what children say when they announce they made something. Encourage them to describe the attributes they see in their creation ("It's round and floppy like a pancake") that led to their conclusion about what it is.

■ Encourage children to observe the attributes of things even when they are not making art. Their improved observational skills will generalize to art-making activities.

## C4 Making simple representations

Young children begin making art with only one or two details. In these creations, they are not concerned with spatial or other representational accuracy. For example, a mouth may be the only feature drawn in a face, or a rectangular shape may represent a house.

*Teaching strategies.* In supporting children's earliest representations, the most important thing teachers can do is accept and take an interest in their initiatives, no matter how simple they are. With appropriate support, children will gradually elaborate on their art ideas. If we pressure children to include more, we imply that what is there is inadequate. Children may then become discouraged and stop making art. Here are some ideas to support children where they are:

■ Accept what children create. Do not request or require them to add more details. They may interpret such requests as negative judgments on their work and lose interest or motivation.

■ Acknowledge the detail children do include in their artwork. Show interest as a means of encouraging the child to elaborate on the image or the process of creating it. For example, when a teacher commented "You drew a big circle with a smaller one inside it," the child said "That's our fish tank

and the new baby fish. There were more, but the big fish ate them all up."

■ Do not presume to know what a child is representing. It is easy to misinterpret, especially when the details are minimal. Instead, invite the child to tell you about it. As a caution, Althouse, Johnson, and Mitchell (2003) relate this embarrassing incident:

> A first-grade teacher said to Maria, "I see a dog in your picture." Maria answered in a frustrated tone, "That's not a dog; that's my mama." Realizing his mistake, Mr. Allen responded, "Tell me more about your mother." This gave the child the opportunity to give more details about the picture. (55)

**A** Adult-guided experience is especially important for learnings such as:

## A1 Naming art materials, tools, and actions

Learning the names of objects and operations in the visual arts is no different than it is in other domains. That is, children need to hear these names explicitly from adults—whether the words are *the letter A, subtraction,* or *sculpting.* With teacher input, young children learn labels and are able to differentiate identifying attributes of materials (crayons, paints, pastels, clay, wood, yarn), tools (cameras, paintbrushes, loom, potters wheel, canvas, frame), and creative actions (painting, dripping, drawing, spinning, weaving, molding, framing).

*Teaching strategies.* Strategies to develop children's vocabulary in the visual arts are comparable to those in other content areas. If teachers supply these terms while children are actively engaged with art, rather than at unrelated times, the terms will be more meaningful to them. For example:

■ Provide the names of art materials, tools, and actions in context and when they are introduced to children. Tie the names to concrete objects and actions as children experience them. Keep the statements simple and factual.

■ Accept the language children use to describe tools, materials, and actions. Then add words to expand their vocabulary. For example, when

Marissa said "I squished my paper," her teacher said "Yes, I see you squished the paper. I'm going to crumple mine, too." Write down what children say about their artwork, in the same way that you would take dictation about other ideas children want you to record (see **Chapter 3**). For example, label how they describe areas, techniques, or subject matter in their artwork. If children do not want you to write directly on their pictures, use sticky notes or make labels such as those found in museums.

■ Ask children open-ended questions about materials, actions, and effects to encourage their use of art language. For example, ask "What happened when you added a big squirt of red paint to your cup?" Or, if a child is comparing dry and wet balls of clay, wonder "How do they feel? What happens when you try to roll them flat?"

## A2 Becoming adept at using two- and three-dimensional art materials and tools

As they get older and have more practice with art materials, young children develop more control. They can use materials on a smaller scale and tools that require greater dexterity such as beads, sequins, glue, and scissors.

*Teaching strategies.* Children need time and practice to enhance their art-making skills. However, left on their own, their level of expertise may not increase. Adults are essential to model techniques, make suggestions, and help children solve problems. As with the mastery of any challenge, adults should be sensitive to children's frustration levels. Sometimes a hint is all that's needed to get a child over a hurdle; other situations call for more explicit instruction. Here are some strategies:

■ Show children that they can use increasingly complex art materials, tools, and techniques. Make them available throughout the day so children have many opportunities to practice and refine their skills. For example, ask children to draw the day's upcoming events at greeting circle, chalk a class mural at large group, or weave yarn and twigs through a fence at outside time. Introduce diverse tools after children have had ample

---

### Open-Ended Questions Encourage Art Talk

Closed-ended or convergent questions (with one right answer) can end rather than extend a conversation. Even open-ended or divergent questions (without a preset "correct" response) can strain conversation if asked too often or mechanically. However, a well-timed inquiry, in which the teacher invites a child's ideas, can lead to an instructive exchange. Here are some ways to phrase questions that will encourage children to respond thoughtfully.

"How do the [beads/clay] [feel/smell]?"

"Does the [straw/paintbrush] make you think of anything else?"

"What do you think we could do with [these shells and pebbles/fingerpaints]?"

"How did you make that [boat/thick line]? Can you tell us what you used to make it?"

"You want to make a [seed box/collage]. How will you make that? What will you need to make it?"

"Can you tell me how you used [the chisel] to make your [bookends]?"

"Jason used the [tapestry hook] today. Will you share with us what you learned about it?"

"How did you make this [shape open at one end and then narrow/dotted line/smudge effect]?" (Teacher points.)

"Do you remember what you mixed to get this [peachy] color?" or "How did you make [all the different shades of green] in your picture?"

"What did you do to make the [paint/string] so [thick in this corner/look like hair]?"

"Tell [me/us/Antoine] about the [materials/tools] you used."

"What made you decide to make a [doghouse/watercolor]?"

"Can you think of a different way to [fold the paper/use that pencil]?"

"What do you suppose would happen if we [dipped the paper in water first]?"

"How do you think you could make the [paper/two coils of clay] to [stand up/stick together]?"

"Can you tell me more about the way you [used these brushes on the wood]?"

"I wonder what's [the same/different] about the [watercolor and acrylic paints/narrow and wide brushes]?"

---

time to explore with their hands and simple implements. Once children are familiar with the raw medium, they can explore more complex transformations with conventional and unconventional tools and techniques. Provide some sophisticated art materials. Research shows, for example, that giving 5-year-olds narrower paintbrushes enabled them to incorporate significantly more detail in their paintings (Seefeldt 1979). Similarly, children fill up more space when given pencils instead of markers (Salome 1967). Don't change tools every day or two for the sake of novelty or variety. Leave artistic media out for a long time so children can experiment and become adept with them before moving on to something else.

■ Challenge children to combine art materials and use tools in unconventional ways. Bring back art materials they used earlier. Encourage them to apply new techniques to "old" materials. For example,

> The children in one preschool class began the year experimenting with paper. They tried tearing, twisting, crumbling, rolling, and other manipulations. Then they used scissors and hole punches, and finally glue and paint. Later in the year, the teacher introduced the class to yarn and fabric. Again the children began working with their hands, then using tools such as scissors, crimpers, and large tapestry needles. They looked at books on weaving and quilting. Finally, they experimented with dyeing. After a few weeks, the teacher brought out the paper again. Children were excited to see an old "friend," but now they applied the stitching and dyeing techniques they had used with fiber to paper. Some tore or cut strips and wove "paper tapestries." Others painted squares of paper and arranged them in "paper quilts."

■ Experiment with the materials yourself to encourage children's exploration. Do not direct them to copy what you are doing, but rather model curiosity and an investigative attitude.

### A3 Making representations using imagination

This creative activity involves portraying things that are not there or that children have never experienced. It includes depicting make-believe (fantastical) objects, people, and events, as well as making representations of real things in fanciful ways that distort proportions, colors, spatial relations, and so on, to emphasize an attribute or idea.

*Teaching strategies.* Imagination is vital to all artistic pursuits. Teachers can employ many techniques to inspire creative representation by incorporating materials and activities from literacy, dramatic arts, mathematics and science, movement and music, or virtually any other domain. In fact, using artistic representation to integrate learning across disciplines is a hallmark of curricula such as Reggio Emilia (Edwards, Gandini, & Forman 1998; Gandini et al. 2005), the Project Approach (Helm & Katz 2001; Katz & Chard 2000), and High/Scope (Epstein 2007; Hohmann & Weikart 2002).

■ Read books, make up stories, and engage in other activities that inspire children to use their imaginations and represent their fantasies. Dramatic play often involves the creation of artwork (props and scenery) to further children's role-play. Ask children to draw things or experiences they would like to have, or people they would like to befriend. Their ideas may range from exotic pets to trips to the moon to cartoon characters.

■ Do not ask children to name or describe what they have made. Sometimes there is no "what" but only an idea or a feeling. Instead, encourage children to talk in their own terms about the process of creating their representations. For example, say "Tell me how you made this." Or note "I saw you carrying lots of paint cups and brushes to the table," which invites the child to talk about the different colors, brush widths, and so on used to create the artwork.

> When Mrs. Shaw commented to Tony, "You're mixing a big tray of blue and black paint," he responded, "I'm making a sad color because my grandma is in the hospital." Tony filled his paper with swirls of dark color and Mrs. Shaw acknowledged, "You made your painting sad because you are sad about your grandmother."

■ Bring in reproductions of nonrepresentational or abstract artwork. Encourage children to talk about what they see or feel in the imagery. Provide comparable materials and tools for them to create artwork of "unreal" or imaginary ideas, images, and events.

## A4 Making intentional representations

In exercising this skill, children decide beforehand what they intend to depict, and then assemble the materials and tools needed to make it. To accomplish this end, children must have a mental image of their final product. They may then alter or refine the artwork to achieve greater representational accuracy, sometimes with remarkable persistence. For example, a child might spend a long time gluing strips of yarn to create the hair on a sculpture.

*Teaching strategies.* Intentionality in children is an indication they are using mental representations to recall prior experiences, make plans, and anticipate problems and outcomes. These cognitive behaviors are important tools that not only enrich the resulting artwork but also can generalize to learning in other content domains. Artistic intentionality is enhanced when teachers encourage children's forethought and reflection using strategies such as those suggested below:

■ Encourage children to plan art projects. Ask them what they will make and how, including what materials, tools, and techniques they will employ; whether they will do it alone or with others; how long it will take; how big it will be; and whether and where they will display it.

■ Engage children in discussing their artwork, including their conscious (intentional) decisions about use of materials and imagery.

■ Encourage the deliberate use of inspiration from other sources. Provide materials and examples of artwork for children to "copy," much as adult artists are inspired by models. The emphasis should be not on making an exact duplication of the model but rather on each child observing the attributes of the model and then representing it in his or her own way. Encourage children to talk to one another about what they draw or sculpt. Children build on one another's ideas, not to copy but to interpret similar experiences in their own way.

## A5 Making complex representations

Just as children's language becomes more complex with development, so do their visual representations. As they get older, children's art increasingly includes details such as facial features (eyes, eyebrows, nose, mouth, ears, hair, jewelry, freckles) and architectural components (doors, windows, stairs, sidewalk, curtains, bricks, plants). Children strive for factual accuracy in their artwork with regard to size, spatial relations, social relationships, time, feelings, and so on. They may work on a single project over several days or even weeks, in order to include the desired level of detail and complexity.

*Teaching strategies.* Any activity that encourages children to be observant will translate into their art activities. In addition, children need time and space to elaborate on their artwork without feeling rushed or confined. For example:

■ Encourage children to observe and describe things in detail, even when they are not making art. Provide opportunities to observe objects and activities from different perspectives. Photograph an art or construction project in progress and encourage the children to talk about each stage—materials and tools used, what was done with them, how the project's appearance or function changed as a result. Observing and describing will heighten children's attention to details, which will be reflected in their artwork. It can also generalize to other content areas, such as recalling more elements in a story (literacy) or analyzing a problem with complex data from various viewpoints (mathematics and science).

■ Encourage children to share observations with one another as they make representations. Children's awareness is enhanced by the details that others call their attention to. They will then add their own. For example, Taunton and Colbert (2000) found that when working together to depict a potted plant, children shared observations about the plant's structure and discussed differences in their artistic approaches to representing the plant. With another method—the Project Approach—Helm and Katz suggest questions teachers can ask in a "motivational dialogue" to encourage children to focus and elaborate on the details in their observational drawings; for example, "What is this called? What is it used for?" and "Which part will you draw first? How will you connect this part?" (2001, 39–40).

■ Encourage teamwork and collaboration on art projects. As each child contributes something, it opens the others' eyes to more possibilities. Their ideas will build on one another's.

■ Label and store projects in a safe place so children can continue to elaborate on them on subsequent days. Works-in-progress can also become focal points for children to share details about their endeavors with peers, teachers, and parents.

■ Display and discuss children's artwork. Seeing their own and others' artwork encourages children to think about the images and process, and to use more detail when creating future art.

# Appreciating visual art

Of the key knowledge and skills in the area of appreciating visual art, child-guided experience seems particularly important for focusing on one aspect of artwork; making simple aesthetic choices; and recognizing and understanding the feelings expressed through artwork. Adult-guided experience seems to be especially significant for naming artistic media, elements, and techniques; focusing on multiple aspects of artwork; articulating the reasons for aesthetic choices; describing and articulating the feelings expressed through artwork; and recognizing cultural and temporal influences on art.

 **Child-guided experience is especially important for learnings such as:**

### C1 Focusing on one aspect of artwork

Young preschoolers pay attention to one dominant or salient feature in a work of art, such as color or line. Even with a complex image, they may focus on just one area rather than on the image as a whole.

*Teaching strategies.* Children's keen interest in a particular feature or section of a piece of artwork

provides teachers with an opening to explore that subject matter in depth. Build on where children are rather than forcing attention or interest. A broader focus will come with time if adults allow young children's detailed focus to thrive too. For example:

■ Provide illustrations and reproductions that highlight one or a limited number of features, such as paintings with large shapes in bold colors or pen-and-ink drawings that emphasize line.

■ Accept children's fascination with one aspect of a more complex artwork. Encourage them to talk about the first or main element they notice. Ask what drew their eye to this feature. For example, if a child focuses on the lower right corner of a painting, learn why it is interesting to him. When children are ready, they will switch their attention to another area.

■ Plan activities where children can focus on a single art element in depth, such as color or line. For example, look at reproductions of work by Color Field artists such as Mark Rothko and Helen Frankenthaler, whose paintings explore color rather than recognizable imagery. Give children pieces of many colors of fabric (or felt, or carpet) to juxtapose and arrange. Look at portraits by caricaturists whose simple ink drawings capture their subjects' features or emotions. Encourage children to trace the lines with their fingers. Use craft sticks and twigs to make line drawings in mud or in patches of snow outdoors, or trace shapes on fogged-up window panes.

### C2 Making simple aesthetic choices

Early visual preferences appear in concrete areas such as color, pattern, or subject matter. Young children express aesthetic choices in clear and simple ways such as deciding what paint color to use or choosing a shirt pattern to wear. However, even when their choices are quite definite, they are often unable to explain the reasoning behind their preferences.

*Teaching strategies.* Young children need opportunities to make choices and to express their preferences and desires. By providing many options and acknowledging children's right to choose,

# Giving Compliments Versus Encouragement

Compliments are well-meaning, but they can actually discourage the child artist, as well as other children who see and overhear the exchange. Instead, communicate interest by taking time to observe and comment on what the artist is doing, even joining in the experience. The likely reward is an authentic conversation about art.

> Martin is painting at the easel. His painting is an array of colors and unrecognizable forms. As the teacher approaches Martin, she pauses, unsure of what to do or say. Should she praise his effort by saying something like "Very beautiful, Martin, you've worked hard on your painting"? Should she ask questions about the colors and shapes she sees in his painting? Should she ask Martin if he wants to talk to her, or should she wait for him to initiate a discussion about his work?

Probably the most common approach adults take to communicating with children about art is to compliment, or praise, their work: "I really liked the way you used the chalk." "That's a beautiful painting." Though such statements are intended to be supportive and encouraging, they can actually have a negative impact. Praise, though positive, is still judgmental, giving the message that it is the adult's role to evaluate the child's artwork. As a result, the child may grow inhibited, afraid to explore or be creative. The result is a climate in which children become "praise junkies," who feel good about their work only when adults tell them it is good, beautiful, or nice.

The alternative to mechanical compliments is to engage in a dialog with children that encourages them to reflect on and discuss their work. Such a dialog develops naturally when adults interact as *partners* with children. In a partnership approach, adults participate in art activities—they truly become "part of" the children's art experience. This can lead to a sustained dialog with children.

To become a partner in children's art, a good first step is to **stop talking so much or thinking so much about what to say. Instead, observe children closely when they are busy in art**. Sit or kneel next to children and simply watch what they are doing. Many times, observation is the best way to start a conversation—the child will begin talking to you about what he or she is doing. The dialog that grows out of this approach is natural, and the questions the adult asks are related to the child's actions and how the child sees and thinks about his or her artwork.

**Using art materials the same way the children do** is another effective strategy for helping you form a partnership with children. Because of the abundance of materials in the art area, it is often easiest to use this strategy here. If the child is making holes in clay, get another piece of clay and do the same. By imitating, you are telling the child nonverbally that you accept and value what she is doing. This type of encouragement often prompts the child to start a conversation.

The conversations that occur during art partnerships are free-flowing and offer the adult many opportunities to talk with children not only about the *process* of making something—the materials, how the child uses them, and the sequence of activities—but also the *elements of art*—color, line, pattern, shape, space, and texture. Because the adult discusses these concepts in the context of the child's project, they are more meaningful than they would be if taught directly.

---

**Source:** M. Tompkins, "A Partnership with Young Artists," in *Supporting Young Learners 2: Ideas for Child Care Providers and Teachers*, ed. N.A. Brickman, 187–92 (Ypsilanti, MI: High/Scope Press, 1996). Adapted, by permission, from pp. 187, 189–90.

teachers support aesthetic development while encouraging decision making in general. Here are some strategies to try:

■ Provide a wide variety of art materials so that children with diverse preferences will find at least one medium or technique they like to work with.

■ Provide materials that foster art appreciation. These could include art from home (photos, weaving, pottery, quilts); storybooks illustrated in differ-ent styles and media; reproductions of fine art (postcards, photos, scale models); posters; exhibit catalogs; art books; artist biographies (written and illustrated for children); and books with art from various cultures and times in history.

■ Encourage, rather than compliment or praise, children's aesthetic choices. For example, say "I see you used lots of blue in your painting" instead of "Blue is my favorite color." When we praise one child, children not praised may think their work is inferior or unworthy. Children who receive praise one day but not another may think their work is no longer any good.

■ Create a warm and supportive atmosphere for all activities and choices in the classroom. An emotionally safe environment will generalize to making and appreciating art.

■ Share your own aesthetic preferences (without downgrading those of others), and express pleasure in viewing art. In this way, the intentional teacher communicates the joy that art can bring to life.

■ Observe art as it occurs in nature, using all the senses. The formal properties of art—such as light, color, form, and texture—have counterparts in the natural world. Helping children consider nature from an aesthetic perspective not only broadens their appreciation of art, it also makes them more sensitive to the environment. Also, simply being in nature encourages children to use all their senses, which is vital to developing a broad artistic appreciation of the world.

### C3 Recognizing and understanding the feelings expressed through artwork

Young children can be aware of and comprehend the underlying feeling an artist is trying to express in a work of art. However, they may not be able to label it or explain this feeling to someone else. Instead, children may convey their emotional understanding through body and facial gestures (a slump or frown to communicate sadness), a dance movement (hopping with glee), or a comparable representation in their own artwork (tight circles of energy).

*Teaching strategies.* Children, like adults, need emotional outlets, whether they are engaged in socializing, solving an intellectual problem, or making art. In fact, art is an excellent way for preverbal and nonverbal children to identify and express feelings and to begin to understand the emotions of others. Teachers can use the natural affinity between art and expression as follows:

■ When you share storybook illustrations and art reproductions with children, provide art materials and ask children to create something that shows how those works make them feel or how they think the artist was feeling when she made the work.

■ Combine visual art with other senses and other arts media, such as music or dance, to focus on the feelings they evoke. For example, play different types of music at large group and give the children scarves to move in different ways inspired by the music's tempo, pitch, or mood. At small group, provide different types of food for the children to smell, and ask them to pick a crayon whose color is like the smell.

■ Let the feelings in a work of art "speak" for themselves. Allow time during the day for quiet and peaceful contemplation.

### A Adult-guided experience is especially important for learnings such as:

### A1 Naming artistic media, elements, and techniques

Children learn from adults the vocabulary words to describe and differentiate forms of representation (e.g., *painting, sculpting, photography, weaving, quilting, ceramics, mixed media*), the formal properties or elements of the visual arts (e.g., *line, color, shape, space, texture*), and the techniques used by artists to create visual effects (e.g., *stretching canvases, dyeing, molding, layering, collaging, stitching, throwing, handbuilding, carving, filtering light*).

*Teaching strategies.* Mastering the language of visual art often takes repeated exposure before children fully grasp the words and concepts and feel confident employing them in their own conversations. Teachers have many options available to introduce this rich vocabulary and give children multiple opportunities to understand and use it in producing and analyzing art. For example:

■ Develop a language to talk about art with children. Engle (1996) suggests teachers look and talk about what the product is made of, what they see (lines, shapes, colors), what it represents, how it is organized, what it is about, and where the ideas came from. Several publications include glossaries of art terms to use with young children (e.g., Althouse, Johnson, & Mitchell 2003, 130–37; Epstein & Trimis 2002, 259–61). Add to these published glossaries the vocabulary words, phrases, and definitions that you and the children use while discussing their art interests, including those that refer to artwork prevalent in their cultures and community.

■ Expose children to the work of different artists through biographies (written for children) and reproductions of their artwork. Begin with subject matter or techniques the children can relate to, such as Vincent van Gogh's sunflowers, an urban scene by Edward Hopper, white plaster figures by George Segal, or a Jackson Pollock drip painting. The reproductions you show should feature a variety of subjects, media, techniques, artistic styles, and moods. Label and describe these. Encourage the children to ask questions and to share their observations about what they see and how they think the artists achieved various visual effects.

■ Provide children with materials similar to those used by the artists they study. As they draw, paint, sculpt, and so on, comment on the similarities between their techniques and styles and those of the artists in the books and reproductions.

## A2 Focusing on multiple aspects of artwork

As children mature in their cognitive and artistic abilities, they can pay attention to the overall work of art and how its components are interconnected. This includes such aesthetic relationships as the way colors play off one another, the use of volume to heighten or diminish emphasis, how shapes are juxtaposed to lead the eye in a certain direction, and the way one or more moods are evoked through color and line in different areas of the artwork.

*Teaching strategies.* Teachers can develop children's ability to attend to aesthetic relationships by exposing them to increasingly complex and evocative works of art. Because their growing awareness depends on analytical abilities, any

teaching strategies that encourage children to reflect on and articulate their observations will help them apply these skills to appreciating visual art. For example:

■ Gradually increase the complexity of artwork displayed in the classroom, from images that all share common content or a common artistic element to a collection of images that portray a variety of subjects and techniques.

■ As you engage children in conversations about artwork, comment on how one aspect relates to another. For example, say "See how the artist put a big blue stripe in this corner and a skinny one over here" or "The red hat next to the green tree makes both colors really stand out."

■ Encourage children to view artwork from various perspectives or positions (e.g., up close, far away, from the side, squinting) and to see whether things look different in relation to one another. Paintings that feature pointillism (Georges Seurat), multiple layers (Mark Rothko, Josef Albers), or squares of color (Chuck Close) work well for this observational exercise.

## A3 Articulating the reasons for aesthetic choices

As children's growing self-awareness is accompanied by an expanding vocabulary, they are increasingly able to give voice to their own and others' aesthetic preferences. They can explain artistic decisions and choices in the formal language of art by discussing elements such as color, pattern, and style and the relevance of the content to themselves.

*Teaching strategies.* Teachers enable children to talk about aesthetics when they provide language specific to art. Strategies such as the following help children observe and express the rationale behind aesthetic decisions:

■ Anchor art in children's lives to help them express personal ideas. For example,

During a project (Kolodziej 1995) in which preschoolers created their own picture museum before visiting the International Museum of Photography in Rochester, New York, the children brought in favorite

## Talking with Children about Visual Art

You don't have to be a trained artist or art professor to talk to young children about art. As in all your conversations with preschoolers, be specific and focus on the present or a recent art experience. Here are some examples of statements you can make to familiarize young children with the formal elements or properties of visual art.

### Color

Colors in everyday objects are all around us, as well as in art. Variations in color provide many opportunities to comment on their array. For example:

**hue**—"Mondrian, the artist, filled this box with blue and that box with yellow."

**intensity**—"Aaron's hair is bright red. Mine is a duller shade of red."

**temperature**—"The orange square in this Albers painting glows with warmth."

**value**—"The leaves in this picture are dark green, just like the pine tree outside."

**tint and tone**—"When you added white paint, the circle got lighter. Then you added black and it got darker."

**relationship**—"The red flower really stands out next to the green leaves in the picture."

### Line

Lines appear in clothing, children's block constructions, walls and windows, and room decorations, as well as in paintings, drawings, weaving, and other art forms. Here are sample observations you can make about the many different properties of lines:

**kind**—"Jackson Pollock liked to drip squiggly lines of paint."

**beginning/end**—"You started your blue line in this corner and it went clear to the other side."

**direction**—"When you follow this wavy line in the painting, it makes your eyes look up."

**quality**—"Mary's sneakers have wide stripes across the toe. John's have narrow ones in back."

**length**—"The lines for the grass are made with short strokes. This one for the tree is longer."

**relationship**—"The blue yarn goes over the red yarn and then under the yellow yarn."

### Form or shape

You can label recognizable geometric shapes, make comments about irregular forms, and describe the interrelationships among them. For example:

**size**—"This statue is carved from a huge rock."

**name**—"You made a necklace with triangles and squares."

**solidity**—"The blue square is all filled in with blue, but the red one has colored dots inside."

**relationship**—"Matisse cut out a yellow shape and put it inside the red one."

---

photographs of themselves. They then titled the pictures, which encouraged reflection and discussion about where and when the pictures were taken and why they were important to each child. The children also labeled the photographs and made an exhibit catalog with their comments about the images. Creating the picture museum involved children in many participatory ways. In choosing a photograph, they expressed an aesthetic preference. By describing the image, they engaged in art criticism. While creating titles, labels, and an exhibit catalog, the children acquired a sense of how museums are organized and operated. As a result, when the children later visited the museum, they had a firsthand basis for understanding the value of museums and such concepts as

"art collection," as well as an appreciation of photography as an art form.

■ Accept children's explanations of their aesthetic preferences. Display their artwork and encourage them to talk about what, how, and why they made something. Ask open-ended questions to elicit reasons for their choice of materials, images, and techniques. Express your own aesthetic preferences (though not in judging children's work) and state why a work of art or other aesthetic item does or does not appeal to you.

■ Provide reproductions of artwork in different media and styles. Encourage children to talk about

open/closed—"Darren scooped out the clay and is sticking paper clips inside."

### Texture

Because they are oriented to sensory impressions, children are attuned to the physical feeling of various textures. Artwork differs not only in its actual texture but also in the apparent textures that artists create with visual effects. You can help children become aware of how the appearance of a surface suggests the feel of the objects depicted. For example:

actual/implied—"The paint on this van Gogh sunflower is so thick your eyes can almost feel the petals."

hardness—"Now that the clay is dry, the pot feels hard."

roughness—"These dots in the Seurat picture make it look bumpy up close."

regularity—"The threads in your skirt are woven tightly on the pocket but they are loose and lacy around the trim."

reflectiveness—"The silver crayon made such a shiny circle that it looks like a mirror."

### Space

Children develop spatial awareness in their everyday encounters with the world. Your comments can help them develop a language to talk about what they see and how they move in that space. These same concepts can be applied to how artists use space. For example:

distance—"You drew the two cats close together."

location—"Georgia O'Keefe painted a flower right in the middle of the canvas."

boundaries—"In this painting, the woman inside the house is looking out through the window."

positive or negative—"Keisha painted a red square and left the rest of her paper white."

### Design

As children gain experience with planning, they begin to do things by intention or design. Your comments can help them see how artists also plan to include different elements in their work and relate these elements to one another. For example:

symmetry—"The pattern on this side matches the pattern on the other side."

repetition—"This basket has three stripes on the bottom and three stripes at the top."

alternation—"Your bracelet has a blue square and then a yellow circle all the way around."

variation—"Kandinsky used a light red up here and a darker red down there."

emphasis—"Picasso made her mouth big. I wonder what the girl in this painting is saying."

Source: A.S. Epstein, "How to Talk with Children About Art," in *Supporting Young Learners 4: Ideas for Child Care Providers and Teachers*, eds. N.A. Brickman, H. Barton, & J. Burd, 181–84 (Ypsilanti, MI: High/Scope Press, 2005). Adapted, by permission, from pp. 181–84.

what they see and what they think is behind the artist's choice of medium, subject matter, and style. For example, ask "Why do you think this artist makes little pictures but that one makes big pictures?"

■ Read storybooks in which different media are used in the illustrations, including pen-and-ink drawings, watercolor and oil paintings, black-and-white and color photographs, collages and mixed media, pastels, charcoal, and so on. When the narrative is familiar to the children, page through the book focusing on the illustrations and discussing the images and techniques.

### A4 Describing and articulating the feelings expressed through artwork

This ability involves explaining what the artist was thinking or feeling in creating a work of art. As children's social-emotional skills and vocabulary expand, together with their understanding of visual art, they have at their disposal the words to describe the emotions that go into creating art and the feelings that artwork evokes in the viewer.

*Teaching strategies.* When we jointly support children's aesthetic and social-emotional growth, we enable them to become more articulate about the expressive qualities of art. Teaching strategies such as the following can simultaneously build linguistic skills, personal confidence, and artistic understanding:

◼ Model descriptive and metaphoric language when talking about art, using comparisons that children will recognize from daily life. For example, make statements such as "This pale blue looks as soft and soothing as a baby's blanket." Use descriptive art terms in daily conversations. Instead of focusing only on functional traits ("Please pass me the red cup"), comment on features that also evoke an aesthetic or emotional response ("Wearing this bright red dress makes me feel like dancing!").

◼ Incorporate into the study of art other, complementary ways to stimulate the senses. For example, play music with varying attributes or moods (tempo, loudness, pitch, major and minor keys) and provide art materials for children to represent the feelings evoked from each. Let them listen to each selection for a while before they begin to paint or draw. Allow sufficient time with each piece before changing to one with a different mood.

◼ When sending children's artwork home, encourage parents to talk to their children about what they were thinking or how they were feeling as they created the art. Holding a workshop for parents in which they practice talking about the feelings represented in and evoked by artwork will make it easier for them to have such discussions at home with their children.

## A5 Recognizing cultural and temporal influences on art

This area of art appreciation entails being aware of how context influences the creation and interpreta-

---

## Using Storybook Illustrations to Promote Art Vocabulary and Appreciation

Children's storybooks feature illustrations in many different artistic media including drawing, painting, photographs, collages, and fiber. They are a natural resource for engaging children in art appreciation.

**1.** Make sure children are very familiar with the story first. Otherwise, their focus will be taken away from the illustrations and back to the narrative. If the children want to read the story, follow their interest. Wait until another time or situation to look at the pictures.

**2.** Don't look at every picture in the book. Decide beforehand which ones to focus on, whether it is because the children have shown a great deal of interest in them or because they illustrate a particular aesthetic concept you want to explore with the class. Be open to looking at pictures you hadn't planned on if those are the ones that capture the children's attention that day.

**3.** For younger children, use books with large pictures and uncomplicated illustrations. Focus on basic concepts such as color, shape, line, and texture. Older preschoolers and school-age children will be able to appreciate more subtle and complicated drawings. They will also be interested in the content and how it relates to them, providing an opportunity to explore why that subject matter was also of interest to the artist.

**4.** Portraits of storybook characters are a good focus for bringing out aesthetic concepts. Help children identify the details the artist pays attention to, such as facial and bodily features or how someone dresses. Portraits done in different media can help children compare how the choice of medium affects how a particular physical characteristic is rendered.

**5.** Choose books that showcase a variety of media; for example, painting, drawing with pencils or pen and ink, photography (photos of real scenes, photos of other artwork), collage, and mixed media. Discuss how the illustrator's choice of medium enhances the book's story.

**6.** Choose books that illustrate a variety of artistic styles, including realistic (representational) and abstract (nonrepresentational), and traditional and modern.

**7.** Include books with artwork that reflects a variety of cultures, especially those represented in the classroom. Just as diversity is a consideration in literacy (the words in the books), so too should it be a factor in visual art (the illustrations).

tion of artwork. Such influences include the personal background, community and cultural beliefs, and geographic setting of the artist or viewer, and also the time in which the art was created or seen. Because children are increasingly aware of their own circumstances, older preschoolers are able to recognize similarities and differences in time, place, and community represented through art.

*Teaching strategies.* Activities that support multicultural awareness in general are also effective in sensitizing young children to the ways in which background influences artistic creation. As long as we draw on familiar experiences to find a point of contact or relevance for young children, they can reflect on the factors that affect how artwork is created and perceived. For example:

■ Provide actual and illustrated examples of visual art from other cultures and times, particularly those that reflect the diversity in the classroom or community now. (Seek books written for children, but if you cannot find them, adult history or anthropology books with many photographs or drawings work well. Focus on the images rather than the text.) Talk about similarities and differences with the children's lives and how these are reflected in the artwork.

■ Encourage families to share artwork from home that reflects their culture or background in its media (e.g., pottery, weaving, woodworking, calligraphy) and subject matter (e.g., architecture and native plants, styles of dress and adornment, portrayals of daily family life and holiday rituals).

■ Connect with artists in the community and invite them to visit the classroom. Take a field trip to their studios. Ask them to demonstrate how they work and to explain where their ideas come from. If possible, arrange for the children to use materials and tools in the studio or bring them back to the classroom or both. This encourages children to think of themselves as artists.

■ Take children to outdoor art fairs, landscaped parks and gardens, statues and monuments, and other public art displays. On your excursions, describe what you see, and ask children to share their observations. Take photos, and in the classroom mount them where children and parents can see and talk about them. Back in the classroom, provide materials for children to represent the experience. Encourage families to visit similar locations in the community with their children.

■ Visit museums and galleries to look at artwork from other times and cultures. Plan ahead with museum docents and gallery directors. To help children heed the "look, don't touch" prohibition, give them something to hold (Epstein 2001). For example, in advance of your trip get four or five postcards showing art the children will see. Make duplicates so each child has a small reproduction to hold and compare with the works hanging on the walls. Children will enjoy making the matches. Back in the classroom, follow up on the experience by providing props to reenact the trip and materials for children to use in exploring the images and techniques they saw at the museum.

\*　　　\*　　　\*

The visual arts can be a vital component in an integrated preschool curriculum if teachers intentionally give the subject matter the respect it deserves. This position is summed up by Taunton and Colbert:

> To have a significant role in early childhood education, art experiences must be authentic in approach and content and include opportunities for children's reflection through extended classroom dialogues. Authentic art experiences in the classroom are organized through a teacher's knowledge of patterns of artistic and aesthetic development, consideration of the intentions of children as they make art, and recognition of the significant content in the subject of art and art's relationship to other disciplines. (2000, 68)

Making and appreciating visual art has the potential to enrich young children's aesthetic and emotional lives, as well as to enhance their perceptual, intellectual, and social development. For this promise to be fulfilled, teachers must treat art as a legitimate discipline. Intentional teachers take it upon themselves to acquire knowledge about early artistic development, provide the resources necessary to advance art exploration and awareness, and hone the active teaching skills that support mastery of this content domain in young children.

## Questions for Further Thought

**1.** What arguments can early childhood advocates use to preserve the arts in the face of budget allocations favoring scholastic disciplines at the expense of other content areas?

**2.** How do we cut through the media hype that alternately overstates or debunks the promise of early art experiences to contribute to young children's later intellectual success?

**3.** Why, after so many years of lip service to "process, not product," do some early childhood teachers still plan and carry out art projects in which young children all make the same thing, work with precut materials, copy adults, and aim toward a finished (and displayable) product?

**4.** What are the barriers to accepting the idea that preschoolers are capable of engaging in art appreciation? How can we overcome the anxieties and inhibitions of practitioners about teaching art appreciation to young children?

# Reflections on Intentional Teaching

Four-year-old Susan is cutting strips of construction paper to make a "gluing picture" of a house. First, she cuts two red strips, each about 10 inches long, and glues one strip on the left of the paper and another on the right. She tries to connect the two vertical red strips by gluing a blue strip horizontally from the top end of the right strip. But the blue strip isn't long enough to reach the left strip, so she cuts another blue strip and pastes it down as an extension. This strip extends beyond the left strip, but this doesn't bother her.

Susan goes through the same process to make the bottom of the house. She then pastes down more strips to subdivide the house into eight rooms. She places a small plastic bear in each room. "Here's my bear house I made by gluing," Susan announces proudly.

\*     \*     \*

Charisse is the waitress and Amy, Kevin, and Bonita are her customers at the "Hot Cocoa and Pies Restaurant" they have built in their preschool's dramatic play area. Charisse uses her order pad to write down what each customer wants. Amy asks for cocoa, and Charisse writes "1C." When Kevin orders cocoa and cherry pie, she writes "1C 1P." Bonita says to bring her a slice of chocolate pie and a slice of cherry pie too; Charisse records "2P" on her pad.

**Teacher:** So two people ordered cocoa and two people asked for pie.

**Charisse:** (She looks puzzled.) But not all the same. How many of each?

**Teacher:** Let's figure it out. How many orders of cocoa?

**Amy:** Kevin and I both want cocoa. So that's two cups of cocoa.

**Bonita:** And I want two pieces of pie. So that's also two.

**Kevin:** But I asked for pie too!

**Teacher:** So Kevin wants one piece of pie and Bonita wants two pieces of pie.

**Charisse:** Three pieces of pie.

**Teacher:** So all together, your customers ordered two cups of cocoa and three pieces of pie.

**Charisse:** (Holds out her hand.) That'll be one dollar and fourteen-two-three cents. And you guys better leave me a big tip!

These young children are engaged in mathematics during everyday activities. In the first vignette, Susan solves an art problem on her own using informal arithmetic when she adds two short horizontal blue strips to transverse the distance across her paper. In the second vignette, the teacher takes advantage of a role-playing situation to help Charisse think about number. The children in both scenarios initiated the activity and were clearly involved in pursuing their interests. But in Susan's case, the teacher provided materials and time; while in the Charisse example, the teacher also offered thoughtful comments and questions to further the children's understanding of mathematical concepts.

The teaching and learning principles illustrated in these examples apply to every content area addressed in this book—whether it is language and literacy, mathematics and scientific inquiry, social skills and understandings, physical movement, or the visual arts. In every domain, the most meaningful and lasting learning occurs when children are interested in the topic and actively engaged in mastering its specific knowledge and skills.

Some of this body of content they can explore and understand through child-guided learning experience, either on their own or through interactions with peers and older children. Examples include filling and emptying containers and playing firefighters with a friend. For children to acquire other information, concepts, and skills, adult-guided learning experience is essential. Examples include teachers supplying the conventional names of numbers and letters, mediating conflicts, coaching physical actions, and raising awareness of artists and genres. Intentional teachers know they have a role to play in both child-guided and adult-guided modes, and they do so using their own knowledge and skills.

# Guiding principles of intentional teaching

It is my hope that teachers can use the framework and examples in this book as a starting point in choosing teaching strategies. There will still be many instances where they have to make their own decisions about whether child- or adult-guided learning experience is more suited to a particular topic, setting, individual child, or group of children. Below are guiding principles to help intentional teachers decide which strategies to use across a range of learnings and situations.

The first set of principles describes the basic characteristics of all intentional *teachers*, that is, what they know and do. The remaining two sets list the conditions, respectively, under which intentional teachers either encourage child-guided experience or engage in instruction that is more adult-guided. The focus of these latter principles is on

*children* because it is in observing and being sensitive to those they teach that adults can best determine the most effective instructional strategy to use.

While these guiding principles are derived from the theory, research, and practices presented in this book, they are offered here as hypotheses rather than proven facts. You are invited to view them critically and think about how these principles can be tested through further study and application. Although the idea of the "intentional teacher" is based on long-held beliefs, the term itself is relatively new. We still have much to learn from additional research and reflection as we strive to make intentionality a standard part of our teacher training and daily work with children.

## To teach with intention, teachers . . .

▶ create a learning environment rich in materials, experiences, and interactions

▶ encourage children to explore materials, experiences, relationships, and ideas

▶ converse respectfully, reciprocally, and frequently with children

▶ consciously promote all areas of learning and development

▶ know the content (concepts, vocabulary, facts, skills) that make up each area of learning

▶ know and use general teaching strategies that are effective with young children

▶ know and use specific teaching strategies that are effective in different content areas

▶ match content with children's developmental levels and emerging abilities

▶ are planful, purposeful, and thoughtful

▶ take advantage of spontaneous, unexpected teaching and learning opportunities

▶ carefully observe children to determine their interests and level of understanding

▶ adjust their instructional strategies to work with different individuals and groups

▶ neither underestimate nor overestimate what children can do and learn

► challenge children to question their own thinking and conclusions

► scaffold learning, with careful consideration of introducing new materials and ideas

► reflect on and change teaching strategies based on children's responses

## Intentional teachers support child-guided learning experiences when children . . .

► are actively exploring materials, actions, and ideas and making connections on their own

► are establishing interpersonal relationships and learning from one another

► are turning to one another for assistance

► are considering and investigating their own questions about materials, events, and ideas

► appear motivated to solve problems on their own

► are so focused on their enterprise that adult intervention would be an interruption

► are challenging themselves and one another to master new skills

► are applying and extending existing knowledge and skills in new ways

Although these behaviors and attitudes signal to teachers that child-guided experience will be particularly fruitful, this does not exclude using other teacher strategies and planned activities. Even when teachers pick up on cues like these, they will likely want to make strategic use of adult-guided experience to optimize children's learning.

## Intentional teachers employ adult-guided learning experiences when children . . .

► have not encountered the material or experience at home or in other settings

► cannot create established systems of knowledge (such as letter names) on their own

► do not see, hear, or otherwise attend to something likely to interest them

► do not engage with something teachers know they will need for further learning

► explicitly ask for information or help

► are bored or distracted and need help focusing

► appear stalled, discouraged, or frustrated

► appear ready for the next level of mastery but are not likely to attain it on their own

► are not aware of the potentially unsafe or hurtful consequences of their actions

► appear to use materials or actions very repetitively over time

► are conscious of and upset about something they cannot yet do but wish to

For knowledgeable teachers, although these child behaviors and attitudes suggest that adult-guided learning experiences will benefit children, this does not mean that child-guided experience will not also be an important part of the full learning picture.

# Final thoughts

I would like to leave you with final thoughts and beliefs, some already expressed implicitly or explicitly in the foregoing pages. Just as this book has attempted to present a balanced approach to teaching and learning, so too are the following thoughts offered in the form of "on-the-one-hand" and "on-the-other-hand" propositions. You may agree fully, partially, or not at all.

The important thing, from my perspective, is that you consider the ideas and reflect on how they apply to you in your capacity as an early childhood practitioner, administrator, researcher, and advocate.

# Respecting teachers

► There is much wisdom in early childhood educators. We should reject the notion that teachers need prescriptive lesson plans to work effectively with young children. If teachers have the proper training, mentoring, and experience in a supportive work atmosphere (admittedly a big "if"), they can be creative and thoughtful in the classroom.

► On the other hand, meaningful learning cannot be left to chance or instinct. There is a body of knowledge that teachers should know regarding how children learn and how best to teach them. Moreover, each content area has a set of knowledge and skills that teachers should study and be familiar with in order to assess what children know and how to scaffold further learning.

## Respecting content

▶ The knowledge and skills young children need to acquire are not limited to language and literacy, mathematics, and science. School readiness also includes social skills and dispositions. Physical education is essential to maintain good health and develop respect for one's body. And the arts not only are integral to other areas of learning but also are inherently gratifying and basic to our sense of community.

▶ Yet, because early childhood educators have traditionally emphasized the social-emotional domain, we need to change public perception that we are "anti-content." When we say that "learning happens through play" and that "play is a child's work," we must be prepared to explain how and why play can be worthwhile. The best play is purposeful and engages children's minds, bodies, and emotions. Random activity is ultimately not satisfying.

## Respecting children

▶ Preschoolers are still small children, not little adults or even scaled-down elementary school students. We should ease up on the pressures for testing and achievement that can label children, parents, teachers, and schools as "failures." Teachers need to follow the developmentally and research-based recommendations we call "best practices." In that way, we can restore early childhood

and stop pushing the early elementary curriculum down into preschool and kindergarten.

▶ Nevertheless, teachers should respect young children's curiosity and eagerness to learn and not be afraid to introduce information, model and coach specific skills, use unusual vocabulary words, or challenge children to solve complex problems. If teachers observe children's thinking and actions, the attempts to scaffold their learning are likely to be on target. And if teachers occasionally introduce something that is over the children's heads, they will be quick to let the teachers know. Teachers can then back up a step or two, but they shouldn't go back to leaving the children on their own.

From the research on child development and real classroom examples in this book, it is clear that teachers can help children learn—and enjoy learning—in all the content areas they will need to be ready for school and succeed in later life. We already know a great deal about what it means to teach with intention, and about the kinds of knowledge and skills we can help young children acquire. There is still more that we as professionals can explore about how to foster child- and adult-guided experience in the early years. Advancing the concept of the intentional teacher will require further theoretical work, research, curriculum development, staff training and mentoring, program evaluation, child observation, administrative leadership, and reflective practice.

We each have one or more roles to play in this research and development process. I hope *The Intentional Teacher* inspires you to take advantage of all we know, to further your own professional growth, and to continue contributing to the wisdom and practice of the field.

# Resources

## Best practices

### Assessment

Almy, M., & C. Genishi. 1979. *Ways of studying children: An observation manual for early childhood teachers*. Rev. ed. New York: Teachers College Press.

Bredekamp, S., & T. Rosegrant, eds. 1992. *Reaching potentials. Vol. 1: Appropriate curriculum and assessment for young children*. Washington, DC: NAEYC.

Bredekamp, S., & T. Rosegrant, eds. 1995. *Reaching potentials. Vol. 2: Transforming early childhood curriculum and assessment*. Washington, DC: NAEYC.

Jablon, J.R., A.L. Dombro, & M.L. Dichtelmiller. 2007. *The power of observation for birth through eight*. 2d ed. Washington, DC: Teaching Strategies; and Washington, DC: NAEYC.

Koralek, D., ed. 2004. *Spotlight on young children and assessment*. Washington, DC: NAEYC.

Matteson, D.M., & D.K. Freeman. 2006. *Assessing and teaching beginning writers: Every picture tells a story*. Katonah, NY: Richard Owen.

McAfee, O., D. Leong, & E. Bodrova. 2004. *Basics of assessment: A primer for early childhood educators*. Washington, DC: NAEYC.

Meisels, S.J., & S. Atkins-Burnett. 2005. *Developmental screening in early childhood: A guide*. 5th ed. Washington, DC: NAEYC.

NAEYC. 2004, January. Resources on assessment. *Beyond the Journal*. Online: www.journal.naeyc.org/btj/200401/PrintResources.pdf. [Books and articles recommended by authors of articles published in *Young Children*'s January 2004 "Assessment" cluster.]

NAEYC & NAECS/SDE (National Association for Early Childhood Specialists in State Departments of Education). 2003. Early childhood curriculum, assessment, and program evaluation: Building an effective, accountable system in programs for children birth through age 8. Joint Position Statement. Washington, DC: NAEYC; and Urbana-Champaign, IL: NAECS/SDE. Online: www.naeyc.org/positionstatements.

### Web sites

**CLAS (Culturally and Linguistically Appropriate Services) Early Childhood Research Institute—** http://clas.uinc.edu. Collects a wide variety of early childhood and early intervention resources for children and families from diverse cultural and linguistic backgrounds.

**Council for Exceptional Children (CEC)—**www.cec. sped.org. An authoritative source for information about assessment of children with special needs.

## Developmentally appropriate practice

Bowman, B.T., M.S. Donovan, & M.S. Burns, eds. 2000. *Eager to learn: Educating our preschoolers*. Washington, DC: National Academies Press. Also online: www.nap. edu.

Bronson, M.B. 1995. *The right stuff for children birth to 8: Selecting play materials to support development*. Washington, DC: NAEYC.

Copple, C., ed. 2003. *A world of difference: Readings on teaching young children in a diverse society*. Washington, DC: NAEYC.

Copple, C., & S. Bredekamp. 2005. *Basics of developmentally appropriate practice: An introduction for teachers of children 3 to 6*. Washington, DC: NAEYC.

Copple, C., & S. Bredekamp, eds. 2009. *Developmentally appropriate practice for early childhood programs serving children from birth through age 8*. 3d ed. Washington, DC: NAEYC.

Derman-Sparks, L., & J. Olsen Edwards. 2010. *Anti-bias education for young children and ourselves*. Washington, DC: NAEYC.

Gestwicki, C. 1999. *Developmentally appropriate practice, curriculum, and development in early education*. Clifton Park, NY: Thomson Delmar Learning.

Gronlund, G. 2006. *Make early learning standards come alive: Connecting your practice and curriculum to state guidelines*. St. Paul, MN: Redleaf Press; and Washington, DC: NAEYC.

Hyson, M., ed. 2003. *Preparing early childhood professionals: NAEYC's standards for programs*. Washington, DC: NAEYC.

Koralek, D., ed. 2004. *Spotlight on young children and play.* Washington, DC: NAEYC.

Kostelnik, M.J., A.K. Soderman, & A.P. Whiren. 2007. *Developmentally appropriate curriculum: Best practices in early childhood education.* 4th ed. Upper Saddle River, NJ: Prentice Hall.

NAEYC. 2005. *NAEYC early childhood program standards and accreditation criteria: The mark of quality in early childhood education.* Washington, DC: Author. (See: Language Development, Criteria 2.21–2.27; Early Literacy Development, Criteria 2.28–2.38; Early Mathematics, Criteria 2.39–2.51; Scientific Inquiry and Knowledge, Criteria 2.52–2.62; Social-Emotional Development, Criteria 2.15–2.20; Understanding Ourselves, Our Communities, and the World, Criteria 2.63–2.75) Standards and criteria also can be accessed at: www.naeyc.org/academy.

### Web sites

**Child Care Information Exchange**—www.childcareexchange.com. Promotes the exchange of ideas among leaders in early childhood programs worldwide.

**Embracing the Child**—www.embracingthechild.org/prek.html. Recommends books on a wide range of topics organized by subject and age. Topics include counting, geometry and shape, estimation, science, alphabet, self-esteem, and more.

**National Association for the Education of Young Children (NAEYC)**—www.naeyc.org. Offers a wide variety of information on the early childhood field, including position statements on critical issues.

## Families

Baker, A.C., & L.A. Manfredi/Pettit. 2004. *Relationships, the heart of quality care: Creating community among adults in early care settings.* Washington, DC: NAEYC.

Diffily, D., & K. Morrison, eds. 1996. *Family-friendly communication for early childhood programs.* Washington, DC: NAEYC.

DiNatale, L. 2002. Developing high-quality family involvement programs in early childhood settings. *Young Children* 57 (5): 90–95.

Dodge, D.T., & J. Phinney. 2006. *A parent's guide to preschool.* Washington, DC: Teaching Strategies.

Keyser, J. 2006. *From parents to partners: Building a family-centered early childhood program.* St. Paul, MN: Redleaf Press; and Washington, DC: NAEYC.

Koralek, D., ed. 2007. *Spotlight on young children and families.* Washington, DC: NAEYC.

Lombardi, J. 2003. *Time to care: Redesigning child care to promote education, support families, and build communities.* Philadelphia, PA: Temple University Press.

Parlakian, R. 2001. *The power of questions: Building quality relationships with families.* Brochure. Washington, DC: Zero to Three.

Swick, K.J. 1991. Teacher-parent partnerships to enhance school success in early childhood education. Washington, DC: National Education Association. ERIC, ED351149. Online: http://eric.ed.gov.

### Web sites

**ChildCareGroup**—www.childcaregroup.org. Provides a holistic model of relationship-centered child care.

**Parent Services Project**—www.parentservices.org. National nonprofit organization dedicated to integrating family support into early childhood programs and schools through training, technical assistance, and education.

**Zero to Three**—www.zerotothree.org. Provides a variety of information on working with families of very young children.

# Learning domains

## Language and literacy

Bowman, B., ed. 2002. *Love to read: Essays in developing and enhancing early literacy skills of African American children.* Washington, DC: National Black Child Development Institute.

Burns, M.S., P. Griffin, & C. Snow, eds. 1999. *Starting out right. A guide to promoting children's reading success.* Washington, DC: National Academies Press.

Christie, J., B.J. Enz, & C. Vukelich. 2007. *Teaching language and literacy: Preschool through the elementary grades.* 3d ed. New York: Allyn & Bacon.

Core Knowledge Foundation. 2000. *Core knowledge preschool sequence: Content and skill guidelines for preschool.* Charlottesville, VA: Author.

DeBruin-Parecki, A., & M. Hohmann. 2003. *Letter links: Alphabet learning with children's names.* Ypsilanti, MI: High/Scope Press.

Dickinson, D., & O. Tabors. 2001. *Beginning literacy with language: Young children learning at home and school.* Baltimore, MD: Brookes.

Hart, B., & T. Risley. 1999. *The social world of children learning to talk.* Baltimore, MD: Brookes.

Hohmann, M. 2002. *Fee, fie, phonemic awareness: 130 prereading activities for preschoolers.* Ypsilanti, MI: High/Scope Press.

McGuinness, D. 2004. *Growing a reader from birth: Your child's path from language to literacy.* New York: Norton.

Morrow, L.M., & L.B. Gambrell. 2004. *Using children's literature in preschool: Comprehending and enjoying books.* Newark, DE: International Reading Association.

Neuman, S.B., C. Copple, & S. Bredekamp. 2000. *Learning to read and write: Developmentally appropriate practices for young children.* Washington, DC: NAEYC.

Ranweiler, L. 2004. *Preschool readers and writers: Early literacy strategies for teachers.* Ypsilanti, MI: High/Scope Press.

Roskos, K.A., P. Tabors, & L. Lenhart. 2004. *Oral language and early literacy in preschool: Talking, reading, and writing.* Newark, DE: International Reading Association.

Schickedanz, J.A. 1999. *Much more than the ABCs.* Washington, DC: NAEYC.

Schickedanz, J.A., & R.M. Casbergue. 2004. *Writing in preschool: Learning to orchestrate meaning and marks.* Newark, DE: International Reading Association.

Strickland, D.S., & J.A. Schickedanz. 2004. *Learning about print in preschool: Working with letters, words, and beginning links with phonemic awareness.* Newark, DE: International Reading Association.

U.S. Department of Education and U.S. Department of Health and Human Services, Early Childhood–Head Start Task Force. 2002. *Teaching our youngest: A guide for preschool teachers and child care and family providers.* Washington, DC: Author.

Vukelich, C., & J. Christie. 2004. *Building a foundation for preschool literacy: Effective instruction for children's reading and writing development.* Newark, DE: International Reading Association.

## Web sites

**Reading Is Fundamental**—www.rif.org. Offers "Ask the Expert," literacy news, resources, and activities/programs to spark children's interest in reading.

# Mathematics and scientific inquiry

Baroody, A.J. 2000, July. Does mathematics instruction for three- to five-year-olds really make sense? *Young Children* 55 (4): 61–67.

Chalufour, I., & K. Worth. 2004. *Building structures with young children.* The Young Scientist Series. St. Paul, MN: Redleaf Press; and Washington, DC: NAEYC.

Charlesworth, R. 2005. *Experiences in math for young children.* 5th ed. Clifton Park, NY: Thomson Delmar Learning.

Clements, D.H. 2001, January. Mathematics in the preschool. *Teaching Children Mathematics* 7 (5): 270–75.

Clements, D.H. 2004. Major themes and recommendations. In *Engaging young children in mathematics: Standards for early childhood mathematics education,* eds. D.H. Clements, J. Sarama, & A.-M. DiBiase, 7–72. Mahwah, NJ: Erlbaum.

Copley, J.V. 2000. *The young child and mathematics.* Washington, DC: NAEYC.

Copley, J.V., ed. 2004. *Showcasing mathematics for the young child: Activities for three-, four-, and five-year-olds.* Reston, VA: National Council of Teachers of Mathematics.

Copley, J.V., C. Jones, & J. Dighe. 2006. *Mathematics: The Creative Curriculum approach.* Washington, DC: Teaching Strategies.

Epstein, A.S., & S. Gainsley. 2005. *I'm older than you, I'm five! Math in the preschool classroom: The teacher's idea book 6.* Ypsilanti, MI: High/Scope Press.

Forman, G. 1989. Helping children ask good questions. In *The wonder of it: Exploring how the world works,* ed. B. Neugebauer, 21–25. Redmond, WA: Child Care Information Exchange.

Koralek, D., ed. 2003. *Spotlight on young children and math.* Washington, DC: NAEYC.

Koralek, D., ed. 2003. *Spotlight on young children and science.* Washington, DC: NAEYC.

NCTM (National Council of Teachers of Mathematics). 2000. *Principles and standards for school mathematics.* Reston, VA: Author. Also online: http://standards.nctm.org/document/index.htm.

Seo, K.-H. 2003, January. What children's play tells us about teaching mathematics. *Young Children* 58 (1): 28–34.

University of California at Los Angeles (UCLA) Early Care and Education. 2005. *Preschool pathways to science.* Los Angeles: Author.

Worth, K., & S. Grollman. 2003. *Worms, shadows, and whirlpools: Science in the early childhood classroom.* Portsmouth, NH: Heinemann; and Washington, DC: NAEYC.

## Web sites

**Mathematical Perspectives Teacher Center**—www.mathperspectives.com/tcenter.html. Provides preK to grade 6 math educators with tools, strategies, and assessments.

**National Council of Teachers of Mathematics**—www.nctm.org. Includes online *Principles and Standards for School Mathematics* and electronic examples of learning experiences. Its "Illuminations" portal (http://illuminations.nctm.org/) provides *Standards*-based resources, including online lesson plans and activities searchable by grade level and keyword.

**National Science Teachers Association**—www.nsta.org. A wealth of online information and teaching ideas.

# Physical movement

Clements, R. 2004. *My neighborhood movement challenges: Narratives, games, and stunts for ages three through eight years.* Reston, VA: AAHPERD.

Gallahue, D., & F. Cleland-Donnelly. 2003. *Developmental physical education for all children.* 4th ed. Champaign, IL: Human Kinetics.

Graham, G., S. Holt/Hale, & M. Parker. 2004. *Children moving: A reflective approach to teaching physical education.* 6th ed. St. Louis, MO: McGraw-Hill.

NASPE (National Association for Sport and Physical Education). 2000. Appropriate practices in movement programs for young children ages 3–5. NASPE Position Statement, developed by the Council on Physical Education for Children (COPEC). Reston, VA: Author.

NASPE. 2002. *Active start: A statement of physical activity guidelines for children birth to five years.* Reston, VA: Author.

Pica, R. 1997, June. Beyond physical development: Why young children need to move. *Young Children* 52 (6): 4–11.

Pica, R. 2004. *Experiences in movement: Birth to age 8.* Clifton Park, NY: Thomson Delmar Learning.

Pica, R. 2006. *Moving and learning across the curriculum: More than 300 activities and games to make learning fun.* 2d ed. Clifton Park, NY: Thomson Delmar Learning.

Sanders, S.W. 1992. *Designing preschool movement programs.* Champaign, IL: Human Kinetics.

Sanders, S.W. 2002. *Active for life: Developmentally appropriate movement programs for young children.* Washington, DC: NAEYC.

Weikart, P.S. 2007. *Round the circle: Key experiences in movement for young children.* 3d ed. Ypsilanti, MI: High/Scope Press.

## Web sites

**National Association for Sport and Physical Education (NASPE)**—www.aahperd.org/naspe. Includes national standards and physical activity guidelines, and a monthly "teacher's tool box" with activities.

# Social skills and understandings

CSEFEL (Center on the Social and Emotional Foundations for Early Learning). 2003. *What works briefs.* Champaign, IL: University of Illinois at Urbana-Champaign. Also online: www.vanderbilt.edu/csefel/wwb.html.

Delpit, L. 2006. *Other people's children: Cultural conflict in the classroom.* 2d ed. New York: The New Press.

Elias, M.J., J.E. Zins, R.P. Weissberg, K.S. Frey, M.T. Greenberg, N.M. Haynes, R. Kessler, M.E. Schwab-Stone, & T.P. Shriver. 1997. *Promoting social and emotional learning: Guidelines for educators.* Alexandria, VA: Association for Supervision and Curriculum Development.

Epstein, A.S. 2009. *Me, you, us: Social-emotional learning in preschool.* Ypsilanti, MI: HighScope Press; and Washington, DC: NAEYC.

Evans, B. 2002. *You can't come to my birthday party! Conflict resolution with young children.* Ypsilanti, MI: High/Scope Press.

Feeney, S., & E. Moravcik. 2005, September. Children's literature: A window to understanding self and others. *Young Children* 60 (5): 20–28.

Gartrell, D. 2004. *The power of guidance: Teaching social-emotional skills in early childhood classrooms.* Clifton Park, NY: Thomson Delmar Learning.

Hyson, M. 2004. *The emotional development of young children: Building an emotion-centered curriculum.* 2d ed. Washington, DC: NAEYC.

Jacobson, T. 2003. *Confronting our discomfort: Clearing the way for anti-bias in early childhood.* Portsmouth, NH: Heinemann.

Katz, L., & D. McClellan. 1997. *Fostering children's social competence: The teacher's role.* Washington, DC: NAEYC.

Koralek, D., ed., with G. Mindes. 2006. *Spotlight on young children and social studies.* Washington, DC: NAEYC.

Levin, D.E. 2003. *Teaching young children in violent times: Building a peaceable classroom.* 2d ed. Washington, DC: Educators for Social Responsibility and NAEYC.

Mindes, G. 2006. *Teaching young children social studies.* Westport, CT: Praeger.

Seefeldt, C., & A. Galper. 2006. *Active experiences for active children: Social studies.* 2d ed. Upper Saddle River, NJ: Prentice Hall.

Shure, M.B. 2001. *I can problem solve: An interpersonal cognitive problem solving program: Kindergarten and primary grades.* 2d ed. Champaign, IL: Research Press.

Stone, J. 2001. *Building classroom community: The early childhood teacher's role.* Washington, DC: NAEYC.

Vance, E., & P.J. Weaver. 2002. *Class meetings: Young children solving problems together.* Washington, DC: NAEYC.

## Web sites

**Zero to Three**—www.zerotothree.org. Provides training resources for professionals to support children's social-emotional development, including tips on play in the "Parenting A-Z" section.

# Visual arts

Althouse, R., M.H. Johnson, & S.T. Mitchell. 2003. *The colors of learning: Integrating the visual arts into the early childhood curriculum.* New York: Teachers College Press.

Colbert, C., & M. Taunton. 1992. *Developmentally appropriate practices for the visual arts education of young children.* Reston, VA: National Art Education Association.

Edwards, C., L. Gandini, & G. Forman. eds. 1998. *The hundred languages of children: The Reggio Emilia approach— Advanced reflections.* 2d ed. Greenwich, CT: Ablex.

Epstein, A.S., & E. Trimis. 2002. *Supporting young artists: The development of the visual arts in young children.* Ypsilanti, MI: High/Scope Press.

Gandini, L., L. Hill, L. Cadwell, & C. Schwall. 2005. *In the spirit of the studio: Learning from the* atelier *of Reggio Emilia.* St. Paul, MN: Redleaf Press.

Koralek, D., ed. 2005. *Spotlight on young children and the creative arts.* Washington, DC: NAEYC.

Seefeldt, C. 1999. Art for young children. In *The early childhood curriculum: Current findings in theory and practice,* 3d ed., ed. C. Seefeldt, 201–17. New York: Teachers College Press.

The Task Force on Children's Learning and the Arts: Birth to Age Eight. 1998. *Young children and the arts: Making creative connections.* Washington, DC: Arts Education Partnership.

Taunton, M., & M. Colbert. 2000. Art in the early childhood classroom: Authentic experiences and extended dialogues. In *Promoting meaningful learning: Innovation in educating early childhood professionals,* ed. N.J. Yelland, 67–76. Washington, DC: NAEYC.

Thompson, C.M. 1995. Transforming curriculum in the visual arts. In *Reaching potentials. Vol. 2: Transforming early childhood curriculum and assessment,* eds. S. Bredekamp & T. Rosegrant, 81–96. Washington, DC: NAEYC.

Thompson, C.M., ed. 1995. *The visual arts and early childhood learning.* Reston, VA: National Art Education Association.

Thompson, S.C. 2005. *Children as illustrators: Making meaning through art and language.* Washington, DC: NAEYC.

## Web sites

**Arts Education Partnership**—http://aep-arts.org/. Provides art education advocacy resources, information on funding opportunities, and art education links.

**International Child Art Foundation (ICAF)**—www.icaf.org/index3.html. Offers educators information on the benefits of creative arts in the classroom and on art programs sponsored by ICAF, including international art festivals.

# References

Althouse, R., M.H. Johnson, & S.T. Mitchell. 2003. *The colors of learning: Integrating the visual arts into the early childhood curriculum.* New York: Teachers College Press; and Washington, DC: NAEYC.

Arnheim, R. 1989. *Thoughts on art education.* Los Angeles: The Getty Center for Education in the Arts.

Arts Education Partnership. 1998. *Young children and the arts: Making creative connections—A report of the Task Force on Children's Learning and the Arts: Birth to Age Eight.* Washington, DC: Author.

Baroody, A.J. 2000, July. Does mathematics instruction for three- to five-year-olds really make sense? *Young Children* 55 (4): 61–67.

Berliner, D.C. 1987. Simple views of effective teaching and a simple theory of classroom instruction. In *Talks to teachers,* eds. D.C. Berliner & B.V. Rosenshine, 99–110. New York: Random House.

Berliner, D.C. 1992. The nature of expertise in teaching. In *Effective and responsible teaching: The new synthesis,* eds. F.K. Oser, A. Dick, & J.L. Patry, 227–48. San Francisco: Jossey-Bass.

Bredekamp, S., & C. Copple, eds. 1997. *Developmentally appropriate practice in early childhood programs.* Rev. ed. Washington, DC: NAEYC.

Bredekamp, S., & T. Rosegrant. 1992. Reaching potentials: Introduction. In *Reaching potentials. Vol. 1: Appropriate curriculum and assessment for young children,* eds. S. Bredekamp & T. Rosegrant, 2–8. Washington, DC: NAEYC.

Buckleitner, W., & C. Hohmann. 1991. Blocks, sand, paint . . . and computers. In *Supporting young learners: Ideas for preschool and day care providers,* eds. N.A. Brickman & L.S. Taylor, 174–83. Ypsilanti, MI: High/Scope Press.

Campbell, P.F. 1999. Fostering each child's understanding of mathematics. In *The early childhood curriculum: Current findings in theory and practice,* 3d ed., ed. C. Seefeldt, 106–32. New York: Teachers College Press.

CSEFEL (Center on the Social and Emotional Foundations for Early Learning). 2003. *What works briefs.* Champaign, IL: University of Illinois at Urbana-Champaign. Also online: http://csefel.uiuc.edu/whatworks.html.

Chalufour, I., & K. Worth. 2004. *Building structures with young children.* The Young Scientist Series. St. Paul, MN: Redleaf Press; and Washington, DC: NAEYC.

Clements, D.H. 1999. The effective use of computers with young children. In *Mathematics in the early years,* ed. J.V. Copley, 119–28. Reston, VA: National Council of Teachers of Mathematics; and Washington, DC: NAEYC.

Clements, D.H. 2001. Mathematics in the preschool. *Teaching Children Mathematics* 7 (5): 270–75.

Clements, D.H. 2002. Computers in early childhood mathematics. *Contemporary Issues in Early Childhood* 3 (2): 160–81.

Clements, D.H. 2004. Major themes and recommendations. In *Engaging young children in mathematics: Standards for early childhood mathematics education,* eds. D.H. Clements, J. Sarama, & A.-M. DiBiase, 7–72. Mahwah, NJ: Erlbaum.

Copley, J.V. 2000. *The young child and mathematics.* Washington, DC: NAEYC.

Copley, J.V., ed. 2004. *Showcasing mathematics for the young child: Activities for three-, four-, and five-year-olds.* Reston, VA: National Council of Teachers of Mathematics.

Copple, C., & S. Bredekamp. 2006. *Basics of developmentally appropriate practice: An introduction for teachers of children 3 to 6.* Washington, DC: NAEYC.

Corsaro, W., & L. Molinari. 2005. *I compagni: Understanding children's transition from preschool to elementary school.* New York: Teachers College Press.

DeBruin-Parecki, A., & M. Hohmann. 2003. *Letter links: Alphabet learning with children's names.* Ypsilanti, MI: High/Scope Press.

Dobbs, S.M. 1998. *Learning in and through art.* Los Angeles: The Getty Education Institute for the Arts.

Edwards, C., L. Gandini, & G. Forman, eds. 1998. *The hundred languages of children: The Reggio Emilia approach—Advanced reflections.* 2d ed. Greenwich, CT: Ablex.

Eisner, E.W. 2004. *The arts and the creation of mind.* New Haven, CT: Yale University Press.

Elias, M.J., J.E. Zins, R.P. Weissberg, K.S. Frey, M.T. Greenberg, N.M. Haynes, R. Kessler, M.E. Schwab-Stone, & T.P. Shriver. 1997. *Promoting social and emo-*

tional learning: Guidelines for educators. Alexandria, VA: Association for Supervision and Curriculum Development.

Engle, B.S. 1996. Learning to look: Appreciating child art. *Young Children* 51 (3): 74–79.

Epstein, A.S. 2001. Thinking about art with young children. In *Supporting young learners 3: Ideas for child care providers and teachers*, ed. N.A. Brickman, 185–93. Ypsilanti, MI: High/Scope Press.

Epstein, A.S. 2003, September. How planning and reflection develop young children's thinking skills. *Young Children* 58 (5): 28–36.

Epstein, A.S. 2005. How to talk with children about art. In *Supporting young learners 4: Ideas for child care providers and teachers*, eds. N.A. Brickman, H. Barton, & J. Burd, 181–84. Ypsilanti, MI: High/Scope Press.

Epstein, A.S. 2007. *Essentials of active learning in preschool: Getting to know the High/Scope curriculum*. Ypsilanti, MI: High/Scope Press.

Epstein, A.S., & E. Trimis. 2002. *Supporting young artists: The development of the visual arts in young children*. Ypsilanti, MI: High/Scope Press.

Eshach, H., & M.N. Fried. 2005, September. Should science be taught in early childhood? *Journal of Science Education and Technology* 14 (3): 315–36.

Espinosa, L. 1992. The process of change: The Redwood City story. In *Reaching potentials. Vol. 1: Appropriate curriculum and assessment for young children*, eds. S. Bredekamp & T. Rosegrant, 159–66. Washington, DC: NAEYC.

Evans, B. 2002. *You can't come to my birthday party! Conflict resolution with young children*. Ypsilanti, MI: High/Scope Press.

Evans, B. 2005. Bye Mommy! Bye Daddy! Easing separations for preschoolers. In *Supporting young learners 4: Ideas for child care providers and teachers*, eds. N.A. Brickman, H. Barton, & J. Burd, 49–57. Ypsilanti, MI: High/Scope Press.

Fight Crime: Invest in Kids. 2000. *America's child care crisis: A crime prevention tragedy*. Washington, DC: Author. Also see: www.fightcrime.org.

Fiske, E.B., ed. 1999. *Champions of change: The impact of the arts on learning*. Washington, DC: Arts Education Partnership and The President's Committee on the Arts and Humanities.

Gallahue, D.L. 1995. Transforming physical education curriculum. In *Reaching potentials. Vol. 2: Transforming early childhood curriculum and assessment*, eds. S. Bredekamp & T. Rosegrant, 125–44. Washington, DC: NAEYC.

Gambrell, L.B., & S.A. Mazzoni. 1999. Emergent literacy: What research reveals about learning to read. In *The early childhood curriculum: Current findings in theory and practice*, 3d ed., ed. C. Seefeldt, 80–105. New York: Teachers College Press.

Gandini, L., L. Hill, L. Cadwell, & C. Schwall. 2005. *In the spirit of the studio: Learning from the* atelier *of Reggio Emilia*. New York: Teachers College Press.

Gardner, H. 1991. *The unschooled mind: How children think and how schools should teach*. New York: Basic Books.

Gelman, R., & K. Brenneman. 2004. Science learning pathways for young children. *Early Childhood Research Quarterly* 19 (1): 150–58.

Gelman, R., & C.R. Gallistel. 1978. *The child's understanding of number*. Cambridge, MA: Harvard University Press.

Genishi, C., & R. Fassler. 1999. Oral language in the early childhood classroom: Building on diverse foundations. In *The early childhood curriculum: Current findings in theory and practice*, 3d ed., ed. C. Seefeldt, 54–79. New York: Teachers College Press.

Gerecke, K., & P. Weatherby. 2001. High/Scope strategies for specific disabilities. In *Supporting young learners 3: Ideas for child care providers and teachers*, ed. N.A. Brickman, 255–66. Ypsilanti, MI: High/Scope Press.

Ginsburg, H.P., N. Inoue, & K.-H. Seo. 1999. Young children doing mathematics: Observations of everyday activities. In *Mathematics in the early years*, ed. J.V. Copley, 88–99. Reston, VA: National Council of Teachers of Mathematics; and Washington, DC: NAEYC.

Graham, G., S. Holt/Hale, & M. Parker. 2004. *Children moving: A reflective approach to teaching physical education*. St. Louis, MO: McGraw-Hill.

Graves, M. 1996. Classification: Collecting, sorting, and organizing. In *Supporting young learners 2: Ideas for child care providers and teachers*, ed. N.A. Brickman, 207–14. Ypsilanti, MI: High/Scope Press.

Greenes, C. 1999. Ready to learn: Developing young children's mathematical powers. In *Mathematics in the early years*, ed. J.V. Copley, 39–47. Reston, VA: National Council of Teachers of Mathematics; and Washington, DC: NAEYC.

Greer, W.D. 1984. Discipline-based art education: Approaching art as a subject of study. *Studies in Art Education* 25 (4): 212–18.

Gronlund, G. 2006. *Make early learning standards come alive: Connecting your practice and curriculum to state guidelines*. St. Paul, MN: Redleaf Press; and Washington, DC: NAEYC.

Harris, V. 1991. The playground: An outdoor setting for learning. In *Supporting young learners: Ideas for preschool and day care providers*, eds. N.A. Brickman & L.S. Taylor, 167–73. Ypsilanti, MI: High/Scope Press.

Hart, B., & T. Risley. 1995. *Meaningful differences in the everyday experience of young American children*. Baltimore, MD: Brookes.

Healy, J.M. 1994. *Your child's growing mind: A practical guide to brain development and learning from birth to adolescence*. New York: Doubleday.

Helm, J.H., & L. Katz. 2001. *Young investigators: The project approach in the early years.* New York: Teachers College Press; and Washington, DC: NAEYC.

High/Scope Educational Research Foundation. 2004. *Growing readers early literacy curriculum.* Ypsilanti, MI: High/Scope Press.

Hildreth, G. 1936. Developmental sequences in name writing. *Child Development* 7: 291–303.

Hoffman, M. 2000. *Empathy and moral development: Implications for caring and justice.* New York: Cambridge University Press.

Hohmann, M. 2005. Vocabulary-building strategies. In *Supporting young learners 4: Ideas for child care providers and teachers,* eds. N.A. Brickman, H. Barton, & J. Burd, 245–52. Ypsilanti, MI: High/Scope Press.

Hohmann, M., & D.P. Weikart. 2002. *Educating young children: Active learning practices for preschool and child care programs.* 2d ed. Ypsilanti, MI: High/Scope Press.

Howes, C. 1988. Peer interactions of young children. *Monographs of the Society for Research in Child Development,* Serial No. 217, 53 (1).

Hyson, M. 2000, November. Is it okay to have calendar time? Look up to the star . . . look within yourself. *Young Children* 55 (6): 60–61.

Hyson, M., ed. 2003. *Preparing early childhood professionals: NAEYC's standards for programs.* Washington, DC: NAEYC.

Hyson, M. 2004. *The emotional development of young children: Building an emotion-centered curriculum.* 2d ed. New York: Teachers College Press.

IRA (International Reading Association) & NAEYC. 1998. Learning to read and write: Developmentally appropriate practices for young children. Joint Position Statement, adopted May 1998. Washington, DC: NAEYC. Online: www.naeyc.org/about/positions/pdf/PSREAD98.PDF.

Jantz, R.K., & C. Seefeldt. 1999. Early childhood social studies. In *The early childhood curriculum: Current findings in theory and practice,* 3d ed., ed. C. Seefeldt, 159–78. New York: Teachers College Press.

Kagan, S.L., E. Moore, & S. Bredekamp, eds. 1995, June. *Reconsidering children's early development and learning: Toward common views and vocabulary.* Goal 1 Technical Planning Group Report 95-03. Washington, DC: National Education Goals Panel.

Kamii, C. 2000. *Young children reinvent arithmetic.* 2d ed. New York: Teachers College Press.

Katz, L.G., & S.C. Chard. 2000. *Engaging children's minds: The Project Approach.* 2d ed. Greenwich, CT: Ablex.

Katz, L.G., & D.E. McClellan. 1997. *Fostering children's social competence: The teacher's role.* Washington, DC: NAEYC.

Kellogg, R., & S. O'Dell. 1967. *The psychology of children's art.* New York: Psychology Today/CRM-Random House.

Kerlavage, M.S. 1995. A bunch of naked ladies and a tiger: Children's responses to adult works of art. In *The visual arts and early childhood learning,* ed. C.M. Thompson, 56–62. Reston, VA: National Art Education Association.

Kindler, A.M. 1995. Significance of adult input in early childhood artistic development. In *The visual arts and early childhood learning,* ed. C.M. Thompson, 1–5. Reston, VA: National Art Education Association.

Kolodziej, S. 1995. The picture museum: Creating a photography museum with children. In *The visual arts and early childhood learning,* ed. C.M. Thompson, 52–55. Reston, VA: National Art Education Association.

Kontos, S., C. Howes, B. Shinn, & E. Galinsky. 1994. *Quality in family child care and relative care.* New York: Teachers College Press.

Landry, C.E., & G.E. Forman. 1999. Research on early science education. In *The early childhood curriculum: Current findings in theory and practice,* 3d ed., ed. C. Seefeldt, 133–57. New York: Teachers College Press.

Levin, D.E. 2003. *Teaching young children in violent times: Building a peaceable classroom.* Washington, DC: Educators for Social Responsibility and NAEYC.

Manross, M.A. 2000. Learning to throw in physical education class: Part 3. *Teaching Elementary Physical Education* 11 (3): 26–29.

Mathews, J. 1997. Manderian for two objects are not the same. *Visual Arts Research* 23 (1): 73–96.

Mindes, G. 2005, September. Social studies in today's early childhood curricula. *Young Children* 60 (5): 12–18. Also online: http://journal.naeyc.org/btj/200509/MindesBTJ905.pdf.

Mix, K.S., S.C. Levine, & J. Huttenlocher. 1999. Early fraction calculation ability. *Developmental Psychology* 35: 164–74.

National Art Education Association. 1982. *Quality goals statement.* Washington, DC: Author.

NAEYC. 2003. NAEYC standards for early childhood professional preparation: Initial licensure programs. Position Statement, adopted July 2001. In *Preparing early childhood professionals: NAEYC's standards for programs,* ed. M. Hyson, 17–63. Washington, DC: Author. Also online: www.naeyc.org/faculty/pdf/2001.pdf.

NAEYC. 2005. *NAEYC early childhood program standards and accreditation criteria: The mark of quality in early childhood education.* Washington, DC: Author. Standards and criteria also can be accessed at: www.naeyc.org/academy/standards/.

NAEYC & NAECS/SDE (National Association of Early Childhood Specialists in State Departments of Education). 1991. Position statement on guidelines for appropriate curriculum content and assessment of children ages 3 through 8. *Young Children* 46 (3): 21–37.

NAEYC & NAECS/SDE. 2003. Early childhood curriculum, assessment, and program evaluation: Building an effective, accountable system in programs for children birth through age 8. Joint Position Statement, adopted November 2003. Washington, DC: Authors. Online: www.naeyc.org/about/positions/pdf/pscape.pdf.

NAEYC & NCTM (National Council of Teachers of Mathematics). 2002. Early childhood mathematics: Promoting good beginnings. Joint Position Statement, adopted April 2002. Washington, DC: NAEYC. Online: www.naeyc.org/about/positions/pdf/psmath.pdf.

NASPE (National Association for Sport and Physical Education). 2000. Appropriate practices in movement programs for young children ages 3–5. NASPE Position Statement, developed by the Council on Physical Education for Children (COPEC). Reston, VA: Author.

NASPE. 2002. *Active start: A statement of physical activity guidelines for children birth to five years.* Reston, VA: Author.

National Center for Health Statistics. 2004. *Health, United States, 2004.* Hyattsville, MD: Author.

NCSESA (National Committee on Science Education Standards and Assessment), National Research Council. 1996. *National Science Education Standards.* Washington, DC: National Academy Press.

NCSS (National Council for the Social Studies). 1984. Social studies for young children. Position Statement, adopted 1984. Silver Spring, MD: Author. Online: www.socialstudies.org/positions/children/.

NCTM (National Council of Teachers of Mathematics). 2000. *Principles and standards for school mathematics.* Reston, VA: Author. Also see: www.nctm.org/standards/.

NCTM. 2006. *Curriculum focal points for prekindergarten through grade 8 mathematics: A quest for coherence.* Reston, VA: Author. Also see: www.nctm.org/focalpoints/.

National Education Goals Panel. 1994. *Goals 2000: Educate America act.* Washington, DC: U.S. Government Printing Office.

National Endowment for the Arts. 1988. *Toward civilization: A report on arts education.* Washington, DC: U.S. Government Printing Office.

NRP (National Reading Panel). 2000. *Teaching children to read: An evidence-based assessment of the scientific research literature on reading and its implications for reading instruction.* Washington, DC: National Institute of Child Health and Human Development, National Institutes of Health.

National Research Council. 2000a. *Eager to learn: Educating our preschoolers.* Washington, DC: National Academy Press.

National Research Council. 2000b. *Neurons to neighborhoods: The science of early childhood development.* Washington, DC: National Academy Press.

Neuman, S.B., C. Copple, & S. Bredekamp. 2000. *Learning to read and write: Developmentally appropriate practices for young children.* Washington, DC: NAEYC.

Olszewski, L. 1998, November 13. Study links arts classes to academic achievement. *San Francisco Chronicle,* A19.

Parsons, M.J. 1987. *How we understand art.* Cambridge, United Kingdom: Cambridge University.

Perrett, B. 1996. Group times: What makes them work? In *Supporting young learners 2: Ideas for child care providers and teachers,* ed. N.A. Brickman, 71–76. Ypsilanti, MI: High/Scope Press.

Piaget, J. 1932/1965. *The moral judgment of the child.* New York: The Free Press.

Pianta, R.C. 2003, August. *Standardized classroom observations from pre-k to 3rd grade: A mechanism for improving access to consistently high quality classroom experiences and practices during the P–3 years.* New York: Foundation for Child Development.

Pica, R. 1997, June. Beyond physical development: Why young children need to move. *Young Children* 52 (6): 4–11.

Ranweiler, L. 2004. *Preschool readers and writers: Early literacy strategies for teachers.* Ypsilanti, MI: High/Scope Press.

Raver, C.C., C. Izard, & C.B. Kopp. 2002. Emotions matter: Making the case for the role of young children's emotional development for early school readiness. *Society for Research in Child Development Social Policy Report* 16 (3): 1–19.

Reynolds, A.J., J.A. Temple, D.L. Robertson, & E.A. Mann. 2001. Long-term effects of an early childhood intervention on educational achievement and juvenile arrest: A 15-year follow-up of low-income children in public schools. *Journal of the American Medical Association* 285 (18): 2339–46.

Rowe, D. 1994. *Preschoolers as authors: Literacy learning in the social world.* Cresskill, NJ: Hampton Press.

Salome, R.A. 1967. A comparative analysis of kindergarten children's drawings in crayon and colored pencil. *Studies in Art Education* 72: 25–27.

Sanders, S.W. 1992. *Designing preschool movement programs.* Champaign, IL: Human Kinetics.

Sanders, S.W. 2002. *Active for life: Developmentally appropriate movement programs for young children.* Washington, DC: NAEYC.

Sanders, S.W. 2006. Physical education in kindergarten. In *K today: Teaching and learning in the kindergarten year,* ed. D. Gullo, 127–37. Washington, DC: NAEYC.

Scott-Kassner, C. 1992. Research on music in early child-hood. In *Handbook of research on music teaching and learning,* ed. R. Colwell, 633–50. Reston, VA: Music Educators National Conference.

Schweinhart, L.J., J. Montie, Z. Xiang, W.S. Barnett, C.R. Belfield, & M. Nores. 2005. *Lifetime effects: The High/Scope Perry Preschool Study through age 40.* Ypsilanti, MI: High/Scope Press.

Seefeldt, C. 1979. The effects of a program designed to increase young children's perception of texture. *Studies in Art Education* 20: 40–44.

Seefeldt, C. 1999. Art for young children. In *The early childhood curriculum: Current findings in theory and practice,* 3d ed., ed. C. Seefeldt, 201–17. New York: Teachers College Press.

Seefeldt, C. 2003. Foreword. In *The colors of learning: Integrating the visual arts into the early childhood curriculum,* eds. R. Althouse, M.H. Johnson, & S.T. Mitchell, ix–x. New York: Teachers College Press; and Washington, DC: NAEYC.

Seo, K.-H. 2003, January. What children's play tells us about teaching mathematics. *Young Children* 58 (1): 28–34.

Snow, C.E., M.S. Burns, & P. Griffin, eds. 1998. *Preventing reading difficulties in young children.* A Report of the Committee on the Prevention of Reading Difficulties in Young Children, National Research Council. Washington, DC: National Academy of Sciences.

Spinrad, T.L., & C.A. Stifter. 2006. Toddlers' empathy-related responding to distress: Predictions from negative emotionality and maternal behavior in infancy. *Infancy* 10 (2): 97–121.

Stellaccio, C.K., & M. McCarthy. 1999. Research in early childhood music and movement education. In *The early childhood curriculum: Current findings in theory and practice,* 3d ed., ed. C. Seefeldt, 179–200. New York: Teachers College Press.

Strubank, R. 1991. Movement and music throughout the daily routine. In *Supporting young learners: Ideas for preschool and day care providers,* eds. N.A. Brickman & L.S. Taylor, 104–11. Ypsilanti, MI: High/Scope Press.

Taunton, M., & M. Colbert. 2000. Art in the early child-hood classroom: Authentic experiences and extended dialogues. In *Promoting meaningful learning: Innovation in educating early childhood professionals,* ed. N.J. Yelland, 67–76. Washington, DC: NAEYC.

Tegano, D., J. Moran, A. DeLong, J. Brickley, & K. Ramanssini. 1996. Designing classroom spaces: Making the most of time. *Early Childhood Education Journal* 23 (3): 135–41.

Thompson, C.M. 1995. Transforming curriculum in the visual arts. In *Reaching potentials. Vol. 2: Transforming early childhood curriculum and assessment,* eds. S. Bredekamp & T. Rosegrant, 81–96. Washington, DC: NAEYC.

Tompkins, M. 1996a. A partnership with young artists. In *Supporting young learners 2: Ideas for child care providers and teachers,* ed. N.A. Brickman, 187–92. Ypsilanti, MI: High/Scope Press.

Tompkins, M. 1996b. Spatial learning: Beyond circles, squares, and triangles. In *Supporting young learners 2: Ideas for child care providers and teachers,* ed. N.A. Brickman, 215–22. Ypsilanti, MI: High/Scope Press.

U.S. Department of Education. 1994. *National standards for arts education: What every young American should know and be able to do in the arts.* Washington, DC: U.S. Government Printing Office.

Vance, E., & P.J. Weaver. 2002. *Class meetings: Young children solving problems together.* Washington, DC: NAEYC.

Vygotsky, L. 1978. *Mind and society: The development of higher psychological processes.* Cambridge, MA: Harvard University Press.

Weikart, P.S. 2000. *Round the circle: Key experiences in movement for young children.* 2d ed. Ypsilanti, MI: High/Scope Press.

Whitebook, M., C. Howes, & D. Phillips. 1989. *The National Child Care Staffing Study: Who cares? Child care teachers and the quality of care in America.* Final Report. Oakland, CA: Child Care Employee Project.

Worth, K., & S. Grollman. 2003. *Worms, shadows, and whirlpools: Science in the early childhood classroom.* Portsmouth, NH: Heinemann; and Washington, DC: NAEYC.

Yoskikawa, H. 1995. Long-term effects of early childhood programs on social outcomes and delinquency. *The Future of Children* 5 (3): 51–75.

# Index

National Research Council, 67
National Reading Panel (NRP), 24, 25
No Child Left Behind Act, vii, 24
notation (numbers), 52
number and operations, 42, 44, 49–54
number sense, 50
numeration, 52–53

obesity, 88
orientation (physical), 55–56
outdoor spaces, 11, 91, 96, 112–113

part-part-whole concept, 50–51
patterns, 45, 60–63
pedagogy, 5–6
phonemic awareness, 24, 28–30
phonological awareness, 24, 26, 28–30
physical education. *See* movement
physical environment, 10–12, 18, 33, 77, 91
physical movement. *See* movement
physical needs, 14–15, 82–84
Piaget, Jean, 73, 109
play, 11, 18, 27, 33, 77–79, 116. *See also* games
praise/compliments (vs. acknowledgment), 5, 17–18, 74, 119–120
print knowledge/awareness, 25, 33–34
problem solving, 18–19, 42
professional development, 21
Project Approach (art), 117–118
punctuation, 39–40

questions (teachers'). *See also* conversation, 28, 115

reading, 20, 23–25, 31–37
    comprehension, 31–32
    readiness, 24
reasoning and proof, 42
representation (art), 109, 113–114, 116–118
representation (math), 42, 64
rhythms (movement), 103–104
rules, classroom, 82–86

safety. *See* physical environment
schedule (for day), 10, 13–14, 74, 76–77, 91
scientific inquiry, 41–65
self-confidence, 73–74
self-identity, 71–72
self-regulation, emotional, 69
seriation, 58–59
shape, 54–57
social skills/understandings, 67–86
Society for Research in Child Development, 68
space. *See* outdoor spaces; physical environment
space awareness, 90, 100–101, 102–103
spatial relationships, 55–56
spatial sense (math), 54–58
special needs, children with, 16–17, 73, 79–80
speech. *See* language
speeds (movement), 101
spelling, 39–40
sports (vs. movement programs), 89–90, 93–94
stability skills, 90, 95–96, 98–99
standards
    for early learning, 5–6, 15, 24, 42, 46, 49, 58, 68, 89–91, 108
    for program accreditation, 11, 43, 68
    for teacher preparation, 20–21, 25
subitizing, 50
symmetry, 54

Task Force on Children's Learning and the Arts, 108
technology. *See* computers
transformation (math), 54–57

U.S. Department of Education, 24

visual arts. *See* arts, visual
visual discrimination skills, 32–33, 111
visualization (math), 54
vocabulary, 25, 29–31, 32, 93, 103, 104, 114–115, 120–121

words. *See* vocabulary
writing, 37–40

# Early years are learning years

## Become a member of NAEYC, and help make them count!

Just as you help young children learn and grow, the National Association for the Education of Young Children—your professional organization—supports you in the work you love. NAEYC is the world's largest early childhood education organization, with a national network of local, state, and regional Affiliates. We are more than 100,000 members working together to bring high-quality early learning opportunities to all children from birth through age eight.

Since 1926, NAEYC has provided educational services and resources for people working with children, including:

• *Young Children*, the award-winning journal (six issues a year) for early childhood educators

• **Books, posters, brochures, and videos** to support your work with young children and families

• **The NAEYC Annual Conference**, which brings tens of thousands of people together from across the country and around the world to share their expertise and ideas on the education of young children

• **Insurance plans** for members and programs

• **A voluntary accreditation system** to help programs reach national standards for high-quality early childhood education

• **Young Children International** to promote global communication and information exchanges

• **www.naeyc.org**—a dynamic Web site with up-to-date information on all of our services and resources

## To join NAEYC

To find a complete list of membership benefits and options or to join NAEYC online, visit **www.naeyc.org/membership.** Or you can mail this form to us.

(Membership must be for an individual, not a center or school.)

Name_____

Address_____

City_____ State_____ ZIP_____

E-mail _____

Phone (H)_____(W) _____

❏ New member   ❏ Renewal ID # _____

Affiliate name/number _____

To determine your dues, you must visit **www.naeyc.org/membership** or call 800-424-2460, ext. 2002.

## Indicate your payment option

❏ VISA   ❏ MasterCard   ❏ AmEx   ❏ Discover

Card # _____Exp. date _____

Cardholder's name_____

Signature _____

*Note:* By joining NAEYC you also become a member of your state and local Affiliates.

## Send this form and payment to

NAEYC
PO Box 97156
Washington, DC 20090-7156